Food

365-day Catholic Planner to pray the Holy
Rosary, read the Holy Bible and
make daily sacrifices.

By: Pablo Claret

Viva Cristo Rey Multimedia – vivacristorey.org
Year of Our Lord Jesus Christ 2020

MY CATHOLIC PLANNER

LONG LIVE CHRIST THE KING!

PROPERTY OF:

_____

IF LOST, CONTACT:

EMAIL: _____

CELLPHONE: _____

MEMENTO MORIS

YOUR SOUL'S GROWTH PLANNER

LONG LIVE CHRIST THE KING!

DATE: MONTH   DAY   YEAR

GOALS OF THE DAY

PRAYING THE ROSARY OF 15 DECADES................... ☐

READING THE HOLY BIBLE (15 MINUTES)............... ☐

DAILY SACRIFICES... ☐

☐ _____   ☐ _____

☐ _____   ☐ _____

☐ _____   ☐ _____

☐ _____   ☐ _____

☐ _____   ☐ _____

☐ _____   ☐ _____

☐ _____   ☐ _____

☐ _____   ☐ _____

☐ _____   ☐ _____

SUGGESTIONS

If you don't know how to pray the Holy Rosary, you can get our book "Rosary for beginners" in the following link: www.vcrey.com/rosary-book

Some sacrifices that you can do include:

- Not drinking water or liquids during a meal.
- Abstain from meat on Fridays (which is also required by Holy Mother Church).
- Not eating candy or dessert during one day.
- Take a cold shower.
- Not eating meat in saturdays in honor of the Blessed Virgin Mary.
- Keep one hour of silence.
- Do not buy or sell in Sunday (which is also a commandment).
- Give food to the hungry.
- Give water to the thirsty.
- Visit the sick, and confort them.

IMPORTANT NOTES

☐ _____

☐ _____

☐ _____

☐ _____

☐ _____

☐ _____

☐ _____

☐ _____

☐ _____

YOUR SOUL'S GROWTH PLANNER

LONG LIVE CHRIST THE KING!

VIVA
CRISTO
REY.ORG

DATE: MONTH   DAY   YEAR

GOALS OF THE DAY

PRAYING THE ROSARY OF 15 DECADES.................. ☐

READING THE HOLY BIBLE (15 MINUTES).............. ☐

DAILY SACRIFICES... ☐

☐ _____   ☐ _____
☐ _____   ☐ _____
☐ _____   ☐ _____
☐ _____   ☐ _____
☐ _____   ☐ _____
☐ _____   ☐ _____
☐ _____   ☐ _____
☐ _____   ☐ _____
☐ _____   ☐ _____

SUGGESTIONS

If you don't know how to pray the Holy Rosary, you can get our book "Rosary for beginners" in the following link: www.vcrey.com/rosary-book

Some sacrifices that you can do include:

- Not drinking water or liquids during a meal.
- Abstain from meat on Fridays (which is also required by Holy Mother Church).
- Not eating candy or dessert during one day.
- Take a cold shower.
- Not eating meat in saturdays in honor of the Blessed Virgin Mary.
- Keep one hour of silence.
- Do not buy or sell in Sunday (which is also a commandment).
- Give food to the hungry.
- Give water to the thirsty.
- Visit the sick, and confort them.

IMPORTANT NOTES

☐ _____
☐ _____
☐ _____
☐ _____
☐ _____
☐ _____
☐ _____
☐ _____
☐ _____

YOUR SOUL'S GROWTH PLANNER

LONG LIVE CHRIST THE KING!

VIVA
CRISTO
REY.ORG

DATE: MONTH   DAY   YEAR

GOALS OF THE DAY

PRAYING THE ROSARY OF 15 DECADES................... ☐

READING THE HOLY BIBLE (15 MINUTES)............... ☐

DAILY SACRIFICES.. ☐

☐ _____ ☐ _____
☐ _____ ☐ _____
☐ _____ ☐ _____
☐ _____ ☐ _____
☐ _____ ☐ _____
☐ _____
☐ _____ ☐ _____
☐ _____ ☐ _____
☐ _____ ☐ _____

SUGGESTIONS

If you don't know how to pray the Holy Rosary, you can get our book "Rosary for beginners" in the following link: www.vcrey.com/rosary-book

Some sacrifices that you can do include:

- Not drinking water or liquids during a meal.
- Abstain from meat on Fridays (which is also required by Holy Mother Church).
- Not eating candy or dessert during one day.
- Take a cold shower.
- Not eating meat in saturdays in honor of the Blessed Virgin Mary.
- Keep one hour of silence.
- Do not buy or sell in Sunday (which is also a commandment).
- Give food to the hungry.
- Give water to the thirsty.
- Visit the sick, and confort them.

IMPORTANT NOTES

☐ _____
☐ _____
☐ _____
☐ _____
☐ _____
☐ _____
☐ _____
☐ _____
☐ _____

YOUR SOUL'S GROWTH PLANNER

LONG LIVE CHRIST THE KING!

VIVA
CRISTO
REY.ORG

DATE: MONTH   DAY   YEAR

GOALS OF THE DAY

PRAYING THE ROSARY OF 15 DECADES................... ☐

READING THE HOLY BIBLE (15 MINUTES)............... ☐

DAILY SACRIFICES.. ☐

☐ _____   ☐ _____
☐ _____   ☐ _____
☐ _____   ☐ _____

☐ _____   ☐ _____
☐ _____   ☐ _____
☐ _____   ☐ _____
☐ _____   ☐ _____

☐ _____   ☐ _____
☐ _____   ☐ _____

SUGGESTIONS

If you don't know how to pray the Holy Rosary, you can get our book "Rosary for beginners" in the following link: www.vcrey.com/rosary-book

Some sacrifices that you can do include:

- Not drinking water or liquids during a meal.
- Abstain from meat on Fridays (which is also required by Holy Mother Church).
- Not eating candy or dessert during one day.
- Take a cold shower.
- Not eating meat in saturdays in honor of the Blessed Virgin Mary.
- Keep one hour of silence.
- Do not buy or sell in Sunday (which is also a commandment).
- Give food to the hungry.
- Give water to the thirsty.
- Visit the sick, and confort them.

IMPORTANT NOTES

☐ _____
☐ _____
☐ _____
☐ _____
☐ _____
☐ _____
☐ _____
☐ _____
☐ _____

YOUR SOUL'S GROWTH PLANNER

LONG LIVE CHRIST THE KING!

VIVA CRISTO REY.ORG

DATE: MONTH   DAY   YEAR

GOALS OF THE DAY

PRAYING THE ROSARY OF 15 DECADES................... ☐

READING THE HOLY BIBLE (15 MINUTES)................ ☐

DAILY SACRIFICES... ☐

☐ _____   ☐ _____
☐ _____   ☐ _____
☐ _____   ☐ _____
☐ _____   ☐ _____
☐ _____   ☐ _____
☐ _____   ☐ _____
☐ _____   ☐ _____
☐ _____   ☐ _____
☐ _____   ☐ _____

SUGGESTIONS

If you don't know how to pray the Holy Rosary, you can get our book "Rosary for beginners" in the following link: www.vcrey.com/rosary-book

Some sacrifices that you can do include:

- Not drinking water or liquids during a meal.
- Abstain from meat on Fridays (which is also required by Holy Mother Church).
- Not eating candy or dessert during one day.
- Take a cold shower.
- Not eating meat in saturdays in honor of the Blessed Virgin Mary.
- Keep one hour of silence.
- Do not buy or sell in Sunday (which is also a commandment).
- Give food to the hungry.
- Give water to the thirsty.
- Visit the sick, and confort them.

IMPORTANT NOTES

☐ _____
☐ _____
☐ _____
☐ _____
☐ _____
☐ _____
☐ _____
☐ _____
☐ _____

YOUR SOUL'S GROWTH PLANNER

LONG LIVE CHRIST THE KING!

VIVA
CRISTO
REY.ORG

DATE: MONTH   DAY   YEAR

GOALS OF THE DAY

PRAYING THE ROSARY OF 15 DECADES................... ☐

READING THE HOLY BIBLE (15 MINUTES)............... ☐

DAILY SACRIFICES.. ☐

☐ _____   ☐ _____
☐ _____   ☐ _____
☐ _____   ☐ _____
☐ _____   ☐ _____
☐ _____   ☐ _____
☐ _____   ☐ _____
☐ _____   ☐ _____
☐ _____   ☐ _____
☐ _____   ☐ _____

SUGGESTIONS

If you don't know how to pray the Holy Rosary, you can get our book "Rosary for beginners" in the following link: www.vcrey.com/rosary-book

Some sacrifices that you can do include:

- Not drinking water or liquids during a meal.
- Abstain from meat on Fridays (which is also required by Holy Mother Church).
- Not eating candy or dessert during one day.
- Take a cold shower.
- Not eating meat in saturdays in honor of the Blessed Virgin Mary.
- Keep one hour of silence.
- Do not buy or sell in Sunday (which is also a commandment).
- Give food to the hungry.
- Give water to the thirsty.
- Visit the sick, and confort them.

IMPORTANT NOTES

☐ _____
☐ _____
☐ _____
☐ _____
☐ _____
☐ _____
☐ _____
☐ _____
☐ _____

YOUR SOUL'S GROWTH PLANNER

LONG LIVE CHRIST THE KING!

VIVA
CRISTO
REY.ORG

DATE: MONTH   DAY   YEAR

GOALS OF THE DAY

PRAYING THE ROSARY OF 15 DECADES................... ☐

READING THE HOLY BIBLE (15 MINUTES)............... ☐

DAILY SACRIFICES... ☐

☐ _____   ☐ _____
☐ _____   ☐ _____
☐ _____   ☐ _____
☐ _____   ☐ _____
☐ _____   ☐ _____
☐ _____   ☐ _____
☐ _____   ☐ _____
☐ _____   ☐ _____
☐ _____   ☐ _____

SUGGESTIONS

If you don't know how to pray the Holy Rosary, you can get our book "Rosary for beginners" in the following link: www.vcrey.com/rosary-book

Some sacrifices that you can do include:

- Not drinking water or liquids during a meal.
- Abstain from meat on Fridays (which is also required by Holy Mother Church).
- Not eating candy or dessert during one day.
- Take a cold shower.
- Not eating meat in saturdays in honor of the Blessed Virgin Mary.
- Keep one hour of silence.
- Do not buy or sell in Sunday (which is also a commandment).
- Give food to the hungry.
- Give water to the thirsty.
- Visit the sick, and confort them.

IMPORTANT NOTES

☐ _____
☐ _____
☐ _____
☐ _____
☐ _____
☐ _____
☐ _____
☐ _____
☐ _____

YOUR SOUL'S GROWTH PLANNER

LONG LIVE CHRIST THE KING!

VIVA CRISTO REY.ORG

DATE: MONTH   DAY   YEAR

GOALS OF THE DAY

PRAYING THE ROSARY OF 15 DECADES................... ☐

READING THE HOLY BIBLE (15 MINUTES)................ ☐

DAILY SACRIFICES... ☐

☐ _____   ☐ _____
☐ _____   ☐ _____
☐ _____   ☐ _____
☐ _____   ☐ _____
☐ _____   ☐ _____
☐ _____   ☐ _____
☐ _____   ☐ _____
☐ _____   ☐ _____
☐ _____   ☐ _____

SUGGESTIONS

If you don't know how to pray the Holy Rosary, you can get our book "Rosary for beginners" in the following link: www.vcrey.com/rosary-book

Some sacrifices that you can do include:

- Not drinking water or liquids during a meal.
- Abstain from meat on Fridays (which is also required by Holy Mother Church).
- Not eating candy or dessert during one day.
- Take a cold shower.
- Not eating meat in saturdays in honor of the Blessed Virgin Mary.
- Keep one hour of silence.
- Do not buy or sell in Sunday (which is also a commandment).
- Give food to the hungry.
- Give water to the thirsty.
- Visit the sick, and confort them.

IMPORTANT NOTES

☐ _____
☐ _____
☐ _____
☐ _____
☐ _____
☐ _____
☐ _____
☐ _____
☐ _____

YOUR SOUL'S GROWTH PLANNER

LONG LIVE CHRIST THE KING!

DATE: MONTH   DAY   YEAR

GOALS OF THE DAY

PRAYING THE ROSARY OF 15 DECADES................... ☐

READING THE HOLY BIBLE (15 MINUTES)............... ☐

DAILY SACRIFICES.. ☐

☐ _____   ☐ _____

☐ _____   ☐ _____

☐ _____   ☐ _____

☐ _____   ☐ _____

☐ _____   ☐ _____

☐ _____   ☐ _____

☐ _____   ☐ _____

☐ _____   ☐ _____

☐ _____   ☐ _____

SUGGESTIONS

If you don't know how to pray the Holy Rosary, you can get our book "Rosary for beginners" in the following link: www.vcrey.com/rosary-book

Some sacrifices that you can do include:

- Not drinking water or liquids during a meal.
- Abstain from meat on Fridays (which is also required by Holy Mother Church).
- Not eating candy or dessert during one day.
- Take a cold shower.
- Not eating meat in saturdays in honor of the Blessed Virgin Mary.
- Keep one hour of silence.
- Do not buy or sell in Sunday (which is also a commandment).
- Give food to the hungry.
- Give water to the thirsty.
- Visit the sick, and confort them.

IMPORTANT NOTES

☐ _____

☐ _____

☐ _____

☐ _____

☐ _____

☐ _____

☐ _____

☐ _____

☐ _____

YOUR SOUL'S GROWTH PLANNER

LONG LIVE CHRIST THE KING!

VIVA CRISTO REY.ORG

DATE: MONTH   DAY   YEAR

GOALS OF THE DAY

PRAYING THE ROSARY OF 15 DECADES................... ☐

READING THE HOLY BIBLE (15 MINUTES)................ ☐

DAILY SACRIFICES.. ☐

☐ _____   ☐ _____
☐ _____   ☐ _____
☐ _____   ☐ _____
☐ _____   ☐ _____
☐ _____   ☐ _____
☐ _____   ☐ _____
☐ _____   ☐ _____
☐ _____   ☐ _____
☐ _____   ☐ _____

SUGGESTIONS

If you don't know how to pray the Holy Rosary, you can get our book "Rosary for beginners" in the following link: www.vcrey.com/rosary-book

Some sacrifices that you can do include:

- Not drinking water or liquids during a meal.
- Abstain from meat on Fridays (which is also required by Holy Mother Church).
- Not eating candy or dessert during one day.
- Take a cold shower.
- Not eating meat in saturdays in honor of the Blessed Virgin Mary.
- Keep one hour of silence.
- Do not buy or sell in Sunday (which is also a commandment).
- Give food to the hungry.
- Give water to the thirsty.
- Visit the sick, and confort them.

IMPORTANT NOTES

☐ _____
☐ _____
☐ _____
☐ _____
☐ _____
☐ _____
☐ _____
☐ _____
☐ _____

YOUR SOUL'S GROWTH PLANNER

LONG LIVE CHRIST THE KING!

VIVA CRISTO REY.ORG

DATE: MONTH   DAY   YEAR

GOALS OF THE DAY

PRAYING THE ROSARY OF 15 DECADES................... ☐

READING THE HOLY BIBLE (15 MINUTES)............... ☐

DAILY SACRIFICES... ☐

☐ _____   ☐ _____

☐ _____   ☐ _____

☐ _____   ☐ _____

☐ _____   ☐ _____

☐ _____   ☐ _____

☐ _____   ☐ _____

☐ _____   ☐ _____

☐ _____   ☐ _____

☐ _____   ☐ _____

SUGGESTIONS

If you don't know how to pray the Holy Rosary, you can get our book "Rosary for beginners" in the following link: www.vcrey.com/rosary-book

Some sacrifices that you can do include:

- Not drinking water or liquids during a meal.
- Abstain from meat on Fridays (which is also required by Holy Mother Church).
- Not eating candy or dessert during one day.
- Take a cold shower.
- Not eating meat in saturdays in honor of the Blessed Virgin Mary.
- Keep one hour of silence.
- Do not buy or sell in Sunday (which is also a commandment).
- Give food to the hungry.
- Give water to the thirsty.
- Visit the sick, and confort them.

IMPORTANT NOTES

☐ _____

☐ _____

☐ _____

☐ _____

☐ _____

☐ _____

☐ _____

☐ _____

☐ _____

YOUR SOUL'S GROWTH PLANNER

LONG LIVE CHRIST THE KING!

VIVA CRISTO REY.ORG

DATE: MONTH   DAY   YEAR

GOALS OF THE DAY

PRAYING THE ROSARY OF 15 DECADES................... ☐

READING THE HOLY BIBLE (15 MINUTES)................ ☐

DAILY SACRIFICES.. ☐

☐ _____   ☐ _____
☐ _____   ☐ _____
☐ _____   ☐ _____
☐ _____   ☐ _____
☐ _____   ☐ _____
☐ _____   ☐ _____
☐ _____   ☐ _____
☐ _____   ☐ _____
☐ _____   ☐ _____

SUGGESTIONS

If you don't know how to pray the Holy Rosary, you can get our book "Rosary for beginners" in the following link: www.vcrey.com/rosary-book

Some sacrifices that you can do include:

- Not drinking water or liquids during a meal.
- Abstain from meat on Fridays (which is also required by Holy Mother Church).
- Not eating candy or dessert during one day.
- Take a cold shower.
- Not eating meat in saturdays in honor of the Blessed Virgin Mary.
- Keep one hour of silence.
- Do not buy or sell in Sunday (which is also a commandment).
- Give food to the hungry.
- Give water to the thirsty.
- Visit the sick, and confort them.

IMPORTANT NOTES

☐ _____
☐ _____
☐ _____
☐ _____
☐ _____
☐ _____
☐ _____
☐ _____
☐ _____

YOUR SOUL'S GROWTH PLANNER

LONG LIVE CHRIST THE KING!

VIVA
CRISTO
REY.ORG

DATE: MONTH   DAY   YEAR

GOALS OF THE DAY

PRAYING THE ROSARY OF 15 DECADES.................. ☐

READING THE HOLY BIBLE (15 MINUTES)............... ☐

DAILY SACRIFICES... ☐

☐ _____   ☐ _____
☐ _____   ☐ _____
☐ _____   ☐ _____
☐ _____   ☐ _____
☐ _____   ☐ _____
☐ _____   ☐ _____
☐ _____   ☐ _____
☐ _____   ☐ _____
☐ _____   ☐ _____

SUGGESTIONS

If you don't know how to pray the Holy Rosary, you can get our book "Rosary for beginners" in the following link: www.vcrey.com/rosary-book

Some sacrifices that you can do include:

- Not drinking water or liquids during a meal.
- Abstain from meat on Fridays (which is also required by Holy Mother Church).
- Not eating candy or dessert during one day.
- Take a cold shower.
- Not eating meat in saturdays in honor of the Blessed Virgin Mary.
- Keep one hour of silence.
- Do not buy or sell in Sunday (which is also a commandment).
- Give food to the hungry.
- Give water to the thirsty.
- Visit the sick, and confort them.

IMPORTANT NOTES

☐ _____
☐ _____
☐ _____
☐ _____
☐ _____
☐ _____
☐ _____
☐ _____
☐ _____

YOUR SOUL'S GROWTH PLANNER

LONG LIVE CHRIST THE KING!

VIVA CRISTO REY.ORG

DATE: MONTH   DAY   YEAR

GOALS OF THE DAY

PRAYING THE ROSARY OF 15 DECADES................... ☐

READING THE HOLY BIBLE (15 MINUTES)............... ☐

DAILY SACRIFICES.. ☐

☐ _____   ☐ _____
☐ _____   ☐ _____
☐ _____   ☐ _____
☐ _____   ☐ _____
☐ _____   ☐ _____
☐ _____   ☐ _____
☐ _____   ☐ _____
☐ _____   ☐ _____
☐ _____   ☐ _____

SUGGESTIONS

If you don't know how to pray the Holy Rosary, you can get our book "Rosary for beginners" in the following link: www.vcrey.com/rosary-book

Some sacrifices that you can do include:

- Not drinking water or liquids during a meal.
- Abstain from meat on Fridays (which is also required by Holy Mother Church).
- Not eating candy or dessert during one day.
- Take a cold shower.
- Not eating meat in saturdays in honor of the Blessed Virgin Mary.
- Keep one hour of silence.
- Do not buy or sell in Sunday (which is also a commandment).
- Give food to the hungry.
- Give water to the thirsty.
- Visit the sick, and confort them.

IMPORTANT NOTES

☐ _____
☐ _____
☐ _____
☐ _____
☐ _____
☐ _____
☐ _____
☐ _____
☐ _____

YOUR SOUL'S GROWTH PLANNER

LONG LIVE CHRIST THE KING!

VIVA CRISTO REY.ORG

DATE: MONTH   DAY   YEAR

GOALS OF THE DAY

PRAYING THE ROSARY OF 15 DECADES................... ☐

READING THE HOLY BIBLE (15 MINUTES)............... ☐

DAILY SACRIFICES... ☐

☐ _____   ☐ _____

☐ _____   ☐ _____

☐ _____   ☐ _____

☐ _____   ☐ _____

☐ _____   ☐ _____

☐ _____   ☐ _____

☐ _____   ☐ _____

☐ _____   ☐ _____

☐ _____   ☐ _____

SUGGESTIONS

If you don't know how to pray the Holy Rosary, you can get our book "Rosary for beginners" in the following link: www.vcrey.com/rosary-book

Some sacrifices that you can do include:

- Not drinking water or liquids during a meal.
- Abstain from meat on Fridays (which is also required by Holy Mother Church).
- Not eating candy or dessert during one day.
- Take a cold shower.
- Not eating meat in saturdays in honor of the Blessed Virgin Mary.
- Keep one hour of silence.
- Do not buy or sell in Sunday (which is also a commandment).
- Give food to the hungry.
- Give water to the thirsty.
- Visit the sick, and confort them.

IMPORTANT NOTES

☐ _____

☐ _____

☐ _____

☐ _____

☐ _____

☐ _____

☐ _____

☐ _____

☐ _____

YOUR SOUL'S GROWTH PLANNER

LONG LIVE CHRIST THE KING!

VIVA CRISTO REY.ORG

DATE: MONTH   DAY   YEAR

GOALS OF THE DAY

PRAYING THE ROSARY OF 15 DECADES.................. ☐

READING THE HOLY BIBLE (15 MINUTES)............... ☐

DAILY SACRIFICES... ☐

☐ _____   ☐ _____
☐ _____   ☐ _____
☐ _____   ☐ _____
☐ _____   ☐ _____
☐ _____   ☐ _____
☐ _____   ☐ _____
☐ _____   ☐ _____
☐ _____   ☐ _____
☐ _____   ☐ _____

SUGGESTIONS

If you don't know how to pray the Holy Rosary, you can get our book "Rosary for beginners" in the following link: www.vcrey.com/rosary-book

Some sacrifices that you can do include:

- Not drinking water or liquids during a meal.
- Abstain from meat on Fridays (which is also required by Holy Mother Church).
- Not eating candy or dessert during one day.
- Take a cold shower.
- Not eating meat in saturdays in honor of the Blessed Virgin Mary.
- Keep one hour of silence.
- Do not buy or sell in Sunday (which is also a commandment).
- Give food to the hungry.
- Give water to the thirsty.
- Visit the sick, and confort them.

IMPORTANT NOTES

☐ _____
☐ _____
☐ _____
☐ _____
☐ _____
☐ _____
☐ _____
☐ _____
☐ _____

YOUR SOUL'S GROWTH PLANNER

LONG LIVE CHRIST THE KING!

VIVA CRISTO REY.ORG

DATE: MONTH   DAY   YEAR

GOALS OF THE DAY

PRAYING THE ROSARY OF 15 DECADES.................. ☐

READING THE HOLY BIBLE (15 MINUTES).............. ☐

DAILY SACRIFICES... ☐

☐ _____   ☐ _____

☐ _____   ☐ _____

☐ _____   ☐ _____

☐ _____   ☐ _____

☐ _____   ☐ _____

☐ _____   ☐ _____

☐ _____   ☐ _____

☐ _____   ☐ _____

☐ _____   ☐ _____

SUGGESTIONS

If you don't know how to pray the Holy Rosary, you can get our book "Rosary for beginners" in the following link: www.vcrey.com/rosary-book

Some sacrifices that you can do include:

- Not drinking water or liquids during a meal.
- Abstain from meat on Fridays (which is also required by Holy Mother Church).
- Not eating candy or dessert during one day.
- Take a cold shower.
- Not eating meat in saturdays in honor of the Blessed Virgin Mary.
- Keep one hour of silence.
- Do not buy or sell in Sunday (which is also a commandment).
- Give food to the hungry.
- Give water to the thirsty.
- Visit the sick, and confort them.

IMPORTANT NOTES

☐ _____

☐ _____

☐ _____

☐ _____

☐ _____

☐ _____

☐ _____

☐ _____

☐ _____

YOUR SOUL'S GROWTH PLANNER

LONG LIVE CHRIST THE KING!

VIVA
CRISTO
REY.ORG

DATE: MONTH   DAY   YEAR

GOALS OF THE DAY

PRAYING THE ROSARY OF 15 DECADES.................. ☐

READING THE HOLY BIBLE (15 MINUTES)............... ☐

DAILY SACRIFICES....................................... ☐

☐ _____   ☐ _____
☐ _____   ☐ _____
☐ _____   ☐ _____
☐ _____   ☐ _____
☐ _____   ☐ _____
☐ _____   ☐ _____
☐ _____   ☐ _____
☐ _____   ☐ _____
☐ _____   ☐ _____

SUGGESTIONS

If you don't know how to pray the Holy Rosary, you can get our book "Rosary for beginners" in the following link: www.vcrey.com/rosary-book

Some sacrifices that you can do include:

- Not drinking water or liquids during a meal.
- Abstain from meat on Fridays (which is also required by Holy Mother Church).
- Not eating candy or dessert during one day.
- Take a cold shower.
- Not eating meat in saturdays in honor of the Blessed Virgin Mary.
- Keep one hour of silence.
- Do not buy or sell in Sunday (which is also a commandment).
- Give food to the hungry.
- Give water to the thirsty.
- Visit the sick, and confort them.

IMPORTANT NOTES

☐ _____
☐ _____
☐ _____
☐ _____
☐ _____
☐ _____
☐ _____
☐ _____
☐ _____

YOUR SOUL'S GROWTH PLANNER

LONG LIVE CHRIST THE KING!

VIVA
CRISTO
REY.ORG

DATE: MONTH   DAY   YEAR

GOALS OF THE DAY

PRAYING THE ROSARY OF 15 DECADES................... ☐

READING THE HOLY BIBLE (15 MINUTES)............... ☐

DAILY SACRIFICES.. ☐

☐ _____   ☐ _____
☐ _____   ☐ _____
☐ _____   ☐ _____

☐ _____   ☐ _____
☐ _____   ☐ _____
☐ _____   ☐ _____

☐ _____   ☐ _____

☐ _____   ☐ _____
☐ _____   ☐ _____

SUGGESTIONS

If you don't know how to pray the Holy Rosary, you can get our book "Rosary for beginners" in the following link: www.vcrey.com/rosary-book

Some sacrifices that you can do include:

- Not drinking water or liquids during a meal.
- Abstain from meat on Fridays (which is also required by Holy Mother Church).
- Not eating candy or dessert during one day.
- Take a cold shower.
- Not eating meat in saturdays in honor of the Blessed Virgin Mary.
- Keep one hour of silence.
- Do not buy or sell in Sunday (which is also a commandment).
- Give food to the hungry.
- Give water to the thirsty.
- Visit the sick, and confort them.

IMPORTANT NOTES

☐ _____
☐ _____
☐ _____
☐ _____
☐ _____
☐ _____
☐ _____
☐ _____
☐ _____
☐ _____

YOUR SOUL'S GROWTH PLANNER

LONG LIVE CHRIST THE KING!

VIVA
CRISTO
REY.ORG

DATE: MONTH   DAY   YEAR

GOALS OF THE DAY

PRAYING THE ROSARY OF 15 DECADES................... ☐

READING THE HOLY BIBLE (15 MINUTES)............... ☐

DAILY SACRIFICES.. ☐

☐ _____   ☐ _____
☐ _____   ☐ _____
☐ _____   ☐ _____

☐ _____   ☐ _____
☐ _____   ☐ _____
☐ _____   ☐ _____
☐ _____   ☐ _____

☐ _____   ☐ _____
☐ _____   ☐ _____

SUGGESTIONS

If you don't know how to pray the Holy Rosary, you can get our book "Rosary for beginners" in the following link: www.vcrey.com/rosary-book

Some sacrifices that you can do include:

- Not drinking water or liquids during a meal.
- Abstain from meat on Fridays (which is also required by Holy Mother Church).
- Not eating candy or dessert during one day.
- Take a cold shower.
- Not eating meat in saturdays in honor of the Blessed Virgin Mary.
- Keep one hour of silence.
- Do not buy or sell in Sunday (which is also a commandment).
- Give food to the hungry.
- Give water to the thirsty.
- Visit the sick, and confort them.

IMPORTANT NOTES

☐ _____
☐ _____
☐ _____
☐ _____
☐ _____
☐ _____
☐ _____
☐ _____
☐ _____

YOUR SOUL'S GROWTH PLANNER

LONG LIVE CHRIST THE KING!

DATE: MONTH   DAY   YEAR

GOALS OF THE DAY

PRAYING THE ROSARY OF 15 DECADES................... ☐

READING THE HOLY BIBLE (15 MINUTES)............... ☐

DAILY SACRIFICES.. ☐

☐ _____   ☐ _____
☐ _____   ☐ _____
☐ _____   ☐ _____
☐ _____   ☐ _____
☐ _____   ☐ _____
☐ _____   ☐ _____
☐ _____   ☐ _____
☐ _____   ☐ _____
☐ _____   ☐ _____

SUGGESTIONS

If you don't know how to pray the Holy Rosary, you can get our book "Rosary for beginners" in the following link: www.vcrey.com/rosary_book

Some sacrifices that you can do include:

- Not drinking water or liquids during a meal.
- Abstain from meat on Fridays (which is also required by Holy Mother Church).
- Not eating candy or dessert during one day.
- Take a cold shower.
- Not eating meat in saturdays in honor of the Blessed Virgin Mary.
- Keep one hour of silence.
- Do not buy or sell in Sunday (which is also a commandment).
- Give food to the hungry.
- Give water to the thirsty.
- Visit the sick, and confort them.

IMPORTANT NOTES

☐ _____
☐ _____
☐ _____
☐ _____
☐ _____
☐ _____
☐ _____
☐ _____
☐ _____

YOUR SOUL'S GROWTH PLANNER

VIVA
CRISTO
REY.ORG

LONG LIVE CHRIST THE KING!

DATE: MONTH   DAY   YEAR

GOALS OF THE DAY

PRAYING THE ROSARY OF 15 DECADES................. ☐

READING THE HOLY BIBLE (15 MINUTES)............... ☐

DAILY SACRIFICES.. ☐

☐ _____   ☐ _____
☐ _____   ☐ _____
☐ _____   ☐ _____
☐ _____   ☐ _____
☐ _____   ☐ _____
☐ _____   ☐ _____
☐ _____   ☐ _____
☐ _____   ☐ _____
☐ _____   ☐ _____

SUGGESTIONS

If you don't know how to pray the Holy Rosary, you can get our book "Rosary for beginners" in the following link: www.vcrey.com/rosary-book

Some sacrifices that you can do include:

- Not drinking water or liquids during a meal.
- Abstain from meat on Fridays (which is also required by Holy Mother Church).
- Not eating candy or dessert during one day.
- Take a cold shower.
- Not eating meat in saturdays in honor of the Blessed Virgin Mary.
- Keep one hour of silence.
- Do not buy or sell in Sunday (which is also a commandment).
- Give food to the hungry.
- Give water to the thirsty.
- Visit the sick, and confort them.

IMPORTANT NOTES

☐ _____
☐ _____
☐ _____
☐ _____
☐ _____
☐ _____
☐ _____
☐ _____
☐ _____

YOUR SOUL'S GROWTH PLANNER

VIVA CRISTO REY.ORG

LONG LIVE CHRIST THE KING!

DATE: MONTH   DAY   YEAR

GOALS OF THE DAY

PRAYING THE ROSARY OF 15 DECADES................... ☐

READING THE HOLY BIBLE (15 MINUTES)................ ☐

DAILY SACRIFICES... ☐

☐ _____   ☐ _____
☐ _____   ☐ _____
☐ _____   ☐ _____

☐ _____   ☐ _____
☐ _____   ☐ _____
☐ _____   ☐ _____

☐ _____   ☐ _____

☐ _____   ☐ _____
☐ _____   ☐ _____

SUGGESTIONS

If you don't know how to pray the Holy Rosary, you can get our book "Rosary for beginners" in the following link: www.vcrey.com/rosary-book

Some sacrifices that you can do include:

- Not drinking water or liquids during a meal.
- Abstain from meat on Fridays (which is also required by Holy Mother Church).
- Not eating candy or dessert during one day.
- Take a cold shower.
- Not eating meat in saturdays in honor of the Blessed Virgin Mary.
- Keep one hour of silence.
- Do not buy or sell in Sunday (which is also a commandment).
- Give food to the hungry.
- Give water to the thirsty.
- Visit the sick, and confort them.

IMPORTANT NOTES

☐ _____
☐ _____
☐ _____
☐ _____
☐ _____
☐ _____
☐ _____
☐ _____
☐ _____

YOUR SOUL'S GROWTH PLANNER

LONG LIVE CHRIST THE KING!

VIVA
CRISTO
REY.ORG

DATE: MONTH   DAY   YEAR

GOALS OF THE DAY

PRAYING THE ROSARY OF 15 DECADES................... ☐

READING THE HOLY BIBLE (15 MINUTES)............... ☐

DAILY SACRIFICES... ☐

☐ _____   ☐ _____
☐ _____   ☐ _____
☐ _____   ☐ _____
☐ _____   ☐ _____
☐ _____   ☐ _____
☐ _____   ☐ _____
☐ _____   ☐ _____
☐ _____   ☐ _____
☐ _____   ☐ _____

SUGGESTIONS

If you don't know how to pray the Holy Rosary, you can get our book "Rosary for beginners" in the following link: www.vcrey.com/rosary-book

Some sacrifices that you can do include:

- Not drinking water or liquids during a meal.
- Abstain from meat on Fridays (which is also required by Holy Mother Church).
- Not eating candy or dessert during one day.
- Take a cold shower.
- Not eating meat in saturdays in honor of the Blessed Virgin Mary.
- Keep one hour of silence.
- Do not buy or sell in Sunday (which is also a commandment).
- Give food to the hungry.
- Give water to the thirsty.
- Visit the sick, and confort them.

IMPORTANT NOTES

☐ _____
☐ _____
☐ _____
☐ _____
☐ _____
☐ _____
☐ _____
☐ _____
☐ _____

YOUR SOUL'S GROWTH PLANNER

LONG LIVE CHRIST THE KING!

VIVA
CRISTO
REY.ORG

DATE: MONTH   DAY   YEAR

GOALS OF THE DAY

PRAYING THE ROSARY OF 15 DECADES.................... ☐

READING THE HOLY BIBLE (15 MINUTES)................ ☐

DAILY SACRIFICES... ☐

☐ _____   ☐ _____

☐ _____   ☐ _____

☐ _____   ☐ _____

☐ _____   ☐ _____

☐ _____   ☐ _____

☐ _____   ☐ _____

☐ _____   ☐ _____

☐ _____   ☐ _____

☐ _____   ☐ _____

SUGGESTIONS

If you don't know how to pray the Holy Rosary, you can get our book "Rosary for beginners" in the following link: www.vcrey.com/rosary-book

Some sacrifices that you can do include:

- Not drinking water or liquids during a meal.
- Abstain from meat on Fridays (which is also required by Holy Mother Church).
- Not eating candy or dessert during one day.
- Take a cold shower.
- Not eating meat in saturdays in honor of the Blessed Virgin Mary.
- Keep one hour of silence.
- Do not buy or sell in Sunday (which is also a commandment).
- Give food to the hungry.
- Give water to the thirsty.
- Visit the sick, and confort them.

IMPORTANT NOTES

☐ _____

☐ _____

☐ _____

☐ _____

☐ _____

☐ _____

☐ _____

☐ _____

☐ _____

YOUR SOUL'S GROWTH PLANNER

VIVA CRISTO REY.ORG

LONG LIVE CHRIST THE KING!

DATE: MONTH   DAY   YEAR

GOALS OF THE DAY

PRAYING THE ROSARY OF 15 DECADES................... ☐

READING THE HOLY BIBLE (15 MINUTES)............... ☐

DAILY SACRIFICES... ☐

☐ _____   ☐ _____
☐ _____   ☐ _____
☐ _____   ☐ _____
☐ _____   ☐ _____
☐ _____   ☐ _____
☐ _____   ☐ _____
☐ _____   ☐ _____
☐ _____   ☐ _____
☐ _____   ☐ _____

SUGGESTIONS

If you don't know how to pray the Holy Rosary, you can get our book "Rosary for beginners" in the following link: www.vcrey.com/rosary-book

Some sacrifices that you can do include:

- Not drinking water or liquids during a meal.
- Abstain from meat on Fridays (which is also required by Holy Mother Church).
- Not eating candy or dessert during one day.
- Take a cold shower.
- Not eating meat in saturdays in honor of the Blessed Virgin Mary.
- Keep one hour of silence.
- Do not buy or sell in Sunday (which is also a commandment).
- Give food to the hungry.
- Give water to the thirsty.
- Visit the sick, and confort them.

IMPORTANT NOTES

☐ _____
☐ _____
☐ _____
☐ _____
☐ _____
☐ _____
☐ _____
☐ _____
☐ _____

YOUR SOUL'S GROWTH PLANNER

LONG LIVE CHRIST THE KING!

VIVA CRISTO REY.ORG

DATE: MONTH DAY YEAR

GOALS OF THE DAY

PRAYING THE ROSARY OF 15 DECADES................... ☐

READING THE HOLY BIBLE (15 MINUTES)................ ☐

DAILY SACRIFICES... ☐

☐ _____   ☐ _____
☐ _____   ☐ _____
☐ _____   ☐ _____
☐ _____   ☐ _____
☐ _____   ☐ _____
☐ _____   ☐ _____
☐ _____   ☐ _____
☐ _____   ☐ _____
☐ _____   ☐ _____

SUGGESTIONS

If you don't know how to pray the Holy Rosary, you can get our book "Rosary for beginners" in the following link: www.vcrey.com/rosary-book

Some sacrifices that you can do include:

- Not drinking water or liquids during a meal.
- Abstain from meat on Fridays (which is also required by Holy Mother Church).
- Not eating candy or dessert during one day.
- Take a cold shower.
- Not eating meat in saturdays in honor of the Blessed Virgin Mary.
- Keep one hour of silence.
- Do not buy or sell in Sunday (which is also a commandment).
- Give food to the hungry.
- Give water to the thirsty.
- Visit the sick, and confort them.

IMPORTANT NOTES

☐ _____
☐ _____
☐ _____
☐ _____
☐ _____
☐ _____
☐ _____
☐ _____
☐ _____

YOUR SOUL'S GROWTH PLANNER

LONG LIVE CHRIST THE KING!

VIVA CRISTO REY.ORG

DATE: MONTH   DAY   YEAR

GOALS OF THE DAY

PRAYING THE ROSARY OF 15 DECADES................... ☐

READING THE HOLY BIBLE (15 MINUTES)............... ☐

DAILY SACRIFICES.. ☐

☐ _____   ☐ _____
☐ _____   ☐ _____
☐ _____   ☐ _____

☐ _____   ☐ _____
☐ _____   ☐ _____
☐ _____   ☐ _____
☐ _____   ☐ _____

☐ _____   ☐ _____
☐ _____   ☐ _____

SUGGESTIONS

If you don't know how to pray the Holy Rosary, you can get our book "Rosary for beginners" in the following link: www.vcrey.com/rosary-book

Some sacrifices that you can do include:

- Not drinking water or liquids during a meal.
- Abstain from meat on Fridays (which is also required by Holy Mother Church).
- Not eating candy or dessert during one day.
- Take a cold shower.
- Not eating meat in saturdays in honor of the Blessed Virgin Mary.
- Keep one hour of silence.
- Do not buy or sell in Sunday (which is also a commandment).
- Give food to the hungry.
- Give water to the thirsty.
- Visit the sick, and confort them.

IMPORTANT NOTES

☐ _____
☐ _____
☐ _____
☐ _____
☐ _____
☐ _____
☐ _____
☐ _____
☐ _____

YOUR SOUL'S GROWTH PLANNER

LONG LIVE CHRIST THE KING!

VIVA
CRISTO
REY.ORG

DATE: MONTH   DAY   YEAR

GOALS OF THE DAY

PRAYING THE ROSARY OF 15 DECADES................... ☐

READING THE HOLY BIBLE (15 MINUTES)............... ☐

DAILY SACRIFICES... ☐

☐ _____   ☐ _____
☐ _____   ☐ _____
☐ _____   ☐ _____
☐ _____   ☐ _____
☐ _____   ☐ _____
☐ _____   ☐ _____
☐ _____   ☐ _____
☐ _____   ☐ _____
☐ _____   ☐ _____

SUGGESTIONS

If you don't know how to pray the Holy Rosary, you can get our book "Rosary for beginners" in the following link: www.vcrey.com/rosary-book

Some sacrifices that you can do include:

- Not drinking water or liquids during a meal.
- Abstain from meat on Fridays (which is also required by Holy Mother Church).
- Not eating candy or dessert during one day.
- Take a cold shower.
- Not eating meat in saturdays in honor of the Blessed Virgin Mary.
- Keep one hour of silence.
- Do not buy or sell in Sunday (which is also a commandment).
- Give food to the hungry.
- Give water to the thirsty.
- Visit the sick, and confort them.

IMPORTANT NOTES

☐ _____
☐ _____
☐ _____
☐ _____
☐ _____
☐ _____
☐ _____
☐ _____

YOUR SOUL'S GROWTH PLANNER

LONG LIVE CHRIST THE KING!

VIVA
CRISTO
REY.ORG

DATE: MONTH   DAY   YEAR

GOALS OF THE DAY

PRAYING THE ROSARY OF 15 DECADES................... ☐

READING THE HOLY BIBLE (15 MINUTES)............... ☐

DAILY SACRIFICES... ☐

☐ _____   ☐ _____
☐ _____   ☐ _____
☐ _____   ☐ _____
☐ _____   ☐ _____
☐ _____   ☐ _____
☐ _____   ☐ _____
☐ _____   ☐ _____
☐ _____   ☐ _____
☐ _____   ☐ _____

SUGGESTIONS

If you don't know how to pray the Holy Rosary, you can get our book "Rosary for beginners" in the following link: www.vcrey.com/rosary-book

Some sacrifices that you can do include:

- Not drinking water or liquids during a meal.
- Abstain from meat on Fridays (which is also required by Holy Mother Church).
- Not eating candy or dessert during one day.
- Take a cold shower.
- Not eating meat in saturdays in honor of the Blessed Virgin Mary.
- Keep one hour of silence.
- Do not buy or sell in Sunday (which is also a commandment).
- Give food to the hungry.
- Give water to the thirsty.
- Visit the sick, and confort them.

IMPORTANT NOTES

☐ _____
☐ _____
☐ _____
☐ _____
☐ _____
☐ _____
☐ _____
☐ _____
☐ _____

YOUR SOUL'S GROWTH PLANNER

LONG LIVE CHRIST THE KING!

VIVA
CRISTO
REY.ORG

DATE: MONTH   DAY   YEAR

GOALS OF THE DAY

PRAYING THE ROSARY OF 15 DECADES................... ☐

READING THE HOLY BIBLE (15 MINUTES)................ ☐

DAILY SACRIFICES... ☐

☐ _____   ☐ _____

☐ _____   ☐ _____

☐ _____   ☐ _____

☐ _____   ☐ _____

☐ _____   ☐ _____

☐ _____   ☐ _____

☐ _____   ☐ _____

☐ _____   ☐ _____

☐ _____   ☐ _____

SUGGESTIONS

If you don't know how to pray the Holy Rosary, you can get our book "Rosary for beginners" in the following link: www.vcrey.com/rosary-book

Some sacrifices that you can do include:

- Not drinking water or liquids during a meal.
- Abstain from meat on Fridays (which is also required by Holy Mother Church).
- Not eating candy or dessert during one day.
- Take a cold shower.
- Not eating meat in saturdays in honor of the Blessed Virgin Mary.
- Keep one hour of silence.
- Do not buy or sell in Sunday (which is also a commandment).
- Give food to the hungry.
- Give water to the thirsty.
- Visit the sick, and confort them.

IMPORTANT NOTES

☐ _____

☐ _____

☐ _____

☐ _____

☐ _____

☐ _____

☐ _____

☐ _____

☐ _____

YOUR SOUL'S GROWTH PLANNER

LONG LIVE CHRIST THE KING!

VIVA CRISTO REY.ORG

DATE: MONTH   DAY   YEAR

GOALS OF THE DAY

PRAYING THE ROSARY OF 15 DECADES................... ☐

READING THE HOLY BIBLE (15 MINUTES)............... ☐

DAILY SACRIFICES.. ☐

☐ _____   ☐ _____
☐ _____   ☐ _____
☐ _____   ☐ _____
☐ _____   ☐ _____
☐ _____   ☐ _____
☐ _____   ☐ _____
☐ _____   ☐ _____
☐ _____   ☐ _____
☐ _____   ☐ _____

SUGGESTIONS

If you don't know how to pray the Holy Rosary, you can get our book "Rosary for beginners" in the following link: www.vcrey.com/rosary-book

Some sacrifices that you can do include:

- Not drinking water or liquids during a meal.
- Abstain from meat on Fridays (which is also required by Holy Mother Church).
- Not eating candy or dessert during one day.
- Take a cold shower.
- Not eating meat in saturdays in honor of the Blessed Virgin Mary.
- Keep one hour of silence.
- Do not buy or sell in Sunday (which is also a commandment).
- Give food to the hungry.
- Give water to the thirsty.
- Visit the sick, and confort them.

IMPORTANT NOTES

☐ _____
☐ _____
☐ _____
☐ _____
☐ _____
☐ _____
☐ _____
☐ _____
☐ _____

YOUR SOUL'S GROWTH PLANNER

LONG LIVE CHRIST THE KING!

VIVA CRISTO REY.ORG

DATE: MONTH   DAY   YEAR

GOALS OF THE DAY

PRAYING THE ROSARY OF 15 DECADES................... ☐

READING THE HOLY BIBLE (15 MINUTES)................ ☐

DAILY SACRIFICES... ☐

☐ _____   ☐ _____
☐ _____   ☐ _____
☐ _____   ☐ _____
☐ _____   ☐ _____
☐ _____   ☐ _____
☐ _____   ☐ _____
☐ _____   ☐ _____
☐ _____   ☐ _____
☐ _____   ☐ _____

SUGGESTIONS

If you don't know how to pray the Holy Rosary, you can get our book "Rosary for beginners" in the following link: www.vcrey.com/rosary-book

Some sacrifices that you can do include:

- Not drinking water or liquids during a meal.
- Abstain from meat on Fridays (which is also required by Holy Mother Church).
- Not eating candy or dessert during one day.
- Take a cold shower.
- Not eating meat in saturdays in honor of the Blessed Virgin Mary.
- Keep one hour of silence.
- Do not buy or sell in Sunday (which is also a commandment).
- Give food to the hungry.
- Give water to the thirsty.
- Visit the sick, and confort them.

IMPORTANT NOTES

☐ _____
☐ _____
☐ _____
☐ _____
☐ _____
☐ _____
☐ _____
☐ _____
☐ _____

YOUR SOUL'S GROWTH PLANNER

VIVA CRISTO REY.ORG

LONG LIVE CHRIST THE KING!

DATE: MONTH   DAY   YEAR

GOALS OF THE DAY

PRAYING THE ROSARY OF 15 DECADES.................. ☐

READING THE HOLY BIBLE (15 MINUTES)................ ☐

DAILY SACRIFICES.. ☐

☐ _____   ☐ _____
☐ _____   ☐ _____
☐ _____   ☐ _____

☐ _____   ☐ _____
☐ _____   ☐ _____
☐ _____   ☐ _____
☐ _____   ☐ _____

☐ _____   ☐ _____
☐ _____   ☐ _____

SUGGESTIONS

If you don't know how to pray the Holy Rosary, you can get our book "Rosary for beginners" in the following link: www.vcrey.com/rosary-book

Some sacrifices that you can do include:

- Not drinking water or liquids during a meal.
- Abstain from meat on Fridays (which is also required by Holy Mother Church).
- Not eating candy or dessert during one day.
- Take a cold shower.
- Not eating meat in saturdays in honor of the Blessed Virgin Mary.
- Keep one hour of silence.
- Do not buy or sell in Sunday (which is also a commandment).
- Give food to the hungry.
- Give water to the thirsty.
- Visit the sick, and confort them.

IMPORTANT NOTES

☐ _____
☐ _____
☐ _____
☐ _____
☐ _____
☐ _____
☐ _____
☐ _____
☐ _____

YOUR SOUL'S GROWTH PLANNER

LONG LIVE CHRIST THE KING!

VIVA CRISTO REY.ORG

DATE: MONTH   DAY   YEAR

GOALS OF THE DAY

PRAYING THE ROSARY OF 15 DECADES................... ☐

READING THE HOLY BIBLE (15 MINUTES)............... ☐

DAILY SACRIFICES... ☐

☐ _____   ☐ _____
☐ _____   ☐ _____
☐ _____   ☐ _____
☐ _____   ☐ _____
☐ _____   ☐ _____
☐ _____   ☐ _____
☐ _____   ☐ _____
☐ _____   ☐ _____
☐ _____   ☐ _____

SUGGESTIONS

If you don't know how to pray the Holy Rosary, you can get our book "Rosary for beginners" in the following link: www.vcrey.com/rosary-book

Some sacrifices that you can do include:

- Not drinking water or liquids during a meal.
- Abstain from meat on Fridays (which is also required by Holy Mother Church).
- Not eating candy or dessert during one day.
- Take a cold shower.
- Not eating meat in saturdays in honor of the Blessed Virgin Mary.
- Keep one hour of silence.
- Do not buy or sell in Sunday (which is also a commandment).
- Give food to the hungry.
- Give water to the thirsty.
- Visit the sick, and confort them.

IMPORTANT NOTES

☐ _____
☐ _____
☐ _____
☐ _____
☐ _____
☐ _____
☐ _____
☐ _____
☐ _____

YOUR SOUL'S GROWTH PLANNER

LONG LIVE CHRIST THE KING!

VIVA CRISTO REY.ORG

DATE: MONTH   DAY   YEAR

GOALS OF THE DAY

PRAYING THE ROSARY OF 15 DECADES................... ☐

READING THE HOLY BIBLE (15 MINUTES)................ ☐

DAILY SACRIFICES... ☐

☐ _____   ☐ _____
☐ _____   ☐ _____
☐ _____   ☐ _____
☐ _____   ☐ _____
☐ _____   ☐ _____
☐ _____   ☐ _____
☐ _____   ☐ _____
☐ _____   ☐ _____
☐ _____   ☐ _____

SUGGESTIONS

If you don't know how to pray the Holy Rosary, you can get our book "Rosary for beginners" in the following link: www.vcrey.com/rosary-book

Some sacrifices that you can do include:

- Not drinking water or liquids during a meal.
- Abstain from meat on Fridays (which is also required by Holy Mother Church).
- Not eating candy or dessert during one day.
- Take a cold shower.
- Not eating meat in saturdays in honor of the Blessed Virgin Mary.
- Keep one hour of silence.
- Do not buy or sell in Sunday (which is also a commandment).
- Give food to the hungry.
- Give water to the thirsty.
- Visit the sick, and confort them.

IMPORTANT NOTES

☐ _____
☐ _____
☐ _____
☐ _____
☐ _____
☐ _____
☐ _____
☐ _____
☐ _____

YOUR SOUL'S GROWTH PLANNER

LONG LIVE CHRIST THE KING!

VIVA CRISTO REY.ORG

DATE: MONTH   DAY   YEAR

GOALS OF THE DAY

PRAYING THE ROSARY OF 15 DECADES................... ☐

READING THE HOLY BIBLE (15 MINUTES)................ ☐

DAILY SACRIFICES... ☐

☐ _____   ☐ _____
☐ _____   ☐ _____
☐ _____   ☐ _____
☐ _____   ☐ _____
☐ _____   ☐ _____
☐ _____   ☐ _____
☐ _____   ☐ _____
☐ _____   ☐ _____
☐ _____   ☐ _____

SUGGESTIONS

If you don't know how to pray the Holy Rosary, you can get our book "Rosary for beginners" in the following link: www.vcrey.com/rosary-book

Some sacrifices that you can do include:

- Not drinking water or liquids during a meal.
- Abstain from meat on Fridays (which is also required by Holy Mother Church).
- Not eating candy or dessert during one day.
- Take a cold shower.
- Not eating meat in saturdays in honor of the Blessed Virgin Mary.
- Keep one hour of silence.
- Do not buy or sell in Sunday (which is also a commandment).
- Give food to the hungry.
- Give water to the thirsty.
- Visit the sick, and confort them.

IMPORTANT NOTES

☐ _____
☐ _____
☐ _____
☐ _____
☐ _____
☐ _____
☐ _____
☐ _____
☐ _____

YOUR SOUL'S GROWTH PLANNER

LONG LIVE CHRIST THE KING!

VIVA CRISTO REY.ORG

DATE: MONTH   DAY   YEAR

GOALS OF THE DAY

PRAYING THE ROSARY OF 15 DECADES.................. ☐

READING THE HOLY BIBLE (15 MINUTES)................ ☐

DAILY SACRIFICES... ☐

☐ _____   ☐ _____
☐ _____   ☐ _____
☐ _____   ☐ _____

☐ _____   ☐ _____
☐ _____   ☐ _____
☐ _____   ☐ _____
☐ _____   ☐ _____

☐ _____   ☐ _____
☐ _____   ☐ _____

SUGGESTIONS

If you don't know how to pray the Holy Rosary, you can get our book "Rosary for beginners" in the following link: www.vcrey.com/rosary-book

Some sacrifices that you can do include:

- Not drinking water or liquids during a meal.
- Abstain from meat on Fridays (which is also required by Holy Mother Church).
- Not eating candy or dessert during one day.
- Take a cold shower.
- Not eating meat in saturdays in honor of the Blessed Virgin Mary.
- Keep one hour of silence.
- Do not buy or sell in Sunday (which is also a commandment).
- Give food to the hungry.
- Give water to the thirsty.
- Visit the sick, and confort them.

IMPORTANT NOTES

☐ _____
☐ _____
☐ _____
☐ _____
☐ _____
☐ _____
☐ _____
☐ _____
☐ _____

YOUR SOUL'S GROWTH PLANNER

LONG LIVE CHRIST THE KING!

VIVA
CRISTO
REY.ORG

DATE: MONTH   DAY   YEAR

GOALS OF THE DAY

PRAYING THE ROSARY OF 15 DECADES.................. ☐

READING THE HOLY BIBLE (15 MINUTES)............... ☐

DAILY SACRIFICES.. ☐

☐ _____   ☐ _____
☐ _____   ☐ _____
☐ _____   ☐ _____
☐ _____   ☐ _____
☐ _____   ☐ _____
☐ _____   ☐ _____
☐ _____   ☐ _____
☐ _____   ☐ _____
☐ _____   ☐ _____

SUGGESTIONS

If you don't know how to pray the Holy Rosary, you can get our book "Rosary for beginners" in the following link: www.vcrey.com/rosary-book

Some sacrifices that you can do include:

- Not drinking water or liquids during a meal.
- Abstain from meat on Fridays (which is also required by Holy Mother Church).
- Not eating candy or dessert during one day.
- Take a cold shower.
- Not eating meat in saturdays in honor of the Blessed Virgin Mary.
- Keep one hour of silence.
- Do not buy or sell in Sunday (which is also a commandment).
- Give food to the hungry.
- Give water to the thirsty.
- Visit the sick, and confort them.

IMPORTANT NOTES

☐ _____
☐ _____
☐ _____
☐ _____
☐ _____
☐ _____
☐ _____
☐ _____
☐ _____

YOUR SOUL'S GROWTH PLANNER

LONG LIVE CHRIST THE KING!

VIVA CRISTO REY.ORG

DATE: MONTH   DAY   YEAR

GOALS OF THE DAY

PRAYING THE ROSARY OF 15 DECADES.................. ☐

READING THE HOLY BIBLE (15 MINUTES)............... ☐

DAILY SACRIFICES.. ☐

☐ _____   ☐ _____
☐ _____   ☐ _____
☐ _____   ☐ _____
☐ _____   ☐ _____
☐ _____   ☐ _____
☐ _____   ☐ _____
☐ _____   ☐ _____
☐ _____   ☐ _____
☐ _____   ☐ _____

SUGGESTIONS

If you don't know how to pray the Holy Rosary, you can get our book "Rosary for beginners" in the following link: www.vcrey.com/rosary-book

Some sacrifices that you can do include:

- Not drinking water or liquids during a meal.
- Abstain from meat on Fridays (which is also required by Holy Mother Church).
- Not eating candy or dessert during one day.
- Take a cold shower.
- Not eating meat in saturdays in honor of the Blessed Virgin Mary.
- Keep one hour of silence.
- Do not buy or sell in Sunday (which is also a commandment).
- Give food to the hungry.
- Give water to the thirsty.
- Visit the sick, and confort them.

IMPORTANT NOTES

☐ _____
☐ _____
☐ _____
☐ _____
☐ _____
☐ _____
☐ _____
☐ _____
☐ _____

YOUR SOUL'S GROWTH PLANNER

LONG LIVE CHRIST THE KING!

VIVA CRISTO REY.ORG

DATE: MONTH   DAY   YEAR

GOALS OF THE DAY

PRAYING THE ROSARY OF 15 DECADES.................. ☐

READING THE HOLY BIBLE (15 MINUTES)................ ☐

DAILY SACRIFICES... ☐

☐ _____   ☐ _____
☐ _____   ☐ _____
☐ _____   ☐ _____
☐ _____   ☐ _____
☐ _____   ☐ _____
☐ _____   ☐ _____
☐ _____   ☐ _____
☐ _____   ☐ _____
☐ _____   ☐ _____

SUGGESTIONS

If you don't know how to pray the Holy Rosary, you can get our book "Rosary for beginners" in the following link: www.vcrey.com/rosary-book

Some sacrifices that you can do include:

- Not drinking water or liquids during a meal.
- Abstain from meat on Fridays (which is also required by Holy Mother Church).
- Not eating candy or dessert during one day.
- Take a cold shower.
- Not eating meat in saturdays in honor of the Blessed Virgin Mary.
- Keep one hour of silence.
- Do not buy or sell in Sunday (which is also a commandment).
- Give food to the hungry.
- Give water to the thirsty.
- Visit the sick, and confort them.

IMPORTANT NOTES

☐ _____
☐ _____
☐ _____
☐ _____
☐ _____
☐ _____
☐ _____
☐ _____
☐ _____

YOUR SOUL'S GROWTH PLANNER

LONG LIVE CHRIST THE KING!

VIVA CRISTO REY.ORG

DATE: MONTH   DAY   YEAR

GOALS OF THE DAY

PRAYING THE ROSARY OF 15 DECADES................... ☐

READING THE HOLY BIBLE (15 MINUTES)................ ☐

DAILY SACRIFICES.. ☐

☐ _____   ☐ _____
☐ _____   ☐ _____
☐ _____   ☐ _____
☐ _____   ☐ _____
☐ _____   ☐ _____
☐ _____   ☐ _____
☐ _____   ☐ _____
☐ _____   ☐ _____
☐ _____   ☐ _____

SUGGESTIONS

If you don't know how to pray the Holy Rosary, you can get our book "Rosary for beginners" in the following link: www.vcrey.com/rosary-book

Some sacrifices that you can do include:

- Not drinking water or liquids during a meal.
- Abstain from meat on Fridays (which is also required by Holy Mother Church).
- Not eating candy or dessert during one day.
- Take a cold shower.
- Not eating meat in saturdays in honor of the Blessed Virgin Mary.
- Keep one hour of silence.
- Do not buy or sell in Sunday (which is also a commandment).
- Give food to the hungry.
- Give water to the thirsty.
- Visit the sick, and confort them.

IMPORTANT NOTES

☐ _____
☐ _____
☐ _____
☐ _____
☐ _____
☐ _____
☐ _____
☐ _____
☐ _____

YOUR SOUL'S GROWTH PLANNER

LONG LIVE CHRIST THE KING!

VIVA CRISTO REY.ORG

DATE: MONTH   DAY   YEAR

GOALS OF THE DAY

PRAYING THE ROSARY OF 15 DECADES................... ☐

READING THE HOLY BIBLE (15 MINUTES)............... ☐

DAILY SACRIFICES... ☐

☐ _____   ☐ _____

☐ _____   ☐ _____

☐ _____   ☐ _____

☐ _____   ☐ _____

☐ _____   ☐ _____

☐ _____   ☐ _____

☐ _____   ☐ _____

☐ _____   ☐ _____

SUGGESTIONS

If you don't know how to pray the Holy Rosary, you can get our book "Rosary for beginners" in the following link: www.vcrey.com/rosary-book

Some sacrifices that you can do include:

- Not drinking water or liquids during a meal.
- Abstain from meat on Fridays (which is also required by Holy Mother Church).
- Not eating candy or dessert during one day.
- Take a cold shower.
- Not eating meat in saturdays in honor of the Blessed Virgin Mary.
- Keep one hour of silence.
- Do not buy or sell in Sunday (which is also a commandment).
- Give food to the hungry.
- Give water to the thirsty.
- Visit the sick, and confort them.

IMPORTANT NOTES

☐ _____

☐ _____

☐ _____

☐ _____

☐ _____

☐ _____

☐ _____

☐ _____

☐ _____

YOUR SOUL'S GROWTH PLANNER

LONG LIVE CHRIST THE KING!

VIVA
CRISTO
REY.ORG

DATE: MONTH   DAY   YEAR

GOALS OF THE DAY

PRAYING THE ROSARY OF 15 DECADES................... ☐

READING THE HOLY BIBLE (15 MINUTES)................ ☐

DAILY SACRIFICES... ☐

☐ _____   ☐ _____

☐ _____   ☐ _____

☐ _____   ☐ _____

☐ _____   ☐ _____

☐ _____   ☐ _____

☐ _____   ☐ _____

☐ _____   ☐ _____

☐ _____   ☐ _____

☐ _____   ☐ _____

SUGGESTIONS

If you don't know how to pray the Holy Rosary, you can get our book "Rosary for beginners" in the following link: www.vcrey.com/rosary-book

Some sacrifices that you can do include:

- Not drinking water or liquids during a meal.
- Abstain from meat on Fridays (which is also required by Holy Mother Church).
- Not eating candy or dessert during one day.
- Take a cold shower.
- Not eating meat in saturdays in honor of the Blessed Virgin Mary.
- Keep one hour of silence.
- Do not buy or sell in Sunday (which is also a commandment).
- Give food to the hungry.
- Give water to the thirsty.
- Visit the sick, and confort them.

IMPORTANT NOTES

☐ _____

☐ _____

☐ _____

☐ _____

☐ _____

☐ _____

☐ _____

☐ _____

☐ _____

YOUR SOUL'S GROWTH PLANNER

LONG LIVE CHRIST THE KING!

VIVA CRISTO REY.ORG

DATE: MONTH   DAY   YEAR

GOALS OF THE DAY

PRAYING THE ROSARY OF 15 DECADES.................. ☐

READING THE HOLY BIBLE (15 MINUTES)............... ☐

DAILY SACRIFICES... ☐

☐ _____   ☐ _____
☐ _____   ☐ _____
☐ _____   ☐ _____
☐ _____   ☐ _____
☐ _____   ☐ _____
☐ _____   ☐ _____
☐ _____   ☐ _____
☐ _____   ☐ _____
☐ _____   ☐ _____

SUGGESTIONS

If you don't know how to pray the Holy Rosary, you can get our book "Rosary for beginners" in the following link: www.vcrey.com/rosary-book

Some sacrifices that you can do include:

- Not drinking water or liquids during a meal.
- Abstain from meat on Fridays (which is also required by Holy Mother Church).
- Not eating candy or dessert during one day.
- Take a cold shower.
- Not eating meat in saturdays in honor of the Blessed Virgin Mary.
- Keep one hour of silence.
- Do not buy or sell in Sunday (which is also a commandment).
- Give food to the hungry.
- Give water to the thirsty.
- Visit the sick, and confort them.

IMPORTANT NOTES

☐ _____
☐ _____
☐ _____
☐ _____
☐ _____
☐ _____
☐ _____
☐ _____
☐ _____

YOUR SOUL'S GROWTH PLANNER

LONG LIVE CHRIST THE KING!

VIVA CRISTO REY.ORG

DATE: MONTH   DAY   YEAR

GOALS OF THE DAY

PRAYING THE ROSARY OF 15 DECADES.................... ☐

READING THE HOLY BIBLE (15 MINUTES)................ ☐

DAILY SACRIFICES... ☐

☐ _____   ☐ _____
☐ _____   ☐ _____
☐ _____   ☐ _____
☐ _____   ☐ _____
☐ _____   ☐ _____
☐ _____   ☐ _____
☐ _____   ☐ _____
☐ _____   ☐ _____
☐ _____   ☐ _____

SUGGESTIONS

If you don't know how to pray the Holy Rosary, you can get our book "Rosary for beginners" in the following link: www.vcrey.com/rosary-book

Some sacrifices that you can do include:

- Not drinking water or liquids during a meal.
- Abstain from meat on Fridays (which is also required by Holy Mother Church).
- Not eating candy or dessert during one day.
- Take a cold shower.
- Not eating meat in saturdays in honor of the Blessed Virgin Mary.
- Keep one hour of silence.
- Do not buy or sell in Sunday (which is also a commandment).
- Give food to the hungry.
- Give water to the thirsty.
- Visit the sick, and confort them.

IMPORTANT NOTES

☐ _____
☐ _____
☐ _____
☐ _____
☐ _____
☐ _____
☐ _____
☐ _____
☐ _____

YOUR SOUL'S GROWTH PLANNER

LONG LIVE CHRIST THE KING!

VIVA
CRISTO
REY.ORG

DATE: MONTH   DAY   YEAR

GOALS OF THE DAY

PRAYING THE ROSARY OF 15 DECADES.................... ☐

READING THE HOLY BIBLE (15 MINUTES)................ ☐

DAILY SACRIFICES... ☐

☐ _____   ☐ _____
☐ _____   ☐ _____
☐ _____   ☐ _____
☐ _____   ☐ _____
☐ _____   ☐ _____
☐ _____   ☐ _____
☐ _____   ☐ _____
☐ _____   ☐ _____
☐ _____   ☐ _____

SUGGESTIONS

If you don't know how to pray the Holy Rosary, you can get our book "Rosary for beginners" in the following link: www.vcrey.com/rosary-book

Some sacrifices that you can do include:

- Not drinking water or liquids during a meal.
- Abstain from meat on Fridays (which is also required by Holy Mother Church).
- Not eating candy or dessert during one day.
- Take a cold shower.
- Not eating meat in saturdays in honor of the Blessed Virgin Mary.
- Keep one hour of silence.
- Do not buy or sell in Sunday (which is also a commandment).
- Give food to the hungry.
- Give water to the thirsty.
- Visit the sick, and confort them.

IMPORTANT NOTES

☐ _____
☐ _____
☐ _____
☐ _____
☐ _____
☐ _____
☐ _____
☐ _____
☐ _____

YOUR SOUL'S GROWTH PLANNER

LONG LIVE CHRIST THE KING!

VIVA
CRISTO
REY.ORG

DATE: MONTH   DAY   YEAR

GOALS OF THE DAY

PRAYING THE ROSARY OF 15 DECADES................... ☐

READING THE HOLY BIBLE (15 MINUTES)............... ☐

DAILY SACRIFICES... ☐

☐ _____   ☐ _____
☐ _____   ☐ _____
☐ _____   ☐ _____
☐ _____   ☐ _____
☐ _____   ☐ _____
☐ _____   ☐ _____
☐ _____   ☐ _____
☐ _____   ☐ _____
☐ _____   ☐ _____

SUGGESTIONS

If you don't know how to pray the Holy Rosary, you can get our book "Rosary for beginners" in the following link: www.vcrey.com/rosary-book

Some sacrifices that you can do include:

- Not drinking water or liquids during a meal.
- Abstain from meat on Fridays (which is also required by Holy Mother Church).
- Not eating candy or dessert during one day.
- Take a cold shower.
- Not eating meat in saturdays in honor of the Blessed Virgin Mary.
- Keep one hour of silence.
- Do not buy or sell in Sunday (which is also a commandment).
- Give food to the hungry.
- Give water to the thirsty.
- Visit the sick, and confort them.

IMPORTANT NOTES

☐ _____
☐ _____
☐ _____
☐ _____
☐ _____
☐ _____
☐ _____
☐ _____
☐ _____

YOUR SOUL'S GROWTH PLANNER

LONG LIVE CHRIST THE KING!

DATE: MONTH   DAY   YEAR

GOALS OF THE DAY

PRAYING THE ROSARY OF 15 DECADES.................. ☐

READING THE HOLY BIBLE (15 MINUTES)............... ☐

DAILY SACRIFICES... ☐

☐ _____   ☐ _____
☐ _____   ☐ _____
☐ _____   ☐ _____
☐ _____   ☐ _____
☐ _____   ☐ _____
☐ _____   ☐ _____
☐ _____   ☐ _____
☐ _____   ☐ _____
☐ _____   ☐ _____

SUGGESTIONS

If you don't know how to pray the Holy Rosary, you can get our book "Rosary for beginners" in the following link: www.vcrey.com/rosary-book

Some sacrifices that you can do include:

- Not drinking water or liquids during a meal.
- Abstain from meat on Fridays (which is also required by Holy Mother Church).
- Not eating candy or dessert during one day.
- Take a cold shower.
- Not eating meat in saturdays in honor of the Blessed Virgin Mary.
- Keep one hour of silence.
- Do not buy or sell in Sunday (which is also a commandment).
- Give food to the hungry.
- Give water to the thirsty.
- Visit the sick, and confort them.

IMPORTANT NOTES

☐ _____
☐ _____
☐ _____
☐ _____
☐ _____
☐ _____
☐ _____
☐ _____
☐ _____

YOUR SOUL'S GROWTH PLANNER

LONG LIVE CHRIST THE KING!

DATE: MONTH   DAY   YEAR

GOALS OF THE DAY

PRAYING THE ROSARY OF 15 DECADES................... ☐

READING THE HOLY BIBLE (15 MINUTES)............... ☐

DAILY SACRIFICES.. ☐

☐ _____   ☐ _____
☐ _____   ☐ _____
☐ _____   ☐ _____

☐ _____   ☐ _____
☐ _____   ☐ _____
☐ _____   ☐ _____
☐ _____   ☐ _____

☐ _____   ☐ _____
☐ _____   ☐ _____

SUGGESTIONS

If you don't know how to pray the Holy Rosary, you can get our book "Rosary for beginners" in the following link: www.vcrey.com/rosary-book

Some sacrifices that you can do include:

- Not drinking water or liquids during a meal.
- Abstain from meat on Fridays (which is also required by Holy Mother Church).
- Not eating candy or dessert during one day.
- Take a cold shower.
- Not eating meat in saturdays in honor of the Blessed Virgin Mary.
- Keep one hour of silence.
- Do not buy or sell in Sunday (which is also a commandment).
- Give food to the hungry.
- Give water to the thirsty.
- Visit the sick, and confort them.

IMPORTANT NOTES

☐ _____
☐ _____
☐ _____
☐ _____
☐ _____
☐ _____
☐ _____
☐ _____
☐ _____

YOUR SOUL'S GROWTH PLANNER

LONG LIVE CHRIST THE KING!

VIVA CRISTO REY.ORG

DATE: MONTH   DAY   YEAR

GOALS OF THE DAY

PRAYING THE ROSARY OF 15 DECADES.................. ☐

READING THE HOLY BIBLE (15 MINUTES)............... ☐

DAILY SACRIFICES... ☐

☐ _____   ☐ _____
☐ _____   ☐ _____
☐ _____   ☐ _____
☐ _____   ☐ _____
☐ _____   ☐ _____
☐ _____   ☐ _____
☐ _____   ☐ _____
☐ _____   ☐ _____
☐ _____   ☐ _____

SUGGESTIONS

If you don't know how to pray the Holy Rosary, you can get our book "Rosary for beginners" in the following link: www.vcrey.com/rosary-book

Some sacrifices that you can do include:

- Not drinking water or liquids during a meal.
- Abstain from meat on Fridays (which is also required by Holy Mother Church).
- Not eating candy or dessert during one day.
- Take a cold shower.
- Not eating meat in saturdays in honor of the Blessed Virgin Mary.
- Keep one hour of silence.
- Do not buy or sell in Sunday (which is also a commandment).
- Give food to the hungry.
- Give water to the thirsty.
- Visit the sick, and confort them.

IMPORTANT NOTES

☐ _____
☐ _____
☐ _____
☐ _____
☐ _____
☐ _____
☐ _____
☐ _____
☐ _____

YOUR SOUL'S GROWTH PLANNER

LONG LIVE CHRIST THE KING!

VIVA
CRISTO
REY.ORG

DATE: MONTH   DAY   YEAR

GOALS OF THE DAY

PRAYING THE ROSARY OF 15 DECADES................... ☐

READING THE HOLY BIBLE (15 MINUTES)................ ☐

DAILY SACRIFICES...................................... ☐

☐ _____   ☐ _____
☐ _____   ☐ _____
☐ _____   ☐ _____
☐ _____   ☐ _____
☐ _____   ☐ _____
☐ _____   ☐ _____
☐ _____   ☐ _____
☐ _____   ☐ _____
☐ _____   ☐ _____

SUGGESTIONS

If you don't know how to pray the Holy Rosary, you can get our book "Rosary for beginners" in the following link: www.vcrey.com/rosary-book

Some sacrifices that you can do include:

- Not drinking water or liquids during a meal.
- Abstain from meat on Fridays (which is also required by Holy Mother Church).
- Not eating candy or dessert during one day.
- Take a cold shower.
- Not eating meat in saturdays in honor of the Blessed Virgin Mary.
- Keep one hour of silence.
- Do not buy or sell in Sunday (which is also a commandment).
- Give food to the hungry.
- Give water to the thirsty.
- Visit the sick, and confort them.

IMPORTANT NOTES

☐ _____
☐ _____
☐ _____
☐ _____
☐ _____
☐ _____
☐ _____
☐ _____
☐ _____

YOUR SOUL'S GROWTH PLANNER

LONG LIVE CHRIST THE KING!

VIVA
CRISTO
REY.ORG

DATE: MONTH   DAY   YEAR

GOALS OF THE DAY

PRAYING THE ROSARY OF 15 DECADES.................... ☐

READING THE HOLY BIBLE (15 MINUTES)................ ☐

DAILY SACRIFICES.. ☐

☐ _____   ☐ _____

☐ _____   ☐ _____

☐ _____   ☐ _____

☐ _____   ☐ _____

☐ _____   ☐ _____

☐ _____   ☐ _____

☐ _____   ☐ _____

☐ _____   ☐ _____

☐ _____   ☐ _____

SUGGESTIONS

If you don't know how to pray the Holy Rosary, you can get our book "Rosary for beginners" in the following link: www.vcrey.com/rosary-book

Some sacrifices that you can do include:

- Not drinking water or liquids during a meal.
- Abstain from meat on Fridays (which is also required by Holy Mother Church).
- Not eating candy or dessert during one day.
- Take a cold shower.
- Not eating meat in saturdays in honor of the Blessed Virgin Mary.
- Keep one hour of silence.
- Do not buy or sell in Sunday (which is also a commandment).
- Give food to the hungry.
- Give water to the thirsty.
- Visit the sick, and confort them.

IMPORTANT NOTES

☐ _____

☐ _____

☐ _____

☐ _____

☐ _____

☐ _____

☐ _____

☐ _____

☐ _____

YOUR SOUL'S GROWTH PLANNER

LONG LIVE CHRIST THE KING!

VIVA CRISTO REY.ORG

DATE: MONTH   DAY   YEAR

GOALS OF THE DAY

PRAYING THE ROSARY OF 15 DECADES................. ☐

READING THE HOLY BIBLE (15 MINUTES)............... ☐

DAILY SACRIFICES.. ☐

☐ _____   ☐ _____
☐ _____   ☐ _____
☐ _____   ☐ _____

☐ _____   ☐ _____
☐ _____   ☐ _____
☐ _____   ☐ _____
☐ _____   ☐ _____

☐ _____   ☐ _____
☐ _____   ☐ _____

SUGGESTIONS

If you don't know how to pray the Holy Rosary, you can get our book "Rosary for beginners" in the following link: www.vcrey.com/rosary-book

Some sacrifices that you can do include:

- Not drinking water or liquids during a meal.
- Abstain from meat on Fridays (which is also required by Holy Mother Church).
- Not eating candy or dessert during one day.
- Take a cold shower.
- Not eating meat in saturdays in honor of the Blessed Virgin Mary.
- Keep one hour of silence.
- Do not buy or sell in Sunday (which is also a commandment).
- Give food to the hungry.
- Give water to the thirsty.
- Visit the sick, and confort them.

IMPORTANT NOTES

☐ _____
☐ _____
☐ _____
☐ _____
☐ _____
☐ _____
☐ _____
☐ _____
☐ _____

YOUR SOUL'S GROWTH PLANNER

LONG LIVE CHRIST THE KING!

VIVA
CRISTO
REY.ORG

DATE: MONTH   DAY   YEAR

GOALS OF THE DAY

PRAYING THE ROSARY OF 15 DECADES................... ☐

READING THE HOLY BIBLE (15 MINUTES)............... ☐

DAILY SACRIFICES.. ☐

☐ _____   ☐ _____
☐ _____   ☐ _____
☐ _____   ☐ _____
☐ _____   ☐ _____
☐ _____   ☐ _____
☐ _____   ☐ _____
☐ _____   ☐ _____
☐ _____   ☐ _____
☐ _____   ☐ _____

SUGGESTIONS

If you don't know how to pray the Holy Rosary, you can get our book "Rosary for beginners" in the following link: www.vcrey.com/rosary-book

Some sacrifices that you can do include:

- Not drinking water or liquids during a meal.
- Abstain from meat on Fridays (which is also required by Holy Mother Church).
- Not eating candy or dessert during one day.
- Take a cold shower.
- Not eating meat in saturdays in honor of the Blessed Virgin Mary.
- Keep one hour of silence.
- Do not buy or sell in Sunday (which is also a commandment).
- Give food to the hungry.
- Give water to the thirsty.
- Visit the sick, and confort them.

IMPORTANT NOTES

☐ _____
☐ _____
☐ _____
☐ _____
☐ _____
☐ _____
☐ _____
☐ _____
☐ _____

YOUR SOUL'S GROWTH PLANNER

LONG LIVE CHRIST THE KING!

VIVA CRISTO REY.ORG

DATE: MONTH   DAY   YEAR

GOALS OF THE DAY

PRAYING THE ROSARY OF 15 DECADES................... ☐

READING THE HOLY BIBLE (15 MINUTES)............... ☐

DAILY SACRIFICES... ☐

☐ _____   ☐ _____
☐ _____   ☐ _____
☐ _____   ☐ _____

☐ _____   ☐ _____
☐ _____   ☐ _____
☐ _____   ☐ _____
☐ _____   ☐ _____

☐ _____   ☐ _____
☐ _____   ☐ _____

SUGGESTIONS

If you don't know how to pray the Holy Rosary, you can get our book "Rosary for beginners" in the following link: www.vcrey.com/rosary-book

Some sacrifices that you can do include:

- Not drinking water or liquids during a meal.
- Abstain from meat on Fridays (which is also required by Holy Mother Church).
- Not eating candy or dessert during one day.
- Take a cold shower.
- Not eating meat in saturdays in honor of the Blessed Virgin Mary.
- Keep one hour of silence.
- Do not buy or sell in Sunday (which is also a commandment).
- Give food to the hungry.
- Give water to the thirsty.
- Visit the sick, and confort them.

IMPORTANT NOTES

☐ _____
☐ _____
☐ _____
☐ _____
☐ _____
☐ _____
☐ _____
☐ _____
☐ _____

YOUR SOUL'S GROWTH PLANNER

LONG LIVE CHRIST THE KING!

VIVA
CRISTO
REY.ORG

DATE: MONTH   DAY   YEAR

GOALS OF THE DAY

PRAYING THE ROSARY OF 15 DECADES.................. ☐

READING THE HOLY BIBLE (15 MINUTES)............... ☐

DAILY SACRIFICES... ☐

☐ _____   ☐ _____

☐ _____   ☐ _____

☐ _____   ☐ _____

☐ _____   ☐ _____

☐ _____   ☐ _____

☐ _____   ☐ _____

☐ _____   ☐ _____

☐ _____   ☐ _____

☐ _____   ☐ _____

SUGGESTIONS

If you don't know how to pray the Holy Rosary, you can get our book "Rosary for beginners" in the following link: www.vcrey.com/rosary-book

Some sacrifices that you can do include:

- Not drinking water or liquids during a meal.
- Abstain from meat on Fridays (which is also required by Holy Mother Church).
- Not eating candy or dessert during one day.
- Take a cold shower.
- Not eating meat in saturdays in honor of the Blessed Virgin Mary.
- Keep one hour of silence.
- Do not buy or sell in Sunday (which is also a commandment).
- Give food to the hungry.
- Give water to the thirsty.
- Visit the sick, and confort them.

IMPORTANT NOTES

☐ _____

☐ _____

☐ _____

☐ _____

☐ _____

☐ _____

☐ _____

☐ _____

☐ _____

YOUR SOUL'S GROWTH PLANNER

LONG LIVE CHRIST THE KING!

VIVA CRISTO REY.ORG

DATE: MONTH   DAY   YEAR

GOALS OF THE DAY

PRAYING THE ROSARY OF 15 DECADES.................. ☐

READING THE HOLY BIBLE (15 MINUTES)............... ☐

DAILY SACRIFICES... ☐

☐ _____   ☐ _____
☐ _____   ☐ _____
☐ _____   ☐ _____

☐ _____   ☐ _____
☐ _____   ☐ _____
☐ _____   ☐ _____
☐ _____   ☐ _____

☐ _____   ☐ _____
☐ _____   ☐ _____

SUGGESTIONS

If you don't know how to pray the Holy Rosary, you can get our book "Rosary for beginners" in the following link: www.vcrey.com/rosary-book

Some sacrifices that you can do include:

- Not drinking water or liquids during a meal.
- Abstain from meat on Fridays (which is also required by Holy Mother Church).
- Not eating candy or dessert during one day.
- Take a cold shower.
- Not eating meat in saturdays in honor of the Blessed Virgin Mary.
- Keep one hour of silence.
- Do not buy or sell in Sunday (which is also a commandment).
- Give food to the hungry.
- Give water to the thirsty.
- Visit the sick, and confort them.

IMPORTANT NOTES

☐ _____
☐ _____
☐ _____
☐ _____
☐ _____
☐ _____
☐ _____
☐ _____
☐ _____

YOUR SOUL'S GROWTH PLANNER

LONG LIVE CHRIST THE KING!

VIVA CRISTO REY.ORG

DATE: MONTH   DAY   YEAR

GOALS OF THE DAY

PRAYING THE ROSARY OF 15 DECADES.................. ☐

READING THE HOLY BIBLE (15 MINUTES)............... ☐

DAILY SACRIFICES... ☐

☐ _____   ☐ _____

☐ _____   ☐ _____

☐ _____   ☐ _____

☐ _____   ☐ _____

☐ _____   ☐ _____

☐ _____   ☐ _____

☐ _____   ☐ _____

☐ _____   ☐ _____

☐ _____   ☐ _____

SUGGESTIONS

If you don't know how to pray the Holy Rosary, you can get our book "Rosary for beginners" in the following link: www.vcrey.com/rosary-book

Some sacrifices that you can do include:

- Not drinking water or liquids during a meal.
- Abstain from meat on Fridays (which is also required by Holy Mother Church).
- Not eating candy or dessert during one day.
- Take a cold shower.
- Not eating meat in saturdays in honor of the Blessed Virgin Mary.
- Keep one hour of silence.
- Do not buy or sell in Sunday (which is also a commandment).
- Give food to the hungry.
- Give water to the thirsty.
- Visit the sick, and confort them.

IMPORTANT NOTES

☐ _____

☐ _____

☐ _____

☐ _____

☐ _____

☐ _____

☐ _____

☐ _____

☐ _____

YOUR SOUL'S GROWTH PLANNER

LONG LIVE CHRIST THE KING!

VIVA CRISTO REY.ORG

DATE: MONTH   DAY   YEAR

GOALS OF THE DAY

PRAYING THE ROSARY OF 15 DECADES................... ☐

READING THE HOLY BIBLE (15 MINUTES)............... ☐

DAILY SACRIFICES... ☐

☐ _____   ☐ _____
☐ _____   ☐ _____
☐ _____   ☐ _____
☐ _____   ☐ _____
☐ _____   ☐ _____
☐ _____   ☐ _____
☐ _____   ☐ _____
☐ _____   ☐ _____
☐ _____   ☐ _____

SUGGESTIONS

If you don't know how to pray the Holy Rosary, you can get our book "Rosary for beginners" in the following link: www.vcrey.com/rosary-book

Some sacrifices that you can do include:

- Not drinking water or liquids during a meal.
- Abstain from meat on Fridays (which is also required by Holy Mother Church).
- Not eating candy or dessert during one day.
- Take a cold shower.
- Not eating meat in saturdays in honor of the Blessed Virgin Mary.
- Keep one hour of silence.
- Do not buy or sell in Sunday (which is also a commandment).
- Give food to the hungry.
- Give water to the thirsty.
- Visit the sick, and confort them.

IMPORTANT NOTES

☐ _____
☐ _____
☐ _____
☐ _____
☐ _____
☐ _____
☐ _____
☐ _____
☐ _____

YOUR SOUL'S GROWTH PLANNER

LONG LIVE CHRIST THE KING!

VIVA
CRISTO
REY.ORG

DATE: MONTH   DAY   YEAR

GOALS OF THE DAY

PRAYING THE ROSARY OF 15 DECADES................... ☐

READING THE HOLY BIBLE (15 MINUTES)................ ☐

DAILY SACRIFICES... ☐

☐ _____   ☐ _____

☐ _____   ☐ _____

☐ _____   ☐ _____

☐ _____   ☐ _____

☐ _____   ☐ _____

☐ _____   ☐ _____

☐ _____   ☐ _____

☐ _____   ☐ _____

☐ _____

SUGGESTIONS

If you don't know how to pray the Holy Rosary, you can get our book "Rosary for beginners" in the following link: www.vcrey.com/rosary-book

Some sacrifices that you can do include:

- Not drinking water or liquids during a meal.
- Abstain from meat on Fridays (which is also required by Holy Mother Church).
- Not eating candy or dessert during one day.
- Take a cold shower.
- Not eating meat in saturdays in honor of the Blessed Virgin Mary.
- Keep one hour of silence.
- Do not buy or sell in Sunday (which is also a commandment).
- Give food to the hungry.
- Give water to the thirsty.
- Visit the sick, and confort them.

IMPORTANT NOTES

☐ _____

☐ _____

☐ _____

☐ _____

☐ _____

☐ _____

☐ _____

☐ _____

☐ _____

YOUR SOUL'S GROWTH PLANNER

LONG LIVE CHRIST THE KING!

VIVA CRISTO REY.ORG

DATE: MONTH   DAY   YEAR

GOALS OF THE DAY

PRAYING THE ROSARY OF 15 DECADES................... ☐

READING THE HOLY BIBLE (15 MINUTES)............... ☐

DAILY SACRIFICES.. ☐

☐ _____   ☐ _____
☐ _____   ☐ _____
☐ _____   ☐ _____
☐ _____   ☐ _____
☐ _____   ☐ _____
☐ _____   ☐ _____
☐ _____   ☐ _____
☐ _____   ☐ _____
☐ _____   ☐ _____

SUGGESTIONS

If you don't know how to pray the Holy Rosary, you can get our book "Rosary for beginners" in the following link: www.vcrey.com/rosary-book

Some sacrifices that you can do include:

- Not drinking water or liquids during a meal.
- Abstain from meat on Fridays (which is also required by Holy Mother Church).
- Not eating candy or dessert during one day.
- Take a cold shower.
- Not eating meat in saturdays in honor of the Blessed Virgin Mary.
- Keep one hour of silence.
- Do not buy or sell in Sunday (which is also a commandment).
- Give food to the hungry.
- Give water to the thirsty.
- Visit the sick, and confort them.

IMPORTANT NOTES

☐ _____
☐ _____
☐ _____
☐ _____
☐ _____
☐ _____
☐ _____
☐ _____
☐ _____

YOUR SOUL'S GROWTH PLANNER

LONG LIVE CHRIST THE KING!

VIVA CRISTO REY.ORG

DATE: MONTH   DAY   YEAR

GOALS OF THE DAY

PRAYING THE ROSARY OF 15 DECADES................... ☐

READING THE HOLY BIBLE (15 MINUTES)................ ☐

DAILY SACRIFICES... ☐

☐ _____   ☐ _____

☐ _____   ☐ _____

☐ _____   ☐ _____

☐ _____   ☐ _____

☐ _____   ☐ _____

☐ _____   ☐ _____

☐ _____   ☐ _____

☐ _____   ☐ _____

☐ _____   ☐ _____

SUGGESTIONS

If you don't know how to pray the Holy Rosary, you can get our book "Rosary for beginners" in the following link: www.vcrey.com/rosary-book

Some sacrifices that you can do include:

- Not drinking water or liquids during a meal.
- Abstain from meat on Fridays (which is also required by Holy Mother Church).
- Not eating candy or dessert during one day.
- Take a cold shower.
- Not eating meat in saturdays in honor of the Blessed Virgin Mary.
- Keep one hour of silence.
- Do not buy or sell in Sunday (which is also a commandment).
- Give food to the hungry.
- Give water to the thirsty.
- Visit the sick, and confort them.

IMPORTANT NOTES

☐ _____

☐ _____

☐ _____

☐ _____

☐ _____

☐ _____

☐ _____

☐ _____

☐ _____

YOUR SOUL'S GROWTH PLANNER

LONG LIVE CHRIST THE KING!

VIVA
CRISTO
REY.ORG

DATE: MONTH   DAY   YEAR

GOALS OF THE DAY

PRAYING THE ROSARY OF 15 DECADES................... ☐

READING THE HOLY BIBLE (15 MINUTES)............... ☐

DAILY SACRIFICES.. ☐

☐ _____   ☐ _____
☐ _____   ☐ _____
☐ _____   ☐ _____
☐ _____   ☐ _____
☐ _____   ☐ _____
☐ _____   ☐ _____
☐ _____   ☐ _____
☐ _____   ☐ _____
☐ _____   ☐ _____

SUGGESTIONS

If you don't know how to pray the Holy Rosary, you can get our book "Rosary for beginners" in the following link: www.vcrey.com/rosary-book

Some sacrifices that you can do include:

- Not drinking water or liquids during a meal.
- Abstain from meat on Fridays (which is also required by Holy Mother Church).
- Not eating candy or dessert during one day.
- Take a cold shower.
- Not eating meat in saturdays in honor of the Blessed Virgin Mary.
- Keep one hour of silence.
- Do not buy or sell in Sunday (which is also a commandment).
- Give food to the hungry.
- Give water to the thirsty.
- Visit the sick, and confort them.

IMPORTANT NOTES

☐ _____
☐ _____
☐ _____
☐ _____
☐ _____
☐ _____
☐ _____
☐ _____
☐ _____

YOUR SOUL'S GROWTH PLANNER

LONG LIVE CHRIST THE KING!

VIVA
CRISTO
REY.ORG

DATE: MONTH   DAY   YEAR

GOALS OF THE DAY

PRAYING THE ROSARY OF 15 DECADES.................. ☐

READING THE HOLY BIBLE (15 MINUTES)............... ☐

DAILY SACRIFICES... ☐

☐ _____   ☐ _____

☐ _____   ☐ _____

☐ _____   ☐ _____

☐ _____   ☐ _____

☐ _____   ☐ _____

☐ _____   ☐ _____

☐ _____   ☐ _____

☐ _____   ☐ _____

☐ _____   ☐ _____

SUGGESTIONS

If you don't know how to pray the Holy Rosary, you can get our book "Rosary for beginners" in the following link: www.vcrey.com/rosary-book

Some sacrifices that you can do include:

- Not drinking water or liquids during a meal.
- Abstain from meat on Fridays (which is also required by Holy Mother Church).
- Not eating candy or dessert during one day.
- Take a cold shower.
- Not eating meat in saturdays in honor of the Blessed Virgin Mary.
- Keep one hour of silence.
- Do not buy or sell in Sunday (which is also a commandment).
- Give food to the hungry.
- Give water to the thirsty.
- Visit the sick, and confort them.

IMPORTANT NOTES

☐ _____

☐ _____

☐ _____

☐ _____

☐ _____

☐ _____

☐ _____

☐ _____

☐ _____

YOUR SOUL'S GROWTH PLANNER

LONG LIVE CHRIST THE KING!

VIVA CRISTO REY.ORG

DATE: MONTH   DAY   YEAR

GOALS OF THE DAY

PRAYING THE ROSARY OF 15 DECADES................... ☐

READING THE HOLY BIBLE (15 MINUTES)................ ☐

DAILY SACRIFICES.. ☐

☐ _____   ☐ _____
☐ _____   ☐ _____
☐ _____   ☐ _____
☐ _____   ☐ _____
☐ _____   ☐ _____
☐ _____   ☐ _____
☐ _____   ☐ _____
☐ _____   ☐ _____
☐ _____   ☐ _____

SUGGESTIONS

If you don't know how to pray the Holy Rosary, you can get our book "Rosary for beginners" in the following link: www.vcrey.com/rosary-book

Some sacrifices that you can do include:

- Not drinking water or liquids during a meal.
- Abstain from meat on Fridays (which is also required by Holy Mother Church).
- Not eating candy or dessert during one day.
- Take a cold shower.
- Not eating meat in saturdays in honor of the Blessed Virgin Mary.
- Keep one hour of silence.
- Do not buy or sell in Sunday (which is also a commandment).
- Give food to the hungry.
- Give water to the thirsty.
- Visit the sick, and confort them.

IMPORTANT NOTES

☐ _____
☐ _____
☐ _____
☐ _____
☐ _____
☐ _____
☐ _____
☐ _____
☐ _____

YOUR SOUL'S GROWTH PLANNER

VIVA CRISTO REY.ORG

LONG LIVE CHRIST THE KING!

DATE: MONTH   DAY   YEAR

GOALS OF THE DAY

PRAYING THE ROSARY OF 15 DECADES................... ☐

READING THE HOLY BIBLE (15 MINUTES)................ ☐

DAILY SACRIFICES... ☐

☐ _____   ☐ _____
☐ _____   ☐ _____
☐ _____   ☐ _____
☐ _____   ☐ _____
☐ _____   ☐ _____
☐ _____   ☐ _____
☐ _____   ☐ _____
☐ _____   ☐ _____
☐ _____   ☐ _____

SUGGESTIONS

If you don't know how to pray the Holy Rosary, you can get our book "Rosary for beginners" in the following link: www.vcrey.com/rosary-book

Some sacrifices that you can do include:

- Not drinking water or liquids during a meal.
- Abstain from meat on Fridays (which is also required by Holy Mother Church).
- Not eating candy or dessert during one day.
- Take a cold shower.
- Not eating meat in saturdays in honor of the Blessed Virgin Mary.
- Keep one hour of silence.
- Do not buy or sell in Sunday (which is also a commandment).
- Give food to the hungry.
- Give water to the thirsty.
- Visit the sick, and confort them.

IMPORTANT NOTES

☐ _____
☐ _____
☐ _____
☐ _____
☐ _____
☐ _____
☐ _____
☐ _____
☐ _____

YOUR SOUL'S GROWTH PLANNER

LONG LIVE CHRIST THE KING!

VIVA CRISTO REY.ORG

DATE: MONTH   DAY   YEAR

GOALS OF THE DAY

PRAYING THE ROSARY OF 15 DECADES................... ☐

READING THE HOLY BIBLE (15 MINUTES)................ ☐

DAILY SACRIFICES....................................... ☐

☐ _____   ☐ _____
☐ _____   ☐ _____
☐ _____   ☐ _____
☐ _____   ☐ _____
☐ _____   ☐ _____
☐ _____   ☐ _____
☐ _____   ☐ _____
☐ _____   ☐ _____
☐ _____   ☐ _____

SUGGESTIONS

If you don't know how to pray the Holy Rosary, you can get our book "Rosary for beginners" in the following link: www.vcrey.com/rosary-book

Some sacrifices that you can do include:

- Not drinking water or liquids during a meal.
- Abstain from meat on Fridays (which is also required by Holy Mother Church).
- Not eating candy or dessert during one day.
- Take a cold shower.
- Not eating meat in saturdays in honor of the Blessed Virgin Mary.
- Keep one hour of silence.
- Do not buy or sell in Sunday (which is also a commandment).
- Give food to the hungry.
- Give water to the thirsty.
- Visit the sick, and confort them.

IMPORTANT NOTES

☐ _____
☐ _____
☐ _____
☐ _____
☐ _____
☐ _____
☐ _____
☐ _____
☐ _____

YOUR SOUL'S GROWTH PLANNER

LONG LIVE CHRIST THE KING!

VIVA CRISTO REY.ORG

DATE: MONTH   DAY   YEAR

GOALS OF THE DAY

PRAYING THE ROSARY OF 15 DECADES................. ☐

READING THE HOLY BIBLE (15 MINUTES)............... ☐

DAILY SACRIFICES... ☐

☐ _____   ☐ _____

☐ _____   ☐ _____

☐ _____   ☐ _____

☐ _____   ☐ _____

☐ _____   ☐ _____

☐ _____   ☐ _____

☐ _____   ☐ _____

☐ _____   ☐ _____

☐ _____   ☐ _____

SUGGESTIONS

If you don't know how to pray the Holy Rosary, you can get our book "Rosary for beginners" in the following link: www.vcrey.com/rosary-book

Some sacrifices that you can do include:

- Not drinking water or liquids during a meal.
- Abstain from meat on Fridays (which is also required by Holy Mother Church).
- Not eating candy or dessert during one day.
- Take a cold shower.
- Not eating meat in saturdays in honor of the Blessed Virgin Mary.
- Keep one hour of silence.
- Do not buy or sell in Sunday (which is also a commandment).
- Give food to the hungry.
- Give water to the thirsty.
- Visit the sick, and confort them.

IMPORTANT NOTES

☐ _____

☐ _____

☐ _____

☐ _____

☐ _____

☐ _____

☐ _____

☐ _____

☐ _____

YOUR SOUL'S GROWTH PLANNER

LONG LIVE CHRIST THE KING!

VIVA
CRISTO
REY.ORG

DATE: MONTH   DAY   YEAR

GOALS OF THE DAY

PRAYING THE ROSARY OF 15 DECADES................... ☐

READING THE HOLY BIBLE (15 MINUTES)............... ☐

DAILY SACRIFICES.. ☐

☐ _____   ☐ _____
☐ _____   ☐ _____
☐ _____   ☐ _____
☐ _____   ☐ _____
☐ _____   ☐ _____
☐ _____   ☐ _____
☐ _____   ☐ _____
☐ _____   ☐ _____
☐ _____   ☐ _____

SUGGESTIONS

If you don't know how to pray the Holy Rosary, you can get our book "Rosary for beginners" in the following link: www.vcrey.com/rosary-book

Some sacrifices that you can do include:

- Not drinking water or liquids during a meal.
- Abstain from meat on Fridays (which is also required by Holy Mother Church).
- Not eating candy or dessert during one day.
- Take a cold shower.
- Not eating meat in saturdays in honor of the Blessed Virgin Mary.
- Keep one hour of silence.
- Do not buy or sell in Sunday (which is also a commandment).
- Give food to the hungry.
- Give water to the thirsty.
- Visit the sick, and confort them.

IMPORTANT NOTES

☐ _____
☐ _____
☐ _____
☐ _____
☐ _____
☐ _____
☐ _____
☐ _____
☐ _____

YOUR SOUL'S GROWTH PLANNER

LONG LIVE CHRIST THE KING!

VIVA
CRISTO
REY.ORG

DATE: MONTH   DAY   YEAR

GOALS OF THE DAY

PRAYING THE ROSARY OF 15 DECADES.................. ☐

READING THE HOLY BIBLE (15 MINUTES)............... ☐

DAILY SACRIFICES... ☐

☐ _____   ☐ _____
☐ _____   ☐ _____
☐ _____   ☐ _____
☐ _____   ☐ _____
☐ _____   ☐ _____
☐ _____   ☐ _____
☐ _____   ☐ _____
☐ _____   ☐ _____
☐ _____   ☐ _____

SUGGESTIONS

If you don't know how to pray the Holy Rosary, you can get our book "Rosary for beginners" in the following link: www.vcrey.com/rosary-book

Some sacrifices that you can do include:

- Not drinking water or liquids during a meal.
- Abstain from meat on Fridays (which is also required by Holy Mother Church).
- Not eating candy or dessert during one day.
- Take a cold shower.
- Not eating meat in saturdays in honor of the Blessed Virgin Mary.
- Keep one hour of silence.
- Do not buy or sell in Sunday (which is also a commandment).
- Give food to the hungry.
- Give water to the thirsty.
- Visit the sick, and confort them.

IMPORTANT NOTES

☐ _____
☐ _____
☐ _____
☐ _____
☐ _____
☐ _____
☐ _____
☐ _____
☐ _____

YOUR SOUL'S GROWTH PLANNER

LONG LIVE CHRIST THE KING!

VIVA CRISTO REY.ORG

DATE: MONTH   DAY   YEAR

GOALS OF THE DAY

PRAYING THE ROSARY OF 15 DECADES................. ☐

READING THE HOLY BIBLE (15 MINUTES)............... ☐

DAILY SACRIFICES....................................... ☐

☐ _____   ☐ _____
☐ _____   ☐ _____
☐ _____   ☐ _____
☐ _____   ☐ _____
☐ _____   ☐ _____
☐ _____   ☐ _____
☐ _____   ☐ _____
☐ _____   ☐ _____
☐ _____   ☐ _____

SUGGESTIONS

If you don't know how to pray the Holy Rosary, you can get our book "Rosary for beginners" in the following link: www.vcrey.com/rosary-book

Some sacrifices that you can do include:

- Not drinking water or liquids during a meal.
- Abstain from meat on Fridays (which is also required by Holy Mother Church).
- Not eating candy or dessert during one day.
- Take a cold shower.
- Not eating meat in saturdays in honor of the Blessed Virgin Mary.
- Keep one hour of silence.
- Do not buy or sell in Sunday (which is also a commandment).
- Give food to the hungry.
- Give water to the thirsty.
- Visit the sick, and confort them.

IMPORTANT NOTES

☐ _____
☐ _____
☐ _____
☐ _____
☐ _____
☐ _____
☐ _____
☐ _____
☐ _____

YOUR SOUL'S GROWTH PLANNER

LONG LIVE CHRIST THE KING!

VIVA CRISTO REY.ORG

DATE: MONTH   DAY   YEAR

GOALS OF THE DAY

PRAYING THE ROSARY OF 15 DECADES................... ☐

READING THE HOLY BIBLE (15 MINUTES)................ ☐

DAILY SACRIFICES... ☐

☐ _____   ☐ _____
☐ _____   ☐ _____
☐ _____   ☐ _____
☐ _____   ☐ _____
☐ _____   ☐ _____
☐ _____   ☐ _____
☐ _____   ☐ _____
☐ _____   ☐ _____
☐ _____   ☐ _____

SUGGESTIONS

If you don't know how to pray the Holy Rosary, you can get our book "Rosary for beginners" in the following link: www.vcrey.com/rosary-book

Some sacrifices that you can do include:

- Not drinking water or liquids during a meal.
- Abstain from meat on Fridays (which is also required by Holy Mother Church).
- Not eating candy or dessert during one day.
- Take a cold shower.
- Not eating meat in saturdays in honor of the Blessed Virgin Mary.
- Keep one hour of silence.
- Do not buy or sell in Sunday (which is also a commandment).
- Give food to the hungry.
- Give water to the thirsty.
- Visit the sick, and confort them.

IMPORTANT NOTES

☐ _____
☐ _____
☐ _____
☐ _____
☐ _____
☐ _____
☐ _____
☐ _____

YOUR SOUL'S GROWTH PLANNER

LONG LIVE CHRIST THE KING!

VIVA CRISTO REY.ORG

DATE: MONTH   DAY   YEAR

GOALS OF THE DAY

PRAYING THE ROSARY OF 15 DECADES.................. ☐

READING THE HOLY BIBLE (15 MINUTES)................ ☐

DAILY SACRIFICES... ☐

☐ _____   ☐ _____
☐ _____   ☐ _____
☐ _____   ☐ _____
☐ _____   ☐ _____
☐ _____   ☐ _____
☐ _____   ☐ _____
☐ _____   ☐ _____
☐ _____   ☐ _____
☐ _____   ☐ _____

SUGGESTIONS

If you don't know how to pray the Holy Rosary, you can get our book "Rosary for beginners" in the following link: www.vcrey.com/rosary-book

Some sacrifices that you can do include:

- Not drinking water or liquids during a meal.
- Abstain from meat on Fridays (which is also required by Holy Mother Church).
- Not eating candy or dessert during one day.
- Take a cold shower.
- Not eating meat in saturdays in honor of the Blessed Virgin Mary.
- Keep one hour of silence.
- Do not buy or sell in Sunday (which is also a commandment).
- Give food to the hungry.
- Give water to the thirsty.
- Visit the sick, and confort them.

IMPORTANT NOTES

☐ _____
☐ _____
☐ _____
☐ _____
☐ _____
☐ _____
☐ _____
☐ _____
☐ _____

YOUR SOUL'S GROWTH PLANNER

LONG LIVE CHRIST THE KING!

VIVA CRISTO REY.ORG

DATE: MONTH   DAY   YEAR

GOALS OF THE DAY

PRAYING THE ROSARY OF 15 DECADES................... ☐

READING THE HOLY BIBLE (15 MINUTES)............... ☐

DAILY SACRIFICES.. ☐

☐ _____   ☐ _____
☐ _____   ☐ _____
☐ _____   ☐ _____
☐ _____   ☐ _____
☐ _____   ☐ _____
☐ _____   ☐ _____
☐ _____   ☐ _____
☐ _____   ☐ _____
☐ _____   ☐ _____

SUGGESTIONS

If you don't know how to pray the Holy Rosary, you can get our book "Rosary for beginners" in the following link: www.vcrey.com/rosary-book

Some sacrifices that you can do include:

- Not drinking water or liquids during a meal.
- Abstain from meat on Fridays (which is also required by Holy Mother Church).
- Not eating candy or dessert during one day.
- Take a cold shower.
- Not eating meat in saturdays in honor of the Blessed Virgin Mary.
- Keep one hour of silence.
- Do not buy or sell in Sunday (which is also a commandment).
- Give food to the hungry.
- Give water to the thirsty.
- Visit the sick, and confort them.

IMPORTANT NOTES

☐ _____
☐ _____
☐ _____
☐ _____
☐ _____
☐ _____
☐ _____
☐ _____
☐ _____

YOUR SOUL'S GROWTH PLANNER

LONG LIVE CHRIST THE KING!

VIVA CRISTO REY.ORG

DATE: MONTH   DAY   YEAR

GOALS OF THE DAY

PRAYING THE ROSARY OF 15 DECADES.................. ☐

READING THE HOLY BIBLE (15 MINUTES)................ ☐

DAILY SACRIFICES.. ☐

☐ _____   ☐ _____
☐ _____   ☐ _____
☐ _____   ☐ _____
☐ _____   ☐ _____
☐ _____   ☐ _____
☐ _____   ☐ _____
☐ _____   ☐ _____
☐ _____   ☐ _____
☐ _____   ☐ _____

SUGGESTIONS

If you don't know how to pray the Holy Rosary, you can get our book "Rosary for beginners" in the following link: www.vcrey.com/rosary-book

Some sacrifices that you can do include:

- Not drinking water or liquids during a meal.
- Abstain from meat on Fridays (which is also required by Holy Mother Church).
- Not eating candy or dessert during one day.
- Take a cold shower.
- Not eating meat in saturdays in honor of the Blessed Virgin Mary.
- Keep one hour of silence.
- Do not buy or sell in Sunday (which is also a commandment).
- Give food to the hungry.
- Give water to the thirsty.
- Visit the sick, and confort them.

IMPORTANT NOTES

☐ _____
☐ _____
☐ _____
☐ _____
☐ _____
☐ _____
☐ _____
☐ _____
☐ _____
☐ _____

YOUR SOUL'S GROWTH PLANNER

LONG LIVE CHRIST THE KING!

VIVA CRISTO REY.ORG

DATE: MONTH   DAY   YEAR

GOALS OF THE DAY

PRAYING THE ROSARY OF 15 DECADES.................. ☐

READING THE HOLY BIBLE (15 MINUTES)................ ☐

DAILY SACRIFICES... ☐

☐ _____   ☐ _____

☐ _____   ☐ _____

☐ _____   ☐ _____

☐ _____   ☐ _____

☐ _____   ☐ _____

☐ _____   ☐ _____

☐ _____   ☐ _____

☐ _____   ☐ _____

☐ _____   ☐ _____

SUGGESTIONS

If you don't know how to pray the Holy Rosary, you can get our book "Rosary for beginners" in the following link: www.vcrey.com/rosary-book

Some sacrifices that you can do include:

- Not drinking water or liquids during a meal.
- Abstain from meat on Fridays (which is also required by Holy Mother Church).
- Not eating candy or dessert during one day.
- Take a cold shower.
- Not eating meat in saturdays in honor of the Blessed Virgin Mary.
- Keep one hour of silence.
- Do not buy or sell in Sunday (which is also a commandment).
- Give food to the hungry.
- Give water to the thirsty.
- Visit the sick, and confort them.

IMPORTANT NOTES

☐ _____

☐ _____

☐ _____

☐ _____

☐ _____

☐ _____

☐ _____

☐ _____

☐ _____

YOUR SOUL'S GROWTH PLANNER

LONG LIVE CHRIST THE KING!

VIVA
CRISTO
REY.ORG

DATE: MONTH   DAY   YEAR

GOALS OF THE DAY

PRAYING THE ROSARY OF 15 DECADES................... ☐

READING THE HOLY BIBLE (15 MINUTES)................ ☐

DAILY SACRIFICES.. ☐

☐ _____   ☐ _____
☐ _____   ☐ _____
☐ _____   ☐ _____

☐ _____   ☐ _____
☐ _____   ☐ _____
☐ _____   ☐ _____
☐ _____   ☐ _____

☐ _____   ☐ _____
☐ _____   ☐ _____

IMPORTANT NOTES

☐ _____
☐ _____
☐ _____
☐ _____
☐ _____
☐ _____
☐ _____
☐ _____
☐ _____

YOUR SOUL'S GROWTH PLANNER

LONG LIVE CHRIST THE KING!

VIVA CRISTO REY.ORG

DATE: MONTH   DAY   YEAR

GOALS OF THE DAY

PRAYING THE ROSARY OF 15 DECADES................... ☐

READING THE HOLY BIBLE (15 MINUTES)............... ☐

DAILY SACRIFICES.. ☐

☐ _____   ☐ _____
☐ _____   ☐ _____
☐ _____   ☐ _____
☐ _____   ☐ _____
☐ _____   ☐ _____
☐ _____   ☐ _____
☐ _____   ☐ _____
☐ _____   ☐ _____
☐ _____   ☐ _____

SUGGESTIONS

If you don't know how to pray the Holy Rosary, you can get our book "Rosary for beginners" in the following link: www.vcrey.com/rosary-book

Some sacrifices that you can do include:

- Not drinking water or liquids during a meal.
- Abstain from meat on Fridays (which is also required by Holy Mother Church).
- Not eating candy or dessert during one day.
- Take a cold shower.
- Not eating meat in saturdays in honor of the Blessed Virgin Mary.
- Keep one hour of silence.
- Do not buy or sell in Sunday (which is also a commandment).
- Give food to the hungry.
- Give water to the thirsty.
- Visit the sick, and confort them.

IMPORTANT NOTES

☐ _____
☐ _____
☐ _____
☐ _____
☐ _____
☐ _____
☐ _____
☐ _____
☐ _____

YOUR SOUL'S GROWTH PLANNER

VIVA CRISTO REY.ORG

LONG LIVE CHRIST THE KING!

DATE: MONTH   DAY   YEAR

GOALS OF THE DAY

PRAYING THE ROSARY OF 15 DECADES................... ☐

READING THE HOLY BIBLE (15 MINUTES)................ ☐

DAILY SACRIFICES.. ☐

☐ _____   ☐ _____
☐ _____   ☐ _____
☐ _____   ☐ _____
☐ _____   ☐ _____
☐ _____   ☐ _____
☐ _____   ☐ _____
☐ _____   ☐ _____
☐ _____   ☐ _____
☐ _____   ☐ _____

SUGGESTIONS

If you don't know how to pray the Holy Rosary, you can get our book "Rosary for beginners" in the following link: www.vcrey.com/rosary-book

Some sacrifices that you can do include:

- Not drinking water or liquids during a meal.
- Abstain from meat on Fridays (which is also required by Holy Mother Church).
- Not eating candy or dessert during one day.
- Take a cold shower.
- Not eating meat in saturdays in honor of the Blessed Virgin Mary.
- Keep one hour of silence.
- Do not buy or sell in Sunday (which is also a commandment).
- Give food to the hungry.
- Give water to the thirsty.
- Visit the sick, and confort them.

IMPORTANT NOTES

☐ _____
☐ _____
☐ _____
☐ _____
☐ _____
☐ _____
☐ _____
☐ _____
☐ _____

YOUR SOUL'S GROWTH PLANNER

LONG LIVE CHRIST THE KING!

VIVA
CRISTO
REY.ORG

DATE: MONTH   DAY   YEAR

GOALS OF THE DAY

PRAYING THE ROSARY OF 15 DECADES.................. ☐

READING THE HOLY BIBLE (15 MINUTES).............. ☐

DAILY SACRIFICES... ☐

☐ _____   ☐ _____
☐ _____   ☐ _____
☐ _____   ☐ _____
☐ _____   ☐ _____
☐ _____   ☐ _____
☐ _____   ☐ _____
☐ _____   ☐ _____
☐ _____   ☐ _____
☐ _____   ☐ _____

SUGGESTIONS

If you don't know how to pray the Holy Rosary, you can get our book "Rosary for beginners" in the following link: www.vcrey.com/rosary-book

Some sacrifices that you can do include:

- Not drinking water or liquids during a meal.
- Abstain from meat on Fridays (which is also required by Holy Mother Church).
- Not eating candy or dessert during one day.
- Take a cold shower.
- Not eating meat in saturdays in honor of the Blessed Virgin Mary.
- Keep one hour of silence.
- Do not buy or sell on Sunday (which is also a commandment).
- Give food to the hungry.
- Give water to the thirsty.
- Visit the sick, and confort them.

IMPORTANT NOTES

☐ _____
☐ _____
☐ _____
☐ _____
☐ _____
☐ _____
☐ _____
☐ _____
☐ _____

YOUR SOUL'S GROWTH PLANNER

LONG LIVE CHRIST THE KING!

VIVA CRISTO REY.ORG

DATE: MONTH   DAY   YEAR

GOALS OF THE DAY

PRAYING THE ROSARY OF 15 DECADES.................. ☐

READING THE HOLY BIBLE (15 MINUTES)............... ☐

DAILY SACRIFICES.. ☐

☐ _____   ☐ _____
☐ _____   ☐ _____
☐ _____   ☐ _____
☐ _____   ☐ _____
☐ _____   ☐ _____
☐ _____   ☐ _____
☐ _____   ☐ _____
☐ _____   ☐ _____
☐ _____   ☐ _____

SUGGESTIONS

If you don't know how to pray the Holy Rosary, you can get our book "Rosary for beginners" in the following link: www.vcrey.com/rosary-book

Some sacrifices that you can do include:

- Not drinking water or liquids during a meal.
- Abstain from meat on Fridays (which is also required by Holy Mother Church).
- Not eating candy or dessert during one day.
- Take a cold shower.
- Not eating meat in saturdays in honor of the Blessed Virgin Mary.
- Keep one hour of silence.
- Do not buy or sell in Sunday (which is also a commandment).
- Give food to the hungry.
- Give water to the thirsty.
- Visit the sick, and confort them.

IMPORTANT NOTES

☐ _____
☐ _____
☐ _____
☐ _____
☐ _____
☐ _____
☐ _____
☐ _____
☐ _____

YOUR SOUL'S GROWTH PLANNER

LONG LIVE CHRIST THE KING!

VIVA CRISTO REY.ORG

DATE: MONTH   DAY   YEAR

GOALS OF THE DAY

PRAYING THE ROSARY OF 15 DECADES................... ☐

READING THE HOLY BIBLE (15 MINUTES)............... ☐

DAILY SACRIFICES.. ☐

☐ _____   ☐ _____
☐ _____   ☐ _____
☐ _____   ☐ _____
☐ _____   ☐ _____
☐ _____   ☐ _____
☐ _____   ☐ _____
☐ _____   ☐ _____
☐ _____   ☐ _____
☐ _____   ☐ _____

SUGGESTIONS

If you don't know how to pray the Holy Rosary, you can get our book "Rosary for beginners" in the following link: www.vcrey.com/rosary-book

Some sacrifices that you can do include:

- Not drinking water or liquids during a meal.
- Abstain from meat on Fridays (which is also required by Holy Mother Church).
- Not eating candy or dessert during one day.
- Take a cold shower.
- Not eating meat in saturdays in honor of the Blessed Virgin Mary.
- Keep one hour of silence.
- Do not buy or sell in Sunday (which is also a commandment).
- Give food to the hungry.
- Give water to the thirsty.
- Visit the sick, and confort them.

IMPORTANT NOTES

☐ _____
☐ _____
☐ _____
☐ _____
☐ _____
☐ _____
☐ _____
☐ _____
☐ _____

YOUR SOUL'S GROWTH PLANNER

LONG LIVE CHRIST THE KING!

VIVA
CRISTO
REY.ORG

DATE: MONTH   DAY   YEAR

GOALS OF THE DAY

PRAYING THE ROSARY OF 15 DECADES................... ☐

READING THE HOLY BIBLE (15 MINUTES)............... ☐

DAILY SACRIFICES... ☐

☐ _____   ☐ _____

☐ _____   ☐ _____

☐ _____   ☐ _____

☐ _____   ☐ _____

☐ _____   ☐ _____

☐ _____   ☐ _____

☐ _____   ☐ _____

☐ _____   ☐ _____

☐ _____   ☐ _____

SUGGESTIONS

If you don't know how to pray the Holy Rosary, you can get our book "Rosary for beginners" in the following link: www.vcrey.com/rosary-book

Some sacrifices that you can do include:

- Not drinking water or liquids during a meal.
- Abstain from meat on Fridays (which is also required by Holy Mother Church).
- Not eating candy or dessert during one day.
- Take a cold shower.
- Not eating meat in saturdays in honor of the Blessed Virgin Mary.
- Keep one hour of silence.
- Do not buy or sell in Sunday (which is also a commandment).
- Give food to the hungry.
- Give water to the thirsty.
- Visit the sick, and confort them.

IMPORTANT NOTES

☐ _____

☐ _____

☐ _____

☐ _____

☐ _____

☐ _____

☐ _____

☐ _____

☐ _____

YOUR SOUL'S GROWTH PLANNER

VIVA CRISTO REY.ORG

LONG LIVE CHRIST THE KING!

DATE: MONTH   DAY   YEAR

GOALS OF THE DAY

PRAYING THE ROSARY OF 15 DECADES.................. ☐

READING THE HOLY BIBLE (15 MINUTES)............... ☐

DAILY SACRIFICES... ☐

☐ _____   ☐ _____
☐ _____   ☐ _____
☐ _____   ☐ _____
☐ _____   ☐ _____
☐ _____   ☐ _____
☐ _____   ☐ _____
☐ _____   ☐ _____
☐ _____   ☐ _____
☐ _____   ☐ _____

SUGGESTIONS

If you don't know how to pray the Holy Rosary, you can get our book "Rosary for beginners" in the following link: www.vcrey.com/rosary-book

Some sacrifices that you can do include:

- Not drinking water or liquids during a meal.
- Abstain from meat on Fridays (which is also required by Holy Mother Church).
- Not eating candy or dessert during one day.
- Take a cold shower.
- Not eating meat in saturdays in honor of the Blessed Virgin Mary.
- Keep one hour of silence.
- Do not buy or sell in Sunday (which is also a commandment).
- Give food to the hungry.
- Give water to the thirsty.
- Visit the sick, and confort them.

IMPORTANT NOTES

☐ _____
☐ _____
☐ _____
☐ _____
☐ _____
☐ _____
☐ _____
☐ _____
☐ _____

YOUR SOUL'S GROWTH PLANNER

LONG LIVE CHRIST THE KING!

VIVA CRISTO REY.ORG

DATE: MONTH   DAY   YEAR

GOALS OF THE DAY

PRAYING THE ROSARY OF 15 DECADES................... ☐

READING THE HOLY BIBLE (15 MINUTES)............... ☐

DAILY SACRIFICES... ☐

☐ _____   ☐ _____

☐ _____   ☐ _____

☐ _____   ☐ _____

☐ _____   ☐ _____

☐ _____   ☐ _____

☐ _____   ☐ _____

☐ _____   ☐ _____

☐ _____   ☐ _____

☐ _____   ☐ _____

SUGGESTIONS

If you don't know how to pray the Holy Rosary, you can get our book "Rosary for beginners" in the following link: www.vcrey.com/rosary-book

Some sacrifices that you can do include:

- Not drinking water or liquids during a meal.
- Abstain from meat on Fridays (which is also required by Holy Mother Church).
- Not eating candy or dessert during one day.
- Take a cold shower.
- Not eating meat in saturdays in honor of the Blessed Virgin Mary.
- Keep one hour of silence.
- Do not buy or sell in Sunday (which is also a commandment).
- Give food to the hungry.
- Give water to the thirsty.
- Visit the sick, and confort them.

IMPORTANT NOTES

☐ _____

☐ _____

☐ _____

☐ _____

☐ _____

☐ _____

☐ _____

☐ _____

☐ _____

YOUR SOUL'S GROWTH PLANNER

LONG LIVE CHRIST THE KING!

VIVA
CRISTO
REY.ORG

DATE: MONTH   DAY   YEAR

GOALS OF THE DAY

PRAYING THE ROSARY OF 15 DECADES.................. ☐

READING THE HOLY BIBLE (15 MINUTES)............... ☐

DAILY SACRIFICES... ☐

☐ _____   ☐ _____
☐ _____   ☐ _____
☐ _____   ☐ _____
☐ _____   ☐ _____
☐ _____   ☐ _____
☐ _____   ☐ _____
☐ _____   ☐ _____
☐ _____   ☐ _____
☐ _____   ☐ _____

SUGGESTIONS

If you don't know how to pray the Holy Rosary, you can get our book "Rosary for beginners" in the following link: www.vcrey.com/rosary-book

Some sacrifices that you can do include:

- Not drinking water or liquids during a meal.
- Abstain from meat on Fridays (which is also required by Holy Mother Church).
- Not eating candy or dessert during one day.
- Take a cold shower.
- Not eating meat in saturdays in honor of the Blessed Virgin Mary.
- Keep one hour of silence.
- Do not buy or sell in Sunday (which is also a commandment).
- Give food to the hungry.
- Give water to the thirsty.
- Visit the sick, and confort them.

IMPORTANT NOTES

☐ _____
☐ _____
☐ _____
☐ _____
☐ _____
☐ _____
☐ _____
☐ _____
☐ _____

YOUR SOUL'S GROWTH PLANNER

VIVA CRISTO REY.ORG

LONG LIVE CHRIST THE KING!

DATE: MONTH   DAY   YEAR

GOALS OF THE DAY

PRAYING THE ROSARY OF 15 DECADES................... ☐

READING THE HOLY BIBLE (15 MINUTES)................ ☐

DAILY SACRIFICES... ☐

☐ _____   ☐ _____
☐ _____   ☐ _____
☐ _____   ☐ _____

☐ _____   ☐ _____
☐ _____   ☐ _____
☐ _____   ☐ _____
☐ _____   ☐ _____

☐ _____   ☐ _____
☐ _____   ☐ _____

SUGGESTIONS

If you don't know how to pray the Holy Rosary, you can get our book "Rosary for beginners" in the following link: www.vcrey.com/rosary-book

Some sacrifices that you can do include:

- Not drinking water or liquids during a meal.
- Abstain from meat on Fridays (which is also required by Holy Mother Church).
- Not eating candy or dessert during one day.
- Take a cold shower.
- Not eating meat in saturdays in honor of the Blessed Virgin Mary.
- Keep one hour of silence.
- Do not buy or sell in Sunday (which is also a commandment).
- Give food to the hungry.
- Give water to the thirsty.
- Visit the sick, and confort them.

IMPORTANT NOTES

☐ _____
☐ _____
☐ _____
☐ _____
☐ _____
☐ _____
☐ _____
☐ _____
☐ _____

YOUR SOUL'S GROWTH PLANNER

LONG LIVE CHRIST THE KING!

DATE: MONTH   DAY   YEAR

GOALS OF THE DAY

PRAYING THE ROSARY OF 15 DECADES.................. ☐

READING THE HOLY BIBLE (15 MINUTES)............... ☐

DAILY SACRIFICES.. ☐

☐ _____   ☐ _____

☐ _____   ☐ _____

☐ _____   ☐ _____

☐ _____   ☐ _____

☐ _____   ☐ _____

☐ _____   ☐ _____

☐ _____   ☐ _____

☐ _____   ☐ _____

☐ _____   ☐ _____

SUGGESTIONS

If you don't know how to pray the Holy Rosary, you can get our book "Rosary for beginners" in the following link: www.vcrey.com/rosary-book

Some sacrifices that you can do include:

- Not drinking water or liquids during a meal.
- Abstain from meat on Fridays (which is also required by Holy Mother Church).
- Not eating candy or dessert during one day.
- Take a cold shower.
- Not eating meat in saturdays in honor of the Blessed Virgin Mary.
- Keep one hour of silence.
- Do not buy or sell in Sunday (which is also a commandment).
- Give food to the hungry.
- Give water to the thirsty.
- Visit the sick, and confort them.

IMPORTANT NOTES

☐ _____

☐ _____

☐ _____

☐ _____

☐ _____

☐ _____

☐ _____

☐ _____

☐ _____

YOUR SOUL'S GROWTH PLANNER

LONG LIVE CHRIST THE KING!

VIVA
CRISTO
REY.ORG

DATE: MONTH   DAY   YEAR

GOALS OF THE DAY

PRAYING THE ROSARY OF 15 DECADES................... ☐

READING THE HOLY BIBLE (15 MINUTES)............... ☐

DAILY SACRIFICES... ☐

☐ _____   ☐ _____
☐ _____   ☐ _____
☐ _____   ☐ _____
☐ _____   ☐ _____
☐ _____   ☐ _____
☐ _____   ☐ _____
☐ _____   ☐ _____
☐ _____   ☐ _____
☐ _____   ☐ _____

SUGGESTIONS

If you don't know how to pray the Holy Rosary, you can get our book "Rosary for beginners" in the following link: www.vcrey.com/rosary-book

Some sacrifices that you can do include:

- Not drinking water or liquids during a meal.
- Abstain from meat on Fridays (which is also required by Holy Mother Church).
- Not eating candy or dessert during one day.
- Take a cold shower.
- Not eating meat in saturdays in honor of the Blessed Virgin Mary.
- Keep one hour of silence.
- Do not buy or sell in Sunday (which is also a commandment).
- Give food to the hungry.
- Give water to the thirsty.
- Visit the sick, and confort them.

IMPORTANT NOTES

☐ _____
☐ _____
☐ _____
☐ _____
☐ _____
☐ _____
☐ _____
☐ _____
☐ _____

YOUR SOUL'S GROWTH PLANNER

LONG LIVE CHRIST THE KING!

VIVA
CRISTO
REY.ORG

DATE: MONTH   DAY   YEAR

GOALS OF THE DAY

PRAYING THE ROSARY OF 15 DECADES................... ☐

READING THE HOLY BIBLE (15 MINUTES)............... ☐

DAILY SACRIFICES... ☐

☐ _____   ☐ _____
☐ _____   ☐ _____
☐ _____   ☐ _____

☐ _____   ☐ _____
☐ _____   ☐ _____
☐ _____   ☐ _____
☐ _____   ☐ _____

☐ _____   ☐ _____
☐ _____   ☐ _____

SUGGESTIONS

If you don't know how to pray the Holy Rosary, you can get our book "Rosary for beginners" in the following link: www.vcrey.com/rosary-book

Some sacrifices that you can do include:

- Not drinking water or liquids during a meal.
- Abstain from meat on Fridays (which is also required by Holy Mother Church).
- Not eating candy or dessert during one day.
- Take a cold shower.
- Not eating meat in saturdays in honor of the Blessed Virgin Mary.
- Keep one hour of silence.
- Do not buy or sell in Sunday (which is also a commandment).
- Give food to the hungry.
- Give water to the thirsty.
- Visit the sick, and confort them.

IMPORTANT NOTES

☐ _____
☐ _____
☐ _____
☐ _____
☐ _____
☐ _____
☐ _____
☐ _____
☐ _____

YOUR SOUL'S GROWTH PLANNER

LONG LIVE CHRIST THE KING!

**VIVA
CRISTO
REY.ORG**

DATE: MONTH   DAY   YEAR

GOALS OF THE DAY

PRAYING THE ROSARY OF 15 DECADES................... ☐

READING THE HOLY BIBLE (15 MINUTES)............... ☐

DAILY SACRIFICES... ☐

☐ _____   ☐ _____
☐ _____   ☐ _____
☐ _____   ☐ _____
☐ _____   ☐ _____
☐ _____   ☐ _____
☐ _____   ☐ _____
☐ _____   ☐ _____
☐ _____   ☐ _____
☐ _____   ☐ _____

SUGGESTIONS

If you don't know how to pray the Holy Rosary, you can get our book "Rosary for beginners" in the following link: www.vcrey.com/rosary-book

Some sacrifices that you can do include:

- Not drinking water or liquids during a meal.
- Abstain from meat on Fridays (which is also required by Holy Mother Church).
- Not eating candy or dessert during one day.
- Take a cold shower.
- Not eating meat in saturdays in honor of the Blessed Virgin Mary.
- Keep one hour of silence.
- Do not buy or sell in Sunday (which is also a commandment).
- Give food to the hungry.
- Give water to the thirsty.
- Visit the sick, and confort them.

IMPORTANT NOTES

☐ _____
☐ _____
☐ _____
☐ _____
☐ _____
☐ _____
☐ _____
☐ _____
☐ _____

YOUR SOUL'S GROWTH PLANNER

LONG LIVE CHRIST THE KING!

VIVA CRISTO REY.ORG

DATE: MONTH   DAY   YEAR

GOALS OF THE DAY

PRAYING THE ROSARY OF 15 DECADES................... ☐

READING THE HOLY BIBLE (15 MINUTES)................ ☐

DAILY SACRIFICES... ☐

☐ _____   ☐ _____

☐ _____   ☐ _____

☐ _____   ☐ _____

☐ _____   ☐ _____

☐ _____   ☐ _____

☐ _____   ☐ _____

☐ _____   ☐ _____

☐ _____   ☐ _____

☐ _____   ☐ _____

SUGGESTIONS

If you don't know how to pray the Holy Rosary, you can get our book "Rosary for beginners" in the following link: www.vcrey.com/rosary-book

Some sacrifices that you can do include:

- Not drinking water or liquids during a meal.
- Abstain from meat on Fridays (which is also required by Holy Mother Church).
- Not eating candy or dessert during one day.
- Take a cold shower.
- Not eating meat in saturdays in honor of the Blessed Virgin Mary.
- Keep one hour of silence.
- Do not buy or sell in Sunday (which is also a commandment).
- Give food to the hungry.
- Give water to the thirsty.
- Visit the sick, and confort them.

IMPORTANT NOTES

☐ _____

☐ _____

☐ _____

☐ _____

☐ _____

☐ _____

☐ _____

☐ _____

☐ _____

YOUR SOUL'S GROWTH PLANNER

LONG LIVE CHRIST THE KING!

VIVA CRISTO REY.ORG

DATE: MONTH   DAY   YEAR

GOALS OF THE DAY

PRAYING THE ROSARY OF 15 DECADES.................. ☐

READING THE HOLY BIBLE (15 MINUTES)............... ☐

DAILY SACRIFICES.. ☐

☐ _____   ☐ _____
☐ _____   ☐ _____
☐ _____   ☐ _____

☐ _____   ☐ _____
☐ _____   ☐ _____
☐ _____   ☐ _____
☐ _____   ☐ _____

☐ _____   ☐ _____
☐ _____   ☐ _____

SUGGESTIONS

If you don't know how to pray the Holy Rosary, you can get our book "Rosary for beginners" in the following link: www.vcrey.com/rosary-book

Some sacrifices that you can do include:

- Not drinking water or liquids during a meal.
- Abstain from meat on Fridays (which is also required by Holy Mother Church).
- Not eating candy or dessert during one day.
- Take a cold shower.
- Not eating meat in saturdays in honor of the Blessed Virgin Mary.
- Keep one hour of silence.
- Do not buy or sell in Sunday (which is also a commandment).
- Give food to the hungry.
- Give water to the thirsty.
- Visit the sick, and confort them.

IMPORTANT NOTES

☐ _____
☐ _____
☐ _____
☐ _____
☐ _____
☐ _____
☐ _____
☐ _____
☐ _____

YOUR SOUL'S GROWTH PLANNER

LONG LIVE CHRIST THE KING!

VIVA
CRISTO
REY.ORG

DATE: MONTH   DAY   YEAR

GOALS OF THE DAY

PRAYING THE ROSARY OF 15 DECADES................... ☐

READING THE HOLY BIBLE (15 MINUTES)............... ☐

DAILY SACRIFICES... ☐

☐ _____ ☐ _____
☐ _____ ☐ _____
☐ _____ ☐ _____
☐ _____ ☐ _____
☐ _____ ☐ _____
☐ _____ ☐ _____
☐ _____ ☐ _____
☐ _____ ☐ _____
☐ _____ ☐ _____

SUGGESTIONS

If you don't know how to pray the Holy Rosary, you can get our book "Rosary for beginners" in the following link: www.vcrey.com/rosary-book

Some sacrifices that you can do include:

- Not drinking water or liquids during a meal.
- Abstain from meat on Fridays (which is also required by Holy Mother Church).
- Not eating candy or dessert during one day.
- Take a cold shower.
- Not eating meat in saturdays in honor of the Blessed Virgin Mary.
- Keep one hour of silence.
- Do not buy or sell in Sunday (which is also a commandment).
- Give food to the hungry.
- Give water to the thirsty.
- Visit the sick, and confort them.

IMPORTANT NOTES

☐ _____
☐ _____
☐ _____
☐ _____
☐ _____
☐ _____
☐ _____
☐ _____
☐ _____

YOUR SOUL'S GROWTH PLANNER

LONG LIVE CHRIST THE KING!

VIVA
CRISTO
REY.ORG

DATE: MONTH   DAY   YEAR

GOALS OF THE DAY

PRAYING THE ROSARY OF 15 DECADES................... ☐

READING THE HOLY BIBLE (15 MINUTES)............... ☐

DAILY SACRIFICES... ☐

☐ _____   ☐ _____
☐ _____   ☐ _____
☐ _____   ☐ _____
☐ _____   ☐ _____
☐ _____   ☐ _____
☐ _____   ☐ _____
☐ _____   ☐ _____
☐ _____   ☐ _____
☐ _____   ☐ _____

SUGGESTIONS

If you don't know how to pray the Holy Rosary, you can get our book "Rosary for beginners" in the following link: www.vcrey.com/rosary-book

Some sacrifices that you can do include:

- Not drinking water or liquids during a meal.
- Abstain from meat on Fridays (which is also required by Holy Mother Church).
- Not eating candy or dessert during one day.
- Take a cold shower.
- Not eating meat in saturdays in honor of the Blessed Virgin Mary.
- Keep one hour of silence.
- Do not buy or sell in Sunday (which is also a commandment).
- Give food to the hungry.
- Give water to the thirsty.
- Visit the sick, and confort them.

IMPORTANT NOTES

☐ _____
☐ _____
☐ _____
☐ _____
☐ _____
☐ _____
☐ _____
☐ _____
☐ _____

YOUR SOUL'S GROWTH PLANNER

LONG LIVE CHRIST THE KING!

VIVA CRISTO REY.ORG

DATE: MONTH   DAY   YEAR

GOALS OF THE DAY

PRAYING THE ROSARY OF 15 DECADES.................. ☐

READING THE HOLY BIBLE (15 MINUTES)................ ☐

DAILY SACRIFICES.. ☐

☐ _____   ☐ _____
☐ _____   ☐ _____
☐ _____   ☐ _____
☐ _____   ☐ _____
☐ _____   ☐ _____
☐ _____   ☐ _____
☐ _____   ☐ _____
☐ _____   ☐ _____
☐ _____   ☐ _____

SUGGESTIONS

If you don't know how to pray the Holy Rosary, you can get our book "Rosary for beginners" in the following link: www.vcrey.com/rosary-book

Some sacrifices that you can do include:

- Not drinking water or liquids during a meal.
- Abstain from meat on Fridays (which is also required by Holy Mother Church).
- Not eating candy or dessert during one day.
- Take a cold shower.
- Not eating meat in saturdays in honor of the Blessed Virgin Mary.
- Keep one hour of silence.
- Do not buy or sell in Sunday (which is also a commandment).
- Give food to the hungry.
- Give water to the thirsty.
- Visit the sick, and confort them.

IMPORTANT NOTES

☐ _____
☐ _____
☐ _____
☐ _____
☐ _____
☐ _____
☐ _____
☐ _____
☐ _____

YOUR SOUL'S GROWTH PLANNER

VIVA CRISTO REY.ORG

LONG LIVE CHRIST THE KING!

DATE: MONTH   DAY   YEAR

GOALS OF THE DAY

PRAYING THE ROSARY OF 15 DECADES................... ☐

READING THE HOLY BIBLE (15 MINUTES)............... ☐

DAILY SACRIFICES.. ☐

☐ _____   ☐ _____
☐ _____   ☐ _____
☐ _____   ☐ _____
☐ _____   ☐ _____
☐ _____   ☐ _____
☐ _____   ☐ _____
☐ _____   ☐ _____
☐ _____   ☐ _____
☐ _____   ☐ _____

SUGGESTIONS

If you don't know how to pray the Holy Rosary, you can get our book "Rosary for beginners" in the following link: www.vcrey.com/rosary-book

Some sacrifices that you can do include:

- Not drinking water or liquids during a meal.
- Abstain from meat on Fridays (which is also required by Holy Mother Church).
- Not eating candy or dessert during one day.
- Take a cold shower.
- Not eating meat in saturdays in honor of the Blessed Virgin Mary.
- Keep one hour of silence.
- Do not buy or sell in Sunday (which is also a commandment).
- Give food to the hungry.
- Give water to the thirsty.
- Visit the sick, and confort them.

IMPORTANT NOTES

☐ _____
☐ _____
☐ _____
☐ _____
☐ _____
☐ _____
☐ _____
☐ _____
☐ _____

YOUR SOUL'S GROWTH PLANNER

LONG LIVE CHRIST THE KING!

VIVA CRISTO REY.ORG

DATE: MONTH   DAY   YEAR

GOALS OF THE DAY

PRAYING THE ROSARY OF 15 DECADES.................. ☐

READING THE HOLY BIBLE (15 MINUTES)............... ☐

DAILY SACRIFICES... ☐

☐ _____   ☐ _____
☐ _____   ☐ _____
☐ _____   ☐ _____
☐ _____   ☐ _____
☐ _____   ☐ _____
☐ _____   ☐ _____
☐ _____   ☐ _____
☐ _____   ☐ _____
☐ _____   ☐ _____

SUGGESTIONS

If you don't know how to pray the Holy Rosary, you can get our book "Rosary for beginners" in the following link: www.vcrey.com/rosary-book

Some sacrifices that you can do include:

- Not drinking water or liquids during a meal.
- Abstain from meat on Fridays (which is also required by Holy Mother Church).
- Not eating candy or dessert during one day.
- Take a cold shower.
- Not eating meat in saturdays in honor of the Blessed Virgin Mary.
- Keep one hour of silence.
- Do not buy or sell in Sunday (which is also a commandment).
- Give food to the hungry.
- Give water to the thirsty.
- Visit the sick, and confort them.

IMPORTANT NOTES

☐ _____
☐ _____
☐ _____
☐ _____
☐ _____
☐ _____
☐ _____
☐ _____
☐ _____

YOUR SOUL'S GROWTH PLANNER

LONG LIVE CHRIST THE KING!

VIVA
CRISTO
REY.ORG

DATE: MONTH   DAY   YEAR

GOALS OF THE DAY

PRAYING THE ROSARY OF 15 DECADES................... ☐

READING THE HOLY BIBLE (15 MINUTES)................ ☐

DAILY SACRIFICES... ☐

☐ _____   ☐ _____

☐ _____   ☐ _____

☐ _____   ☐ _____

☐ _____   ☐ _____

☐ _____   ☐ _____

☐ _____   ☐ _____

☐ _____   ☐ _____

☐ _____   ☐ _____

☐ _____   ☐ _____

SUGGESTIONS

If you don't know how to pray the Holy Rosary, you can get our book "Rosary for beginners" in the following link: www.vcrey.com/rosary-book

Some sacrifices that you can do include:

- Not drinking water or liquids during a meal.
- Abstain from meat on Fridays (which is also required by Holy Mother Church).
- Not eating candy or dessert during one day.
- Take a cold shower.
- Not eating meat in saturdays in honor of the Blessed Virgin Mary.
- Keep one hour of silence.
- Do not buy or sell in Sunday (which is also a commandment).
- Give food to the hungry.
- Give water to the thirsty.
- Visit the sick, and confort them.

IMPORTANT NOTES

☐ _____

☐ _____

☐ _____

☐ _____

☐ _____

☐ _____

☐ _____

☐ _____

☐ _____

YOUR SOUL'S GROWTH PLANNER

LONG LIVE CHRIST THE KING!

VIVA
CRISTO
REY.ORG

DATE: MONTH   DAY   YEAR

GOALS OF THE DAY

PRAYING THE ROSARY OF 15 DECADES................. ☐

READING THE HOLY BIBLE (15 MINUTES)............... ☐

DAILY SACRIFICES... ☐

☐ _____   ☐ _____
☐ _____   ☐ _____
☐ _____   ☐ _____
☐ _____   ☐ _____
☐ _____   ☐ _____
☐ _____   ☐ _____
☐ _____   ☐ _____
☐ _____   ☐ _____
☐ _____   ☐ _____

SUGGESTIONS

If you don't know how to pray the Holy Rosary, you can get our book "Rosary for beginners" in the following link: www.vcrey.com/rosary-book

Some sacrifices that you can do include:

- Not drinking water or liquids during a meal.
- Abstain from meat on Fridays (which is also required by Holy Mother Church).
- Not eating candy or dessert during one day.
- Take a cold shower.
- Not eating meat in saturdays in honor of the Blessed Virgin Mary.
- Keep one hour of silence.
- Do not buy or sell in Sunday (which is also a commandment).
- Give food to the hungry.
- Give water to the thirsty.
- Visit the sick, and confort them.

IMPORTANT NOTES

☐ _____
☐ _____
☐ _____
☐ _____
☐ _____
☐ _____
☐ _____
☐ _____
☐ _____

YOUR SOUL'S GROWTH PLANNER

LONG LIVE CHRIST THE KING!

VIVA CRISTO REY.ORG

DATE: MONTH   DAY   YEAR

GOALS OF THE DAY

PRAYING THE ROSARY OF 15 DECADES................... ☐

READING THE HOLY BIBLE (15 MINUTES)................ ☐

DAILY SACRIFICES... ☐

☐ _____   ☐ _____
☐ _____   ☐ _____
☐ _____   ☐ _____
☐ _____   ☐ _____
☐ _____   ☐ _____
☐ _____   ☐ _____
☐ _____   ☐ _____
☐ _____   ☐ _____
☐ _____   ☐ _____

SUGGESTIONS

If you don't know how to pray the Holy Rosary, you can get our book "Rosary for beginners" in the following link: www.vcrey.com/rosary-book

Some sacrifices that you can do include:

- Not drinking water or liquids during a meal.
- Abstain from meat on Fridays (which is also required by Holy Mother Church).
- Not eating candy or dessert during one day.
- Take a cold shower.
- Not eating meat in saturdays in honor of the Blessed Virgin Mary.
- Keep one hour of silence.
- Do not buy or sell in Sunday (which is also a commandment).
- Give food to the hungry.
- Give water to the thirsty.
- Visit the sick, and confort them.

IMPORTANT NOTES

☐ _____
☐ _____
☐ _____
☐ _____
☐ _____
☐ _____
☐ _____
☐ _____
☐ _____

YOUR SOUL'S GROWTH PLANNER

VIVA CRISTO REY.ORG

LONG LIVE CHRIST THE KING!

DATE: MONTH   DAY   YEAR

GOALS OF THE DAY

PRAYING THE ROSARY OF 15 DECADES................... ☐

READING THE HOLY BIBLE (15 MINUTES)............... ☐

DAILY SACRIFICES.. ☐

☐ _____   ☐ _____
☐ _____   ☐ _____
☐ _____   ☐ _____
☐ _____   ☐ _____
☐ _____   ☐ _____
☐ _____   ☐ _____
☐ _____   ☐ _____
☐ _____   ☐ _____
☐ _____   ☐ _____

SUGGESTIONS

If you don't know how to pray the Holy Rosary, you can get our book "Rosary for beginners" in the following link: www.vcrey.com/rosary-book

Some sacrifices that you can do include:

- Not drinking water or liquids during a meal.
- Abstain from meat on Fridays (which is also required by Holy Mother Church).
- Not eating candy or dessert during one day.
- Take a cold shower.
- Not eating meat in saturdays in honor of the Blessed Virgin Mary.
- Keep one hour of silence.
- Do not buy or sell in Sunday (which is also a commandment).
- Give food to the hungry.
- Give water to the thirsty.
- Visit the sick, and confort them.

IMPORTANT NOTES

☐ _____
☐ _____
☐ _____
☐ _____
☐ _____
☐ _____
☐ _____
☐ _____
☐ _____

YOUR SOUL'S GROWTH PLANNER

LONG LIVE CHRIST THE KING!

VIVA CRISTO REY.ORG

DATE: MONTH   DAY   YEAR

GOALS OF THE DAY

PRAYING THE ROSARY OF 15 DECADES.................... ☐

READING THE HOLY BIBLE (15 MINUTES)................ ☐

DAILY SACRIFICES... ☐

☐ _____   ☐ _____
☐ _____   ☐ _____
☐ _____   ☐ _____
☐ _____   ☐ _____
☐ _____   ☐ _____
☐ _____   ☐ _____
☐ _____   ☐ _____
☐ _____   ☐ _____
☐ _____   ☐ _____

SUGGESTIONS

If you don't know how to pray the Holy Rosary, you can get our book "Rosary for beginners" in the following link: www.vcrey.com/rosary-book

Some sacrifices that you can do include:

- Not drinking water or liquids during a meal.
- Abstain from meat on Fridays (which is also required by Holy Mother Church).
- Not eating candy or dessert during one day.
- Take a cold shower.
- Not eating meat in saturdays in honor of the Blessed Virgin Mary.
- Keep one hour of silence.
- Do not buy or sell in Sunday (which is also a commandment).
- Give food to the hungry.
- Give water to the thirsty.
- Visit the sick, and confort them.

IMPORTANT NOTES

☐ _____
☐ _____
☐ _____
☐ _____
☐ _____
☐ _____
☐ _____
☐ _____
☐ _____

YOUR SOUL'S GROWTH PLANNER

LONG LIVE CHRIST THE KING!

VIVA CRISTO REY.ORG

DATE: MONTH   DAY   YEAR

GOALS OF THE DAY

PRAYING THE ROSARY OF 15 DECADES.................. ☐

READING THE HOLY BIBLE (15 MINUTES)............... ☐

DAILY SACRIFICES... ☐

☐ _____   ☐ _____
☐ _____   ☐ _____
☐ _____   ☐ _____
☐ _____   ☐ _____
☐ _____   ☐ _____
☐ _____   ☐ _____
☐ _____   ☐ _____
☐ _____   ☐ _____
☐ _____   ☐ _____

SUGGESTIONS

If you don't know how to pray the Holy Rosary, you can get our book "Rosary for beginners" in the following link: www.vcrey.com/rosary-book

Some sacrifices that you can do include:

- Not drinking water or liquids during a meal.
- Abstain from meat on Fridays (which is also required by Holy Mother Church).
- Not eating candy or dessert during one day.
- Take a cold shower.
- Not eating meat in saturdays in honor of the Blessed Virgin Mary.
- Keep one hour of silence.
- Do not buy or sell in Sunday (which is also a commandment).
- Give food to the hungry.
- Give water to the thirsty.
- Visit the sick, and confort them.

IMPORTANT NOTES

☐ _____
☐ _____
☐ _____
☐ _____
☐ _____
☐ _____
☐ _____
☐ _____
☐ _____

YOUR SOUL'S GROWTH PLANNER

LONG LIVE CHRIST THE KING!

VIVA CRISTO REY.ORG

DATE: MONTH   DAY   YEAR

GOALS OF THE DAY

PRAYING THE ROSARY OF 15 DECADES................... ☐

READING THE HOLY BIBLE (15 MINUTES)............... ☐

DAILY SACRIFICES... ☐

☐ _____   ☐ _____
☐ _____   ☐ _____
☐ _____   ☐ _____
☐ _____   ☐ _____
☐ _____   ☐ _____
☐ _____   ☐ _____
☐ _____   ☐ _____
☐ _____   ☐ _____
☐ _____   ☐ _____

SUGGESTIONS

If you don't know how to pray the Holy Rosary, you can get our book "Rosary for beginners" in the following link: www.vcrey.com/rosary-book

Some sacrifices that you can do include:

- Not drinking water or liquids during a meal.
- Abstain from meat on Fridays (which is also required by Holy Mother Church).
- Not eating candy or dessert during one day.
- Take a cold shower.
- Not eating meat in saturdays in honor of the Blessed Virgin Mary.
- Keep one hour of silence.
- Do not buy or sell in Sunday (which is also a commandment).
- Give food to the hungry.
- Give water to the thirsty.
- Visit the sick, and confort them.

IMPORTANT NOTES

☐ _____
☐ _____
☐ _____
☐ _____
☐ _____
☐ _____
☐ _____
☐ _____
☐ _____

YOUR SOUL'S GROWTH PLANNER

VIVA
CRISTO
REY.ORG

LONG LIVE CHRIST THE KING!

DATE: MONTH   DAY   YEAR

GOALS OF THE DAY

PRAYING THE ROSARY OF 15 DECADES.................. ☐

READING THE HOLY BIBLE (15 MINUTES)................ ☐

DAILY SACRIFICES... ☐

☐ _____   ☐ _____
☐ _____   ☐ _____
☐ _____   ☐ _____
☐ _____   ☐ _____
☐ _____   ☐ _____
☐ _____
☐ _____   ☐ _____
☐ _____   ☐ _____
☐ _____

SUGGESTIONS

If you don't know how to pray the Holy Rosary, you can get our book "Rosary for beginners" in the following link: www.vcrey.com/rosary-book

Some sacrifices that you can do include:

- Not drinking water or liquids during a meal.
- Abstain from meat on Fridays (which is also required by Holy Mother Church).
- Not eating candy or dessert during one day.
- Take a cold shower.
- Not eating meat in saturdays in honor of the Blessed Virgin Mary.
- Keep one hour of silence.
- Do not buy or sell in Sunday (which is also a commandment).
- Give food to the hungry.
- Give water to the thirsty.
- Visit the sick, and confort them.

IMPORTANT NOTES

☐ _____
☐ _____
☐ _____
☐ _____
☐ _____
☐ _____
☐ _____
☐ _____
☐ _____

YOUR SOUL'S GROWTH PLANNER

LONG LIVE CHRIST THE KING!

VIVA
CRISTO
REY.ORG

DATE: MONTH   DAY   YEAR

GOALS OF THE DAY

PRAYING THE ROSARY OF 15 DECADES.................. ☐

READING THE HOLY BIBLE (15 MINUTES)............... ☐

DAILY SACRIFICES.. ☐

☐ _____   ☐ _____
☐ _____   ☐ _____
☐ _____   ☐ _____
☐ _____   ☐ _____
☐ _____   ☐ _____
☐ _____   ☐ _____
☐ _____   ☐ _____
☐ _____   ☐ _____
☐ _____   ☐ _____

SUGGESTIONS

If you don't know how to pray the Holy Rosary, you can get our book "Rosary for beginners" in the following link: www.vcrey.com/rosary-book

Some sacrifices that you can do include:

- Not drinking water or liquids during a meal.
- Abstain from meat on Fridays (which is also required by Holy Mother Church).
- Not eating candy or dessert during one day.
- Take a cold shower.
- Not eating meat in saturdays in honor of the Blessed Virgin Mary.
- Keep one hour of silence.
- Do not buy or sell in Sunday (which is also a commandment).
- Give food to the hungry.
- Give water to the thirsty.
- Visit the sick, and confort them.

IMPORTANT NOTES

☐ _____
☐ _____
☐ _____
☐ _____
☐ _____
☐ _____
☐ _____
☐ _____
☐ _____

YOUR SOUL'S GROWTH PLANNER

LONG LIVE CHRIST THE KING!

VIVA
CRISTO
REY.ORG

DATE: MONTH   DAY   YEAR

GOALS OF THE DAY

PRAYING THE ROSARY OF 15 DECADES.................... ☐

READING THE HOLY BIBLE (15 MINUTES)................ ☐

DAILY SACRIFICES.. ☐

☐ _____   ☐ _____
☐ _____   ☐ _____
☐ _____   ☐ _____
☐ _____   ☐ _____
☐ _____   ☐ _____
☐ _____   ☐ _____
☐ _____   ☐ _____
☐ _____   ☐ _____
☐ _____   ☐ _____

SUGGESTIONS

If you don't know how to pray the Holy Rosary, you can get our book "Rosary for beginners" in the following link: www.vcrey.com/rosary-book

Some sacrifices that you can do include:

- Not drinking water or liquids during a meal.
- Abstain from meat on Fridays (which is also required by Holy Mother Church).
- Not eating candy or dessert during one day.
- Take a cold shower.
- Not eating meat in saturdays in honor of the Blessed Virgin Mary.
- Keep one hour of silence.
- Do not buy or sell in Sunday (which is also a commandment).
- Give food to the hungry.
- Give water to the thirsty.
- Visit the sick, and confort them.

IMPORTANT NOTES

☐ _____
☐ _____
☐ _____
☐ _____
☐ _____
☐ _____
☐ _____
☐ _____
☐ _____

YOUR SOUL'S GROWTH PLANNER

VIVA CRISTO REY.ORG

LONG LIVE CHRIST THE KING!

DATE: MONTH   DAY   YEAR

GOALS OF THE DAY

PRAYING THE ROSARY OF 15 DECADES.................. ☐

READING THE HOLY BIBLE (15 MINUTES)............... ☐

DAILY SACRIFICES.. ☐

☐ _____   ☐ _____
☐ _____   ☐ _____
☐ _____   ☐ _____
☐ _____   ☐ _____
☐ _____   ☐ _____
☐ _____   ☐ _____
☐ _____   ☐ _____
☐ _____   ☐ _____
☐ _____   ☐ _____

SUGGESTIONS

If you don't know how to pray the Holy Rosary, you can get our book "Rosary for beginners" in the following link: www.vcrey.com/rosary-book

Some sacrifices that you can do include:

- Not drinking water or liquids during a meal.
- Abstain from meat on Fridays (which is also required by Holy Mother Church).
- Not eating candy or dessert during one day.
- Take a cold shower.
- Not eating meat in saturdays in honor of the Blessed Virgin Mary.
- Keep one hour of silence.
- Do not buy or sell in Sunday (which is also a commandment).
- Give food to the hungry.
- Give water to the thirsty.
- Visit the sick, and confort them.

IMPORTANT NOTES

☐ _____
☐ _____
☐ _____
☐ _____
☐ _____
☐ _____
☐ _____
☐ _____
☐ _____

YOUR SOUL'S GROWTH PLANNER

LONG LIVE CHRIST THE KING!

VIVA CRISTO REY.ORG

DATE: MONTH   DAY   YEAR

GOALS OF THE DAY

PRAYING THE ROSARY OF 15 DECADES.................. ☐

READING THE HOLY BIBLE (15 MINUTES)............... ☐

DAILY SACRIFICES.. ☐

☐ _____   ☐ _____
☐ _____   ☐ _____
☐ _____   ☐ _____
☐ _____   ☐ _____
☐ _____   ☐ _____
☐ _____   ☐ _____
☐ _____   ☐ _____
☐ _____   ☐ _____
☐ _____   ☐ _____

SUGGESTIONS

If you don't know how to pray the Holy Rosary, you can get our book "Rosary for beginners" in the following link: www.vcrey.com/rosary-book

Some sacrifices that you can do include:

- Not drinking water or liquids during a meal.
- Abstain from meat on Fridays (which is also required by Holy Mother Church).
- Not eating candy or dessert during one day.
- Take a cold shower.
- Not eating meat in saturdays in honor of the Blessed Virgin Mary.
- Keep one hour of silence.
- Do not buy or sell in Sunday (which is also a commandment).
- Give food to the hungry.
- Give water to the thirsty.
- Visit the sick, and confort them.

IMPORTANT NOTES

☐ _____
☐ _____
☐ _____
☐ _____
☐ _____
☐ _____
☐ _____
☐ _____
☐ _____

YOUR SOUL'S GROWTH PLANNER

LONG LIVE CHRIST THE KING!

DATE: MONTH   DAY   YEAR

GOALS OF THE DAY

PRAYING THE ROSARY OF 15 DECADES.................. ☐

READING THE HOLY BIBLE (15 MINUTES)................ ☐

DAILY SACRIFICES... ☐

☐ _____   ☐ _____

☐ _____   ☐ _____

☐ _____   ☐ _____

☐ _____   ☐ _____

☐ _____   ☐ _____
☐ _____   ☐ _____

☐ _____   ☐ _____

☐ _____   ☐ _____
☐ _____   ☐ _____

SUGGESTIONS

If you don't know how to pray the Holy Rosary, you can get our book "Rosary for beginners" in the following link: www.vcrey.com/rosary-book

Some sacrifices that you can do include:

- Not drinking water or liquids during a meal.
- Abstain from meat on Fridays (which is also required by Holy Mother Church).
- Not eating candy or dessert during one day.
- Take a cold shower.
- Not eating meat in saturdays in honor of the Blessed Virgin Mary.
- Keep one hour of silence.
- Do not buy or sell in Sunday (which is also a commandment).
- Give food to the hungry.
- Give water to the thirsty.
- Visit the sick, and confort them.

IMPORTANT NOTES

☐ _____

☐ _____

☐ _____

☐ _____

☐ _____

☐ _____

☐ _____

☐ _____

☐ _____

YOUR SOUL'S GROWTH PLANNER

LONG LIVE CHRIST THE KING!

VIVA CRISTO REY.ORG

DATE: MONTH   DAY   YEAR

GOALS OF THE DAY

PRAYING THE ROSARY OF 15 DECADES................... ☐

READING THE HOLY BIBLE (15 MINUTES)................ ☐

DAILY SACRIFICES.. ☐

☐ _____   ☐ _____
☐ _____   ☐ _____
☐ _____   ☐ _____
☐ _____   ☐ _____
☐ _____   ☐ _____
☐ _____   ☐ _____
☐ _____   ☐ _____
☐ _____   ☐ _____
☐ _____   ☐ _____

SUGGESTIONS

If you don't know how to pray the Holy Rosary, you can get our book "Rosary for beginners" in the following link: www.vcrey.com/rosary-book

Some sacrifices that you can do include:

- Not drinking water or liquids during a meal.
- Abstain from meat on Fridays (which is also required by Holy Mother Church).
- Not eating candy or dessert during one day.
- Take a cold shower.
- Not eating meat in saturdays in honor of the Blessed Virgin Mary.
- Keep one hour of silence.
- Do not buy or sell in Sunday (which is also a commandment).
- Give food to the hungry.
- Give water to the thirsty.
- Visit the sick, and confort them.

IMPORTANT NOTES

☐ _____
☐ _____
☐ _____
☐ _____
☐ _____
☐ _____
☐ _____
☐ _____
☐ _____

YOUR SOUL'S GROWTH PLANNER

LONG LIVE CHRIST THE KING!

VIVA
CRISTO
REY.ORG

DATE: MONTH   DAY   YEAR

GOALS OF THE DAY

PRAYING THE ROSARY OF 15 DECADES................... ☐

READING THE HOLY BIBLE (15 MINUTES)............... ☐

DAILY SACRIFICES.. ☐

☐ _____   ☐ _____
☐ _____   ☐ _____
☐ _____   ☐ _____
☐ _____   ☐ _____
☐ _____   ☐ _____
☐ _____   ☐ _____
☐ _____   ☐ _____
☐ _____   ☐ _____
☐ _____   ☐ _____

SUGGESTIONS

If you don't know how to pray the Holy Rosary, you can get our book "Rosary for beginners" in the following link: www.vcrey.com/rosary-book

Some sacrifices that you can do include:

- Not drinking water or liquids during a meal.
- Abstain from meat on Fridays (which is also required by Holy Mother Church).
- Not eating candy or dessert during one day.
- Take a cold shower.
- Not eating meat in saturdays in honor of the Blessed Virgin Mary.
- Keep one hour of silence.
- Do not buy or sell in Sunday (which is also a commandment).
- Give food to the hungry.
- Give water to the thirsty.
- Visit the sick, and confort them.

IMPORTANT NOTES

☐ _____
☐ _____
☐ _____
☐ _____
☐ _____
☐ _____
☐ _____
☐ _____
☐ _____

YOUR SOUL'S GROWTH PLANNER

LONG LIVE CHRIST THE KING!

VIVA
CRISTO
REY.ORG

DATE: MONTH   DAY   YEAR

GOALS OF THE DAY

PRAYING THE ROSARY OF 15 DECADES.................. ☐

READING THE HOLY BIBLE (15 MINUTES)............... ☐

DAILY SACRIFICES... ☐

☐ _____   ☐ _____
☐ _____   ☐ _____
☐ _____   ☐ _____
☐ _____   ☐ _____
☐ _____   ☐ _____
☐ _____   ☐ _____
☐ _____   ☐ _____
☐ _____   ☐ _____
☐ _____   ☐ _____

SUGGESTIONS

If you don't know how to pray the Holy Rosary, you can get our book "Rosary for beginners" in the following link: www.vcrey.com/rosary-book

Some sacrifices that you can do include:

- Not drinking water or liquids during a meal.
- Abstain from meat on Fridays (which is also required by Holy Mother Church).
- Not eating candy or dessert during one day.
- Take a cold shower.
- Not eating meat in saturdays in honor of the Blessed Virgin Mary.
- Keep one hour of silence.
- Do not buy or sell in Sunday (which is also a commandment).
- Give food to the hungry.
- Give water to the thirsty.
- Visit the sick, and confort them.

IMPORTANT NOTES

☐ _____
☐ _____
☐ _____
☐ _____
☐ _____
☐ _____
☐ _____
☐ _____
☐ _____

YOUR SOUL'S GROWTH PLANNER

LONG LIVE CHRIST THE KING!

VIVA
CRISTO
REY.ORG

DATE: MONTH   DAY   YEAR

GOALS OF THE DAY

PRAYING THE ROSARY OF 15 DECADES................... ☐

READING THE HOLY BIBLE (15 MINUTES)................ ☐

DAILY SACRIFICES.. ☐

☐ _____   ☐ _____
☐ _____   ☐ _____
☐ _____   ☐ _____
☐ _____   ☐ _____
☐ _____   ☐ _____
☐ _____   ☐ _____
☐ _____   ☐ _____
☐ _____   ☐ _____
☐ _____   ☐ _____

SUGGESTIONS

If you don't know how to pray the Holy Rosary, you can get our book "Rosary for beginners" in the following link: www.vcrey.com/rosary-book

Some sacrifices that you can do include:

- Not drinking water or liquids during a meal.
- Abstain from meat on Fridays (which is also required by Holy Mother Church).
- Not eating candy or dessert during one day.
- Take a cold shower.
- Not eating meat in saturdays in honor of the Blessed Virgin Mary.
- Keep one hour of silence.
- Do not buy or sell in Sunday (which is also a commandment).
- Give food to the hungry.
- Give water to the thirsty.
- Visit the sick, and confort them.

IMPORTANT NOTES

☐ _____
☐ _____
☐ _____
☐ _____
☐ _____
☐ _____
☐ _____
☐ _____
☐ _____

YOUR SOUL'S GROWTH PLANNER

LONG LIVE CHRIST THE KING!

VIVA CRISTO REY.ORG

DATE: MONTH   DAY   YEAR

GOALS OF THE DAY

PRAYING THE ROSARY OF 15 DECADES.................. ☐

READING THE HOLY BIBLE (15 MINUTES)............... ☐

DAILY SACRIFICES... ☐

☐ _____   ☐ _____
☐ _____   ☐ _____
☐ _____   ☐ _____
☐ _____   ☐ _____
☐ _____   ☐ _____
☐ _____   ☐ _____
☐ _____   ☐ _____
☐ _____   ☐ _____
☐ _____   ☐ _____

SUGGESTIONS

If you don't know how to pray the Holy Rosary, you can get our book "Rosary for beginners" in the following link: www.vcrey.com/rosary-book

Some sacrifices that you can do include:

- Not drinking water or liquids during a meal.
- Abstain from meat on Fridays (which is also required by Holy Mother Church).
- Not eating candy or dessert during one day.
- Take a cold shower.
- Not eating meat in saturdays in honor of the Blessed Virgin Mary.
- Keep one hour of silence.
- Do not buy or sell in Sunday (which is also a commandment).
- Give food to the hungry.
- Give water to the thirsty.
- Visit the sick, and confort them.

IMPORTANT NOTES

☐ _____
☐ _____
☐ _____
☐ _____
☐ _____
☐ _____
☐ _____
☐ _____
☐ _____

YOUR SOUL'S GROWTH PLANNER

LONG LIVE CHRIST THE KING!

VIVA CRISTO REY.ORG

DATE: MONTH   DAY   YEAR

GOALS OF THE DAY

PRAYING THE ROSARY OF 15 DECADES.................. ☐

READING THE HOLY BIBLE (15 MINUTES).............. ☐

DAILY SACRIFICES.. ☐

☐ _____   ☐ _____
☐ _____   ☐ _____
☐ _____   ☐ _____
☐ _____   ☐ _____
☐ _____   ☐ _____
☐ _____   ☐ _____
☐ _____   ☐ _____
☐ _____   ☐ _____
☐ _____   ☐ _____

SUGGESTIONS

If you don't know how to pray the Holy Rosary, you can get our book "Rosary for beginners" in the following link: www.vcrey.com/rosary-book

Some sacrifices that you can do include:

- Not drinking water or liquids during a meal.
- Abstain from meat on Fridays (which is also required by Holy Mother Church).
- Not eating candy or dessert during one day.
- Take a cold shower.
- Not eating meat in saturdays in honor of the Blessed Virgin Mary.
- Keep one hour of silence.
- Do not buy or sell in Sunday (which is also a commandment).
- Give food to the hungry.
- Give water to the thirsty.
- Visit the sick, and confort them.

IMPORTANT NOTES

☐ _____
☐ _____
☐ _____
☐ _____
☐ _____
☐ _____
☐ _____
☐ _____
☐ _____

YOUR SOUL'S GROWTH PLANNER

LONG LIVE CHRIST THE KING!

VIVA CRISTO REY.ORG

DATE: MONTH   DAY   YEAR

GOALS OF THE DAY

PRAYING THE ROSARY OF 15 DECADES.................. ☐

READING THE HOLY BIBLE (15 MINUTES)............... ☐

DAILY SACRIFICES... ☐

☐ _____   ☐ _____
☐ _____   ☐ _____
☐ _____   ☐ _____
☐ _____   ☐ _____
☐ _____   ☐ _____
☐ _____
☐ _____   ☐ _____
☐ _____   ☐ _____
☐ _____   ☐ _____

SUGGESTIONS

If you don't know how to pray the Holy Rosary, you can get our book "Rosary for beginners" in the following link: www.vcrey.com/rosary-book

Some sacrifices that you can do include:

- Not drinking water or liquids during a meal.
- Abstain from meat on Fridays (which is also required by Holy Mother Church).
- Not eating candy or dessert during one day.
- Take a cold shower.
- Not eating meat in saturdays in honor of the Blessed Virgin Mary.
- Keep one hour of silence.
- Do not buy or sell in Sunday (which is also a commandment).
- Give food to the hungry.
- Give water to the thirsty.
- Visit the sick, and confort them.

IMPORTANT NOTES

☐ _____
☐ _____
☐ _____
☐ _____
☐ _____
☐ _____
☐ _____
☐ _____
☐ _____

YOUR SOUL'S GROWTH PLANNER

LONG LIVE CHRIST THE KING!

VIVA
CRISTO
REY.ORG

DATE: MONTH   DAY   YEAR

GOALS OF THE DAY

PRAYING THE ROSARY OF 15 DECADES.................. ☐

READING THE HOLY BIBLE (15 MINUTES)............... ☐

DAILY SACRIFICES... ☐

☐ _____   ☐ _____

☐ _____   ☐ _____

☐ _____   ☐ _____

☐ _____   ☐ _____

☐ _____   ☐ _____

☐ _____   ☐ _____

☐ _____   ☐ _____

☐ _____   ☐ _____

☐ _____   ☐ _____

SUGGESTIONS

If you don't know how to pray the Holy Rosary, you can get our book "Rosary for beginners" in the following link: www.vcrey.com/rosary-book

Some sacrifices that you can do include:

- Not drinking water or liquids during a meal.
- Abstain from meat on Fridays (which is also required by Holy Mother Church).
- Not eating candy or dessert during one day.
- Take a cold shower.
- Not eating meat in saturdays in honor of the Blessed Virgin Mary.
- Keep one hour of silence.
- Do not buy or sell in Sunday (which is also a commandment).
- Give food to the hungry.
- Give water to the thirsty.
- Visit the sick, and confort them.

IMPORTANT NOTES

☐ _____

☐ _____

☐ _____

☐ _____

☐ _____

☐ _____

☐ _____

☐ _____

☐ _____

YOUR SOUL'S GROWTH PLANNER

LONG LIVE CHRIST THE KING!

VIVA CRISTO REY.ORG

DATE: MONTH   DAY   YEAR

GOALS OF THE DAY

PRAYING THE ROSARY OF 15 DECADES................... ☐

READING THE HOLY BIBLE (15 MINUTES)............... ☐

DAILY SACRIFICES... ☐

☐ _____   ☐ _____

☐ _____   ☐ _____

☐ _____   ☐ _____

☐ _____   ☐ _____

☐ _____   ☐ _____

☐ _____   ☐ _____

☐ _____   ☐ _____

☐ _____   ☐ _____

☐ _____   ☐ _____

SUGGESTIONS

If you don't know how to pray the Holy Rosary, you can get our book "Rosary for beginners" in the following link: www.vcrey.com/rosary-book

Some sacrifices that you can do include:

- Not drinking water or liquids during a meal.
- Abstain from meat on Fridays (which is also required by Holy Mother Church).
- Not eating candy or dessert during one day.
- Take a cold shower.
- Not eating meat in saturdays in honor of the Blessed Virgin Mary.
- Keep one hour of silence.
- Do not buy or sell in Sunday (which is also a commandment).
- Give food to the hungry.
- Give water to the thirsty.
- Visit the sick, and confort them.

IMPORTANT NOTES

☐ _____

☐ _____

☐ _____

☐ _____

☐ _____

☐ _____

☐ _____

☐ _____

☐ _____

YOUR SOUL'S GROWTH PLANNER

LONG LIVE CHRIST THE KING!

VIVA CRISTO REY.ORG

DATE: MONTH   DAY   YEAR

GOALS OF THE DAY

PRAYING THE ROSARY OF 15 DECADES................... ☐

READING THE HOLY BIBLE (15 MINUTES)................ ☐

DAILY SACRIFICES.. ☐

☐ _____   ☐ _____

☐ _____   ☐ _____

☐ _____   ☐ _____

☐ _____   ☐ _____

☐ _____   ☐ _____

☐ _____   ☐ _____

☐ _____   ☐ _____

☐ _____   ☐ _____

☐ _____   ☐ _____

SUGGESTIONS

If you don't know how to pray the Holy Rosary, you can get our book "Rosary for beginners" in the following link: www.vcrey.com/rosary-book

Some sacrifices that you can do include:

- Not drinking water or liquids during a meal.
- Abstain from meat on Fridays (which is also required by Holy Mother Church).
- Not eating candy or dessert during one day.
- Take a cold shower.
- Not eating meat in saturdays in honor of the Blessed Virgin Mary.
- Keep one hour of silence.
- Do not buy or sell in Sunday (which is also a commandment).
- Give food to the hungry.
- Give water to the thirsty.
- Visit the sick, and confort them.

IMPORTANT NOTES

☐ _____

☐ _____

☐ _____

☐ _____

☐ _____

☐ _____

☐ _____

☐ _____

☐ _____

YOUR SOUL'S GROWTH PLANNER

VIVA
CRISTO
REY.ORG

LONG LIVE CHRIST THE KING!

DATE: MONTH   DAY   YEAR

GOALS OF THE DAY

PRAYING THE ROSARY OF 15 DECADES................... ☐

READING THE HOLY BIBLE (15 MINUTES)................ ☐

DAILY SACRIFICES.. ☐

☐ _____   ☐ _____
☐ _____   ☐ _____
☐ _____   ☐ _____

☐ _____   ☐ _____
☐ _____   ☐ _____
☐ _____   ☐ _____

☐ _____   ☐ _____

☐ _____   ☐ _____
☐ _____   ☐ _____

SUGGESTIONS

If you don't know how to pray the Holy Rosary, you can get our book "Rosary for beginners" in the following link: www.vcrey.com/rosary-book

Some sacrifices that you can do include:

- Not drinking water or liquids during a meal.
- Abstain from meat on Fridays (which is also required by Holy Mother Church).
- Not eating candy or dessert during one day.
- Take a cold shower.
- Not eating meat in saturdays in honor of the Blessed Virgin Mary.
- Keep one hour of silence.
- Do not buy or sell in Sunday (which is also a commandment).
- Give food to the hungry.
- Give water to the thirsty.
- Visit the sick, and confort them.

IMPORTANT NOTES

☐ _____
☐ _____
☐ _____
☐ _____
☐ _____
☐ _____
☐ _____
☐ _____
☐ _____
☐ _____

YOUR SOUL'S GROWTH PLANNER

LONG LIVE CHRIST THE KING!

VIVA CRISTO REY.ORG

DATE: MONTH   DAY   YEAR

GOALS OF THE DAY

PRAYING THE ROSARY OF 15 DECADES................... ☐

READING THE HOLY BIBLE (15 MINUTES)................ ☐

DAILY SACRIFICES... ☐

☐ _____   ☐ _____
☐ _____   ☐ _____
☐ _____   ☐ _____
☐ _____   ☐ _____
☐ _____   ☐ _____
☐ _____   ☐ _____
☐ _____   ☐ _____
☐ _____   ☐ _____
☐ _____   ☐ _____

SUGGESTIONS

If you don't know how to pray the Holy Rosary, you can get our book "Rosary for beginners" in the following link: www.vcrey.com/rosary-book

Some sacrifices that you can do include:

- Not drinking water or liquids during a meal.
- Abstain from meat on Fridays (which is also required by Holy Mother Church).
- Not eating candy or dessert during one day.
- Take a cold shower.
- Not eating meat in saturdays in honor of the Blessed Virgin Mary.
- Keep one hour of silence.
- Do not buy or sell in Sunday (which is also a commandment).
- Give food to the hungry.
- Give water to the thirsty.
- Visit the sick, and confort them.

IMPORTANT NOTES

☐ _____
☐ _____
☐ _____
☐ _____
☐ _____
☐ _____
☐ _____
☐ _____
☐ _____

YOUR SOUL'S GROWTH PLANNER

LONG LIVE CHRIST THE KING!

VIVA CRISTO REY.ORG

DATE: MONTH   DAY   YEAR

GOALS OF THE DAY

PRAYING THE ROSARY OF 15 DECADES................. ☐

READING THE HOLY BIBLE (15 MINUTES)................ ☐

DAILY SACRIFICES... ☐

☐ _____   ☐ _____
☐ _____   ☐ _____
☐ _____   ☐ _____
☐ _____   ☐ _____
☐ _____   ☐ _____
☐ _____   ☐ _____
☐ _____   ☐ _____
☐ _____   ☐ _____

SUGGESTIONS

If you don't know how to pray the Holy Rosary, you can get our book "Rosary for beginners" in the following link: www.vcrey.com/rosary-book

Some sacrifices that you can do include:

- Not drinking water or liquids during a meal.
- Abstain from meat on Fridays (which is also required by Holy Mother Church).
- Not eating candy or dessert during one day.
- Take a cold shower.
- Not eating meat in saturdays in honor of the Blessed Virgin Mary.
- Keep one hour of silence.
- Do not buy or sell in Sunday (which is also a commandment).
- Give food to the hungry.
- Give water to the thirsty.
- Visit the sick, and confort them.

IMPORTANT NOTES

☐ _____
☐ _____
☐ _____
☐ _____
☐ _____
☐ _____
☐ _____
☐ _____
☐ _____

YOUR SOUL'S GROWTH PLANNER

LONG LIVE CHRIST THE KING!

VIVA
CRISTO
REY.ORG

DATE: MONTH   DAY   YEAR

GOALS OF THE DAY

PRAYING THE ROSARY OF 15 DECADES................... ☐

READING THE HOLY BIBLE (15 MINUTES)............... ☐

DAILY SACRIFICES.. ☐

☐ _____   ☐ _____

☐ _____   ☐ _____

☐ _____   ☐ _____

☐ _____   ☐ _____

☐ _____   ☐ _____

☐ _____   ☐ _____

☐ _____   ☐ _____

☐ _____   ☐ _____

☐ _____   ☐ _____

SUGGESTIONS

If you don't know how to pray the Holy Rosary, you can get our book "Rosary for beginners" in the following link: www.vcrey.com/rosary-book

Some sacrifices that you can do include:

- Not drinking water or liquids during a meal.
- Abstain from meat on Fridays (which is also required by Holy Mother Church).
- Not eating candy or dessert during one day.
- Take a cold shower.
- Not eating meat in saturdays in honor of the Blessed Virgin Mary.
- Keep one hour of silence.
- Do not buy or sell in Sunday (which is also a commandment).
- Give food to the hungry.
- Give water to the thirsty.
- Visit the sick, and confort them.

IMPORTANT NOTES

☐ _____

☐ _____

☐ _____

☐ _____

☐ _____

☐ _____

☐ _____

☐ _____

☐ _____

YOUR SOUL'S GROWTH PLANNER

LONG LIVE CHRIST THE KING!

VIVA
CRISTO
REY.ORG

DATE: MONTH   DAY   YEAR

GOALS OF THE DAY

PRAYING THE ROSARY OF 15 DECADES................... ☐

READING THE HOLY BIBLE (15 MINUTES)................ ☐

DAILY SACRIFICES.. ☐

☐ _____   ☐ _____

☐ _____   ☐ _____

☐ _____   ☐ _____

☐ _____   ☐ _____

☐ _____   ☐ _____

☐ _____   ☐ _____

☐ _____   ☐ _____

☐ _____   ☐ _____

☐ _____   ☐ _____

SUGGESTIONS

If you don't know how to pray the Holy Rosary, you can get our book "Rosary for beginners" in the following link: www.vcrey.com/rosary-book

Some sacrifices that you can do include:

- Not drinking water or liquids during a meal.
- Abstain from meat on Fridays (which is also required by Holy Mother Church).
- Not eating candy or dessert during one day.
- Take a cold shower.
- Not eating meat in saturdays in honor of the Blessed Virgin Mary.
- Keep one hour of silence.
- Do not buy or sell in Sunday (which is also a commandment).
- Give food to the hungry.
- Give water to the thirsty.
- Visit the sick, and confort them.

IMPORTANT NOTES

☐ _____

☐ _____

☐ _____

☐ _____

☐ _____

☐ _____

☐ _____

☐ _____

☐ _____

YOUR SOUL'S GROWTH PLANNER

LONG LIVE CHRIST THE KING!

VIVA
CRISTO
REY.ORG

DATE: MONTH   DAY   YEAR

GOALS OF THE DAY

PRAYING THE ROSARY OF 15 DECADES................... ☐

READING THE HOLY BIBLE (15 MINUTES)................ ☐

DAILY SACRIFICES.. ☐

☐ _____   ☐ _____
☐ _____   ☐ _____
☐ _____   ☐ _____
☐ _____   ☐ _____
☐ _____   ☐ _____
☐ _____   ☐ _____
☐ _____   ☐ _____
☐ _____   ☐ _____
☐ _____   ☐ _____

SUGGESTIONS

If you don't know how to pray the Holy Rosary, you can get our book "Rosary for beginners" in the following link: www.vcrey.com/rosary-book

Some sacrifices that you can do include:

- Not drinking water or liquids during a meal.
- Abstain from meat on Fridays (which is also required by Holy Mother Church).
- Not eating candy or dessert during one day.
- Take a cold shower.
- Not eating meat in saturdays in honor of the Blessed Virgin Mary.
- Keep one hour of silence.
- Do not buy or sell in Sunday (which is also a commandment).
- Give food to the hungry.
- Give water to the thirsty.
- Visit the sick, and confort them.

IMPORTANT NOTES

☐ _____
☐ _____
☐ _____
☐ _____
☐ _____
☐ _____
☐ _____
☐ _____
☐ _____

YOUR SOUL'S GROWTH PLANNER

LONG LIVE CHRIST THE KING!

VIVA CRISTO REY.ORG

DATE: MONTH   DAY   YEAR

GOALS OF THE DAY

PRAYING THE ROSARY OF 15 DECADES................... ☐

READING THE HOLY BIBLE (15 MINUTES)............... ☐

DAILY SACRIFICES... ☐

☐ _____   ☐ _____

☐ _____   ☐ _____

☐ _____   ☐ _____

☐ _____   ☐ _____

☐ _____   ☐ _____

☐ _____   ☐ _____

☐ _____   ☐ _____

☐ _____   ☐ _____

☐ _____   ☐ _____

SUGGESTIONS

If you don't know how to pray the Holy Rosary, you can get our book "Rosary for beginners" in the following link: www.vcrey.com/rosary-book

Some sacrifices that you can do include:

- Not drinking water or liquids during a meal.
- Abstain from meat on Fridays (which is also required by Holy Mother Church).
- Not eating candy or dessert during one day.
- Take a cold shower.
- Not eating meat in saturdays in honor of the Blessed Virgin Mary.
- Keep one hour of silence.
- Do not buy or sell in Sunday (which is also a commandment).
- Give food to the hungry.
- Give water to the thirsty.
- Visit the sick, and confort them.

IMPORTANT NOTES

☐ _____

☐ _____

☐ _____

☐ _____

☐ _____

☐ _____

☐ _____

☐ _____

☐ _____

YOUR SOUL'S GROWTH PLANNER

VIVA CRISTO REY.ORG

LONG LIVE CHRIST THE KING!

DATE: MONTH   DAY   YEAR

GOALS OF THE DAY

PRAYING THE ROSARY OF 15 DECADES................... ☐

READING THE HOLY BIBLE (15 MINUTES)................ ☐

DAILY SACRIFICES... ☐

☐ _____   ☐ _____

☐ _____   ☐ _____

☐ _____   ☐ _____

☐ _____   ☐ _____

☐ _____   ☐ _____

☐ _____   ☐ _____

☐ _____   ☐ _____

☐ _____   ☐ _____

☐ _____   ☐ _____

SUGGESTIONS

If you don't know how to pray the Holy Rosary, you can get our book "Rosary for beginners" in the following link: www.vcrey.com/rosary-book

Some sacrifices that you can do include:

- Not drinking water or liquids during a meal.
- Abstain from meat on Fridays (which is also required by Holy Mother Church).
- Not eating candy or dessert during one day.
- Take a cold shower.
- Not eating meat in saturdays in honor of the Blessed Virgin Mary.
- Keep one hour of silence.
- Do not buy or sell in Sunday (which is also a commandment).
- Give food to the hungry.
- Give water to the thirsty.
- Visit the sick, and confort them.

IMPORTANT NOTES

☐ _____

☐ _____

☐ _____

☐ _____

☐ _____

☐ _____

☐ _____

☐ _____

☐ _____

YOUR SOUL'S GROWTH PLANNER

LONG LIVE CHRIST THE KING!

VIVA CRISTO REY.ORG

DATE: MONTH   DAY   YEAR

GOALS OF THE DAY

PRAYING THE ROSARY OF 15 DECADES.................. ☐

READING THE HOLY BIBLE (15 MINUTES)............... ☐

DAILY SACRIFICES... ☐

☐ _____   ☐ _____

☐ _____   ☐ _____

☐ _____   ☐ _____

☐ _____   ☐ _____

☐ _____   ☐ _____

☐ _____   ☐ _____

☐ _____   ☐ _____

☐ _____   ☐ _____

☐ _____   ☐ _____

SUGGESTIONS

If you don't know how to pray the Holy Rosary, you can get our book "Rosary for beginners" in the following link: www.vcrey.com/rosary-book

Some sacrifices that you can do include:

- Not drinking water or liquids during a meal.
- Abstain from meat on Fridays (which is also required by Holy Mother Church).
- Not eating candy or dessert during one day.
- Take a cold shower.
- Not eating meat in saturdays in honor of the Blessed Virgin Mary.
- Keep one hour of silence.
- Do not buy or sell in Sunday (which is also a commandment).
- Give food to the hungry.
- Give water to the thirsty.
- Visit the sick, and confort them.

IMPORTANT NOTES

☐ _____

☐ _____

☐ _____

☐ _____

☐ _____

☐ _____

☐ _____

☐ _____

YOUR SOUL'S GROWTH PLANNER

LONG LIVE CHRIST THE KING!

VIVA
CRISTO
REY.ORG

DATE: MONTH   DAY   YEAR

GOALS OF THE DAY

PRAYING THE ROSARY OF 15 DECADES................... ☐

READING THE HOLY BIBLE (15 MINUTES)................ ☐

DAILY SACRIFICES.. ☐

☐ _____   ☐ _____
☐ _____   ☐ _____
☐ _____   ☐ _____
☐ _____   ☐ _____
☐ _____   ☐ _____
☐ _____   ☐ _____
☐ _____   ☐ _____
☐ _____   ☐ _____
☐ _____   ☐ _____

SUGGESTIONS

If you don't know how to pray the Holy Rosary, you can get our book "Rosary for beginners" in the following link: www.vcrey.com/rosary-book

Some sacrifices that you can do include:

- Not drinking water or liquids during a meal.
- Abstain from meat on Fridays (which is also required by Holy Mother Church).
- Not eating candy or dessert during one day.
- Take a cold shower.
- Not eating meat in saturdays in honor of the Blessed Virgin Mary.
- Keep one hour of silence.
- Do not buy or sell in Sunday (which is also a commandment).
- Give food to the hungry.
- Give water to the thirsty.
- Visit the sick, and confort them.

IMPORTANT NOTES

☐ _____
☐ _____
☐ _____
☐ _____
☐ _____
☐ _____
☐ _____
☐ _____
☐ _____

YOUR SOUL'S GROWTH PLANNER

LONG LIVE CHRIST THE KING!

VIVA
CRISTO
REY.ORG

DATE: MONTH   DAY   YEAR

GOALS OF THE DAY

PRAYING THE ROSARY OF 15 DECADES.................. ☐

READING THE HOLY BIBLE (15 MINUTES)............... ☐

DAILY SACRIFICES... ☐

☐ _____   ☐ _____
☐ _____   ☐ _____
☐ _____   ☐ _____
☐ _____   ☐ _____
☐ _____   ☐ _____
☐ _____   ☐ _____
☐ _____   ☐ _____
☐ _____   ☐ _____
☐ _____   ☐ _____

SUGGESTIONS

If you don't know how to pray the Holy Rosary, you can get our book "Rosary for beginners" in the following link: www.vcrey.com/rosary-book

Some sacrifices that you can do include:

- Not drinking water or liquids during a meal.
- Abstain from meat on Fridays (which is also required by Holy Mother Church).
- Not eating candy or dessert during one day.
- Take a cold shower.
- Not eating meat in saturdays in honor of the Blessed Virgin Mary.
- Keep one hour of silence.
- Do not buy or sell in Sunday (which is also a commandment).
- Give food to the hungry.
- Give water to the thirsty.
- Visit the sick, and confort them.

IMPORTANT NOTES

☐ _____
☐ _____
☐ _____
☐ _____
☐ _____
☐ _____
☐ _____
☐ _____
☐ _____

YOUR SOUL'S GROWTH PLANNER

LONG LIVE CHRIST THE KING!

VIVA
CRISTO
REY.ORG

DATE: MONTH   DAY   YEAR

GOALS OF THE DAY

PRAYING THE ROSARY OF 15 DECADES.................... ☐

READING THE HOLY BIBLE (15 MINUTES)................ ☐

DAILY SACRIFICES... ☐

☐ _____   ☐ _____

☐ _____   ☐ _____

☐ _____   ☐ _____

☐ _____   ☐ _____

☐ _____   ☐ _____
☐ _____   ☐ _____

☐ _____   ☐ _____

☐ _____   ☐ _____
☐ _____   ☐ _____

SUGGESTIONS

If you don't know how to pray the Holy Rosary, you can get our book "Rosary for beginners" in the following link: www.vcrey.com/rosary-book

Some sacrifices that you can do include:

- Not drinking water or liquids during a meal.
- Abstain from meat on Fridays (which is also required by Holy Mother Church).
- Not eating candy or dessert during one day.
- Take a cold shower.
- Not eating meat in saturdays in honor of the Blessed Virgin Mary.
- Keep one hour of silence.
- Do not buy or sell in Sunday (which is also a commandment).
- Give food to the hungry.
- Give water to the thirsty.
- Visit the sick, and confort them.

IMPORTANT NOTES

☐ _____

☐ _____

☐ _____

☐ _____

☐ _____

☐ _____

☐ _____

☐ _____

☐ _____

YOUR SOUL'S GROWTH PLANNER

LONG LIVE CHRIST THE KING!

VIVA CRISTO REY.ORG

DATE: MONTH   DAY   YEAR

GOALS OF THE DAY

PRAYING THE ROSARY OF 15 DECADES................... ☐

READING THE HOLY BIBLE (15 MINUTES)............... ☐

DAILY SACRIFICES.. ☐

☐ _____   ☐ _____
☐ _____   ☐ _____
☐ _____   ☐ _____

☐ _____   ☐ _____
☐ _____   ☐ _____
☐ _____   ☐ _____
☐ _____   ☐ _____

☐ _____   ☐ _____
☐ _____   ☐ _____

SUGGESTIONS

If you don't know how to pray the Holy Rosary, you can get our book "Rosary for beginners" in the following link: www.vcrey.com/rosary-book

Some sacrifices that you can do include:

- Not drinking water or liquids during a meal.
- Abstain from meat on Fridays (which is also required by Holy Mother Church).
- Not eating candy or dessert during one day.
- Take a cold shower.
- Not eating meat in saturdays in honor of the Blessed Virgin Mary.
- Keep one hour of silence.
- Do not buy or sell in Sunday (which is also a commandment).
- Give food to the hungry.
- Give water to the thirsty.
- Visit the sick, and confort them.

IMPORTANT NOTES

☐ _____
☐ _____
☐ _____
☐ _____
☐ _____
☐ _____
☐ _____
☐ _____
☐ _____

YOUR SOUL'S GROWTH PLANNER

LONG LIVE CHRIST THE KING!

VIVA CRISTO REY.ORG

DATE: MONTH   DAY   YEAR

GOALS OF THE DAY

PRAYING THE ROSARY OF 15 DECADES................... ☐

READING THE HOLY BIBLE (15 MINUTES)............... ☐

DAILY SACRIFICES... ☐

☐ _____   ☐ _____
☐ _____   ☐ _____
☐ _____   ☐ _____

☐ _____   ☐ _____
☐ _____   ☐ _____
☐ _____   ☐ _____
☐ _____   ☐ _____

☐ _____   ☐ _____
☐ _____   ☐ _____

SUGGESTIONS

If you don't know how to pray the Holy Rosary, you can get our book "Rosary for beginners" in the following link: www.vcrey.com/rosary-book

Some sacrifices that you can do include:

- Not drinking water or liquids during a meal.
- Abstain from meat on Fridays (which is also required by Holy Mother Church).
- Not eating candy or dessert during one day.
- Take a cold shower.
- Not eating meat in saturdays in honor of the Blessed Virgin Mary.
- Keep one hour of silence.
- Do not buy or sell in Sunday (which is also a commandment).
- Give food to the hungry.
- Give water to the thirsty.
- Visit the sick, and confort them.

IMPORTANT NOTES

☐ _____
☐ _____
☐ _____
☐ _____
☐ _____
☐ _____
☐ _____
☐ _____
☐ _____

YOUR SOUL'S GROWTH PLANNER

LONG LIVE CHRIST THE KING!

VIVA
CRISTO
REY.ORG

DATE: MONTH   DAY   YEAR

GOALS OF THE DAY

PRAYING THE ROSARY OF 15 DECADES................... ☐

READING THE HOLY BIBLE (15 MINUTES)................ ☐

DAILY SACRIFICES... ☐

☐ _____   ☐ _____

☐ _____   ☐ _____

☐ _____   ☐ _____

☐ _____   ☐ _____

☐ _____   ☐ _____

☐ _____   ☐ _____

☐ _____   ☐ _____

☐ _____   ☐ _____

☐ _____   ☐ _____

SUGGESTIONS

If you don't know how to pray the Holy Rosary, you can get our book "Rosary for beginners" in the following link: www.vcrey.com/rosary-book

Some sacrifices that you can do include:

- Not drinking water or liquids during a meal.
- Abstain from meat on Fridays (which is also required by Holy Mother Church).
- Not eating candy or dessert during one day.
- Take a cold shower.
- Not eating meat in saturdays in honor of the Blessed Virgin Mary.
- Keep one hour of silence.
- Do not buy or sell in Sunday (which is also a commandment).
- Give food to the hungry.
- Give water to the thirsty.
- Visit the sick, and confort them.

IMPORTANT NOTES

☐ _____

☐ _____

☐ _____

☐ _____

☐ _____

☐ _____

☐ _____

☐ _____

☐ _____

YOUR SOUL'S GROWTH PLANNER

LONG LIVE CHRIST THE KING!

VIVA
CRISTO
REY.ORG

DATE: MONTH   DAY   YEAR

GOALS OF THE DAY

PRAYING THE ROSARY OF 15 DECADES.................. ☐

READING THE HOLY BIBLE (15 MINUTES)............... ☐

DAILY SACRIFICES.. ☐

☐ _____   ☐ _____
☐ _____   ☐ _____
☐ _____   ☐ _____
☐ _____   ☐ _____
☐ _____   ☐ _____
☐ _____   ☐ _____
☐ _____   ☐ _____
☐ _____   ☐ _____
☐ _____   ☐ _____

SUGGESTIONS

If you don't know how to pray the Holy Rosary, you can get our book "Rosary for beginners" in the following link: www.vcrey.com/rosary-book

Some sacrifices that you can do include:

- Not drinking water or liquids during a meal.
- Abstain from meat on Fridays (which is also required by Holy Mother Church).
- Not eating candy or dessert during one day.
- Take a cold shower.
- Not eating meat in saturdays in honor of the Blessed Virgin Mary.
- Keep one hour of silence.
- Do not buy or sell in Sunday (which is also a commandment).
- Give food to the hungry.
- Give water to the thirsty.
- Visit the sick, and confort them.

IMPORTANT NOTES

☐ _____
☐ _____
☐ _____
☐ _____
☐ _____
☐ _____
☐ _____
☐ _____
☐ _____

YOUR SOUL'S GROWTH PLANNER

LONG LIVE CHRIST THE KING!

VIVA
CRISTO
REY.ORG

DATE: MONTH   DAY   YEAR

GOALS OF THE DAY

PRAYING THE ROSARY OF 15 DECADES................... ☐

READING THE HOLY BIBLE (15 MINUTES)................ ☐

DAILY SACRIFICES.. ☐

☐ _____   ☐ _____
☐ _____   ☐ _____
☐ _____   ☐ _____

☐ _____   ☐ _____
☐ _____   ☐ _____
☐ _____   ☐ _____
☐ _____   ☐ _____

☐ _____   ☐ _____
☐ _____   ☐ _____

IMPORTANT NOTES

☐ _____
☐ _____
☐ _____
☐ _____
☐ _____
☐ _____
☐ _____
☐ _____
☐ _____

YOUR SOUL'S GROWTH PLANNER

LONG LIVE CHRIST THE KING!

VIVA
CRISTO
REY.ORG

DATE: MONTH   DAY   YEAR

GOALS OF THE DAY

PRAYING THE ROSARY OF 15 DECADES.................... ☐

READING THE HOLY BIBLE (15 MINUTES)................ ☐

DAILY SACRIFICES... ☐

☐ _____   ☐ _____

☐ _____   ☐ _____

☐ _____   ☐ _____

☐ _____   ☐ _____

☐ _____   ☐ _____

☐ _____   ☐ _____

☐ _____   ☐ _____

☐ _____   ☐ _____

☐ _____   ☐ _____

SUGGESTIONS

If you don't know how to pray the Holy Rosary, you can get our book "Rosary for beginners" in the following link: www.vcrey.com/rosary-book

Some sacrifices that you can do include:

- Not drinking water or liquids during a meal.
- Abstain from meat on Fridays (which is also required by Holy Mother Church).
- Not eating candy or dessert during one day.
- Take a cold shower.
- Not eating meat in saturdays in honor of the Blessed Virgin Mary.
- Keep one hour of silence.
- Do not buy or sell in Sunday (which is also a commandment).
- Give food to the hungry.
- Give water to the thirsty.
- Visit the sick, and confort them.

IMPORTANT NOTES

☐ _____

☐ _____

☐ _____

☐ _____

☐ _____

☐ _____

☐ _____

☐ _____

☐ _____

YOUR SOUL'S GROWTH PLANNER

LONG LIVE CHRIST THE KING!

VIVA
CRISTO
REY.ORG

DATE: MONTH   DAY   YEAR

GOALS OF THE DAY

PRAYING THE ROSARY OF 15 DECADES.................. ☐

READING THE HOLY BIBLE (15 MINUTES)............... ☐

DAILY SACRIFICES... ☐

☐ _____   ☐ _____

☐ _____   ☐ _____

☐ _____   ☐ _____

☐ _____   ☐ _____

☐ _____   ☐ _____

☐ _____   ☐ _____

☐ _____   ☐ _____

☐ _____   ☐ _____

☐ _____   ☐ _____

SUGGESTIONS

If you don't know how to pray the Holy Rosary, you can get our book "Rosary for beginners" in the following link: www.vcrey.com/rosary-book

Some sacrifices that you can do include:

- Not drinking water or liquids during a meal.
- Abstain from meat on Fridays (which is also required by Holy Mother Church).
- Not eating candy or dessert during one day.
- Take a cold shower.
- Not eating meat in saturdays in honor of the Blessed Virgin Mary.
- Keep one hour of silence.
- Do not buy or sell in Sunday (which is also a commandment).
- Give food to the hungry.
- Give water to the thirsty.
- Visit the sick, and confort them.

IMPORTANT NOTES

☐ _____

☐ _____

☐ _____

☐ _____

☐ _____

☐ _____

☐ _____

☐ _____

☐ _____

YOUR SOUL'S GROWTH PLANNER

LONG LIVE CHRIST THE KING!

VIVA CRISTO REY.ORG

DATE: MONTH   DAY   YEAR

GOALS OF THE DAY

PRAYING THE ROSARY OF 15 DECADES................... ☐

READING THE HOLY BIBLE (15 MINUTES)................ ☐

DAILY SACRIFICES.. ☐

☐ _____   ☐ _____
☐ _____   ☐ _____
☐ _____   ☐ _____
☐ _____   ☐ _____
☐ _____   ☐ _____
☐ _____   ☐ _____
☐ _____   ☐ _____
☐ _____   ☐ _____
☐ _____   ☐ _____

SUGGESTIONS

If you don't know how to pray the Holy Rosary, you can get our book "Rosary for beginners" in the following link: www.vcrey.com/rosary-book

Some sacrifices that you can do include:

- Not drinking water or liquids during a meal.
- Abstain from meat on Fridays (which is also required by Holy Mother Church).
- Not eating candy or dessert during one day.
- Take a cold shower.
- Not eating meat in saturdays in honor of the Blessed Virgin Mary.
- Keep one hour of silence.
- Do not buy or sell in Sunday (which is also a commandment).
- Give food to the hungry.
- Give water to the thirsty.
- Visit the sick, and confort them.

IMPORTANT NOTES

☐ _____
☐ _____
☐ _____
☐ _____
☐ _____
☐ _____
☐ _____
☐ _____
☐ _____

YOUR SOUL'S GROWTH PLANNER

LONG LIVE CHRIST THE KING!

DATE: MONTH   DAY   YEAR

GOALS OF THE DAY

PRAYING THE ROSARY OF 15 DECADES................... ☐

READING THE HOLY BIBLE (15 MINUTES)................ ☐

DAILY SACRIFICES... ☐

☐ _____   ☐ _____

☐ _____   ☐ _____

☐ _____   ☐ _____

☐ _____   ☐ _____

☐ _____   ☐ _____

☐ _____   ☐ _____

☐ _____   ☐ _____

☐ _____   ☐ _____

☐ _____   ☐ _____

SUGGESTIONS

If you don't know how to pray the Holy Rosary, you can get our book "Rosary for beginners" in the following link: www.vcrey.com/rosary-book

Some sacrifices that you can do include:

- Not drinking water or liquids during a meal.
- Abstain from meat on Fridays (which is also required by Holy Mother Church).
- Not eating candy or dessert during one day.
- Take a cold shower.
- Not eating meat in saturdays in honor of the Blessed Virgin Mary.
- Keep one hour of silence.
- Do not buy or sell in Sunday (which is also a commandment).
- Give food to the hungry.
- Give water to the thirsty.
- Visit the sick, and confort them.

IMPORTANT NOTES

☐ _____

☐ _____

☐ _____

☐ _____

☐ _____

☐ _____

☐ _____

☐ _____

☐ _____

YOUR SOUL'S GROWTH PLANNER

LONG LIVE CHRIST THE KING!

VIVA
CRISTO
REY.ORG

DATE: MONTH   DAY   YEAR

GOALS OF THE DAY

PRAYING THE ROSARY OF 15 DECADES................... ☐

READING THE HOLY BIBLE (15 MINUTES)............... ☐

DAILY SACRIFICES.. ☐

☐ _____ ☐ _____

☐ _____ ☐ _____

☐ _____ ☐ _____

☐ _____ ☐ _____

☐ _____ ☐ _____

☐ _____ ☐ _____

☐ _____ ☐ _____

☐ _____ ☐ _____

☐ _____ ☐ _____

SUGGESTIONS

If you don't know how to pray the Holy Rosary, you can get our book "Rosary for beginners" in the following link: www.vcrey.com/rosary-book

Some sacrifices that you can do include:

- Not drinking water or liquids during a meal.
- Abstain from meat on Fridays (which is also required by Holy Mother Church).
- Not eating candy or dessert during one day.
- Take a cold shower.
- Not eating meat in saturdays in honor of the Blessed Virgin Mary.
- Keep one hour of silence.
- Do not buy or sell in Sunday (which is also a commandment).
- Give food to the hungry.
- Give water to the thirsty.
- Visit the sick, and confort them.

IMPORTANT NOTES

☐ _____

☐ _____

☐ _____

☐ _____

☐ _____

☐ _____

☐ _____

☐ _____

☐ _____

YOUR SOUL'S GROWTH PLANNER

LONG LIVE CHRIST THE KING!

VIVA CRISTO REY.ORG

DATE: MONTH   DAY   YEAR

GOALS OF THE DAY

PRAYING THE ROSARY OF 15 DECADES................... ☐

READING THE HOLY BIBLE (15 MINUTES)............... ☐

DAILY SACRIFICES.. ☐

☐ _____   ☐ _____
☐ _____   ☐ _____
☐ _____   ☐ _____
☐ _____   ☐ _____
☐ _____   ☐ _____
☐ _____   ☐ _____
☐ _____   ☐ _____
☐ _____   ☐ _____
☐ _____   ☐ _____

SUGGESTIONS

If you don't know how to pray the Holy Rosary, you can get our book "Rosary for beginners" in the following link: www.vcrey.com/rosary-book

Some sacrifices that you can do include:

- Not drinking water or liquids during a meal.
- Abstain from meat on Fridays (which is also required by Holy Mother Church).
- Not eating candy or dessert during one day.
- Take a cold shower.
- Not eating meat in saturdays in honor of the Blessed Virgin Mary.
- Keep one hour of silence.
- Do not buy or sell in Sunday (which is also a commandment).
- Give food to the hungry.
- Give water to the thirsty.
- Visit the sick, and confort them.

IMPORTANT NOTES

☐ _____
☐ _____
☐ _____
☐ _____
☐ _____
☐ _____
☐ _____
☐ _____
☐ _____

YOUR SOUL'S GROWTH PLANNER

LONG LIVE CHRIST THE KING!

VIVA CRISTO REY.ORG

DATE: MONTH   DAY   YEAR

GOALS OF THE DAY

PRAYING THE ROSARY OF 15 DECADES................... ☐

READING THE HOLY BIBLE (15 MINUTES)................ ☐

DAILY SACRIFICES.. ☐

☐ _____   ☐ _____

☐ _____   ☐ _____

☐ _____   ☐ _____

☐ _____   ☐ _____

☐ _____   ☐ _____

☐ _____   ☐ _____

☐ _____   ☐ _____

☐ _____   ☐ _____

☐ _____   ☐ _____

SUGGESTIONS

If you don't know how to pray the Holy Rosary, you can get our book "Rosary for beginners" in the following link: www.vcrey.com/rosary-book

Some sacrifices that you can do include:

- Not drinking water or liquids during a meal.
- Abstain from meat on Fridays (which is also required by Holy Mother Church).
- Not eating candy or dessert during one day.
- Take a cold shower.
- Not eating meat in saturdays in honor of the Blessed Virgin Mary.
- Keep one hour of silence.
- Do not buy or sell in Sunday (which is also a commandment).
- Give food to the hungry.
- Give water to the thirsty.
- Visit the sick, and confort them.

IMPORTANT NOTES

☐ _____

☐ _____

☐ _____

☐ _____

☐ _____

☐ _____

☐ _____

☐ _____

☐ _____

YOUR SOUL'S GROWTH PLANNER

LONG LIVE CHRIST THE KING!

VIVA CRISTO REY.ORG

DATE: MONTH   DAY   YEAR

GOALS OF THE DAY

PRAYING THE ROSARY OF 15 DECADES.................... ☐

READING THE HOLY BIBLE (15 MINUTES)................ ☐

DAILY SACRIFICES... ☐

☐ _____   ☐ _____
☐ _____   ☐ _____
☐ _____   ☐ _____
☐ _____   ☐ _____
☐ _____   ☐ _____
☐ _____   ☐ _____
☐ _____   ☐ _____
☐ _____   ☐ _____
☐ _____   ☐ _____

SUGGESTIONS

If you don't know how to pray the Holy Rosary, you can get our book "Rosary for beginners" in the following link: www.vcrey.com/rosary-book

Some sacrifices that you can do include:

- Not drinking water or liquids during a meal.
- Abstain from meat on Fridays (which is also required by Holy Mother Church).
- Not eating candy or dessert during one day.
- Take a cold shower.
- Not eating meat in saturdays in honor of the Blessed Virgin Mary.
- Keep one hour of silence.
- Do not buy or sell in Sunday (which is also a commandment).
- Give food to the hungry.
- Give water to the thirsty.
- Visit the sick, and confort them.

IMPORTANT NOTES

☐ _____
☐ _____
☐ _____
☐ _____
☐ _____
☐ _____
☐ _____
☐ _____
☐ _____

YOUR SOUL'S GROWTH PLANNER

LONG LIVE CHRIST THE KING!

VIVA
CRISTO
REY.ORG

DATE: MONTH   DAY   YEAR

GOALS OF THE DAY

PRAYING THE ROSARY OF 15 DECADES................... ☐

READING THE HOLY BIBLE (15 MINUTES)................ ☐

DAILY SACRIFICES... ☐

☐ _____   ☐ _____
☐ _____   ☐ _____
☐ _____   ☐ _____

☐ _____   ☐ _____
☐ _____   ☐ _____
☐ _____   ☐ _____
☐ _____   ☐ _____

☐ _____   ☐ _____
☐ _____   ☐ _____

SUGGESTIONS

If you don't know how to pray the Holy Rosary, you can get our book "Rosary for beginners" in the following link: www.vcrey.com/rosary-book

Some sacrifices that you can do include:

- Not drinking water or liquids during a meal.
- Abstain from meat on Fridays (which is also required by Holy Mother Church).
- Not eating candy or dessert during one day.
- Take a cold shower.
- Not eating meat in saturdays in honor of the Blessed Virgin Mary.
- Keep one hour of silence.
- Do not buy or sell in Sunday (which is also a commandment).
- Give food to the hungry.
- Give water to the thirsty.
- Visit the sick, and confort them.

IMPORTANT NOTES

☐ _____
☐ _____
☐ _____
☐ _____
☐ _____
☐ _____
☐ _____
☐ _____
☐ _____

YOUR SOUL'S GROWTH PLANNER

LONG LIVE CHRIST THE KING!

VIVA
CRISTO
REY.ORG

DATE: MONTH   DAY   YEAR

GOALS OF THE DAY

PRAYING THE ROSARY OF 15 DECADES.................. ☐

READING THE HOLY BIBLE (15 MINUTES)................ ☐

DAILY SACRIFICES.. ☐

☐ _____   ☐ _____

☐ _____   ☐ _____

☐ _____   ☐ _____

☐ _____   ☐ _____

☐ _____   ☐ _____

☐ _____   ☐ _____

☐ _____   ☐ _____

☐ _____   ☐ _____

☐ _____   ☐ _____

SUGGESTIONS

If you don't know how to pray the Holy Rosary, you can get our book "Rosary for beginners" in the following link: www.vcrey.com/rosary-book

Some sacrifices that you can do include:

- Not drinking water or liquids during a meal.
- Abstain from meat on Fridays (which is also required by Holy Mother Church).
- Not eating candy or dessert during one day.
- Take a cold shower.
- Not eating meat in saturdays in honor of the Blessed Virgin Mary.
- Keep one hour of silence.
- Do not buy or sell in Sunday (which is also a commandment).
- Give food to the hungry.
- Give water to the thirsty.
- Visit the sick, and confort them.

IMPORTANT NOTES

☐ _____

☐ _____

☐ _____

☐ _____

☐ _____

☐ _____

☐ _____

☐ _____

☐ _____

YOUR SOUL'S GROWTH PLANNER

LONG LIVE CHRIST THE KING!

VIVA
CRISTO
REY.ORG

DATE: MONTH   DAY   YEAR

GOALS OF THE DAY

PRAYING THE ROSARY OF 15 DECADES................... ☐

READING THE HOLY BIBLE (15 MINUTES)............... ☐

DAILY SACRIFICES... ☐

☐ _____   ☐ _____
☐ _____   ☐ _____
☐ _____   ☐ _____
☐ _____   ☐ _____
☐ _____   ☐ _____
☐ _____   ☐ _____
☐ _____   ☐ _____
☐ _____   ☐ _____
☐ _____   ☐ _____

SUGGESTIONS

If you don't know how to pray the Holy Rosary, you can get our book "Rosary for beginners" in the following link: www.vcrey.com/rosary-book

Some sacrifices that you can do include:

- Not drinking water or liquids during a meal.
- Abstain from meat on Fridays (which is also required by Holy Mother Church).
- Not eating candy or dessert during one day.
- Take a cold shower.
- Not eating meat in saturdays in honor of the Blessed Virgin Mary.
- Keep one hour of silence.
- Do not buy or sell in Sunday (which is also a commandment).
- Give food to the hungry.
- Give water to the thirsty.
- Visit the sick, and confort them.

IMPORTANT NOTES

☐ _____
☐ _____
☐ _____
☐ _____
☐ _____
☐ _____
☐ _____
☐ _____
☐ _____

YOUR SOUL'S GROWTH PLANNER

LONG LIVE CHRIST THE KING!

VIVA
CRISTO
REY.ORG

DATE: MONTH   DAY   YEAR

GOALS OF THE DAY

PRAYING THE ROSARY OF 15 DECADES................... ☐

READING THE HOLY BIBLE (15 MINUTES)............... ☐

DAILY SACRIFICES... ☐

☐ _____   ☐ _____
☐ _____   ☐ _____
☐ _____   ☐ _____
☐ _____   ☐ _____
☐ _____   ☐ _____
☐ _____   ☐ _____
☐ _____   ☐ _____
☐ _____   ☐ _____
☐ _____   ☐ _____

SUGGESTIONS

If you don't know how to pray the Holy Rosary, you can get our book "Rosary for beginners" in the following link: www.vcrey.com/rosary-book

Some sacrifices that you can do include:

- Not drinking water or liquids during a meal.
- Abstain from meat on Fridays (which is also required by Holy Mother Church).
- Not eating candy or dessert during one day.
- Take a cold shower.
- Not eating meat in saturdays in honor of the Blessed Virgin Mary.
- Keep one hour of silence.
- Do not buy or sell in Sunday (which is also a commandment).
- Give food to the hungry.
- Give water to the thirsty.
- Visit the sick, and confort them.

IMPORTANT NOTES

☐ _____
☐ _____
☐ _____
☐ _____
☐ _____
☐ _____
☐ _____
☐ _____
☐ _____

YOUR SOUL'S GROWTH PLANNER

LONG LIVE CHRIST THE KING!

VIVA
CRISTO
REY.ORG

DATE: MONTH   DAY   YEAR

GOALS OF THE DAY

PRAYING THE ROSARY OF 15 DECADES................... ☐

READING THE HOLY BIBLE (15 MINUTES)................ ☐

DAILY SACRIFICES.. ☐

☐ _____   ☐ _____

☐ _____   ☐ _____

☐ _____   ☐ _____

☐ _____   ☐ _____

☐ _____   ☐ _____
☐ _____   ☐ _____

☐ _____   ☐ _____

☐ _____   ☐ _____

☐ _____   ☐ _____

SUGGESTIONS

If you don't know how to pray the Holy Rosary, you can get our book "Rosary for beginners" in the following link: www.vcrey.com/rosary-book

Some sacrifices that you can do include:

- Not drinking water or liquids during a meal.
- Abstain from meat on Fridays (which is also required by Holy Mother Church).
- Not eating candy or dessert during one day.
- Take a cold shower.
- Not eating meat in saturdays in honor of the Blessed Virgin Mary.
- Keep one hour of silence.
- Do not buy or sell in Sunday (which is also a commandment).
- Give food to the hungry.
- Give water to the thirsty.
- Visit the sick, and confort them.

IMPORTANT NOTES

☐ _____

☐ _____

☐ _____

☐ _____

☐ _____

☐ _____

☐ _____

☐ _____

☐ _____

YOUR SOUL'S GROWTH PLANNER

LONG LIVE CHRIST THE KING!

VIVA
CRISTO
REY.ORG

DATE: MONTH   DAY   YEAR

GOALS OF THE DAY

PRAYING THE ROSARY OF 15 DECADES.................... ☐

READING THE HOLY BIBLE (15 MINUTES)................. ☐

DAILY SACRIFICES....................................... ☐

☐ _____   ☐ _____
☐ _____   ☐ _____
☐ _____   ☐ _____

☐ _____   ☐ _____
☐ _____   ☐ _____
☐ _____   ☐ _____

☐ _____   ☐ _____

☐ _____   ☐ _____
☐ _____   ☐ _____

SUGGESTIONS

If you don't know how to pray the Holy Rosary, you can get our book "Rosary for beginners" in the following link: www.vcrey.com/rosary-book

Some sacrifices that you can do include:

- Not drinking water or liquids during a meal.
- Abstain from meat on Fridays (which is also required by Holy Mother Church).
- Not eating candy or dessert during one day.
- Take a cold shower.
- Not eating meat in saturdays in honor of the Blessed Virgin Mary.
- Keep one hour of silence.
- Do not buy or sell in Sunday (which is also a commandment).
- Give food to the hungry.
- Give water to the thirsty.
- Visit the sick, and confort them.

IMPORTANT NOTES

☐ _____
☐ _____
☐ _____
☐ _____
☐ _____
☐ _____
☐ _____
☐ _____
☐ _____

YOUR SOUL'S GROWTH PLANNER

LONG LIVE CHRIST THE KING!

VIVA
CRISTO
REY.ORG

DATE: MONTH   DAY   YEAR

GOALS OF THE DAY

PRAYING THE ROSARY OF 15 DECADES................... ☐

READING THE HOLY BIBLE (15 MINUTES)............... ☐

DAILY SACRIFICES....................................... ☐

☐ _____   ☐ _____
☐ _____   ☐ _____
☐ _____   ☐ _____

☐ _____   ☐ _____
☐ _____   ☐ _____
☐ _____   ☐ _____
☐ _____   ☐ _____

☐ _____   ☐ _____
☐ _____   ☐ _____

SUGGESTIONS

If you don't know how to pray the Holy Rosary, you can get our book "Rosary for beginners" in the following link: www.vcrey.com/rosary-book

Some sacrifices that you can do include:

- Not drinking water or liquids during a meal.
- Abstain from meat on Fridays (which is also required by Holy Mother Church).
- Not eating candy or dessert during one day.
- Take a cold shower.
- Not eating meat in saturdays in honor of the Blessed Virgin Mary.
- Keep one hour of silence.
- Do not buy or sell in Sunday (which is also a commandment).
- Give food to the hungry.
- Give water to the thirsty.
- Visit the sick, and confort them.

IMPORTANT NOTES

☐ _____
☐ _____
☐ _____
☐ _____
☐ _____
☐ _____
☐ _____
☐ _____
☐ _____

YOUR SOUL'S GROWTH PLANNER

LONG LIVE CHRIST THE KING!

DATE: MONTH   DAY   YEAR

GOALS OF THE DAY

PRAYING THE ROSARY OF 15 DECADES................... ☐

READING THE HOLY BIBLE (15 MINUTES)............... ☐

DAILY SACRIFICES... ☐

☐ _____   ☐ _____
☐ _____   ☐ _____
☐ _____   ☐ _____
☐ _____   ☐ _____
☐ _____   ☐ _____
☐ _____   ☐ _____
☐ _____   ☐ _____
☐ _____   ☐ _____
☐ _____   ☐ _____

SUGGESTIONS

If you don't know how to pray the Holy Rosary, you can get our book "Rosary for beginners" in the following link: www.vcrey.com/rosary-book

Some sacrifices that you can do include:

- Not drinking water or liquids during a meal.
- Abstain from meat on Fridays (which is also required by Holy Mother Church).
- Not eating candy or dessert during one day.
- Take a cold shower.
- Not eating meat in saturdays in honor of the Blessed Virgin Mary.
- Keep one hour of silence.
- Do not buy or sell in Sunday (which is also a commandment).
- Give food to the hungry.
- Give water to the thirsty.
- Visit the sick, and confort them.

IMPORTANT NOTES

☐ _____
☐ _____
☐ _____
☐ _____
☐ _____
☐ _____
☐ _____
☐ _____
☐ _____

YOUR SOUL'S GROWTH PLANNER

LONG LIVE CHRIST THE KING!

DATE: MONTH   DAY   YEAR

GOALS OF THE DAY

PRAYING THE ROSARY OF 15 DECADES.................. ☐

READING THE HOLY BIBLE (15 MINUTES)................ ☐

DAILY SACRIFICES.. ☐

☐ _____   ☐ _____
☐ _____   ☐ _____
☐ _____   ☐ _____
☐ _____   ☐ _____
☐ _____   ☐ _____
☐ _____   ☐ _____
☐ _____   ☐ _____
☐ _____   ☐ _____
☐ _____   ☐ _____

SUGGESTIONS

If you don't know how to pray the Holy Rosary, you can get our book "Rosary for beginners" in the following link: www.vcrey.com/rosary-book

Some sacrifices that you can do include:

- Not drinking water or liquids during a meal.
- Abstain from meat on Fridays (which is also required by Holy Mother Church).
- Not eating candy or dessert during one day.
- Take a cold shower.
- Not eating meat in saturdays in honor of the Blessed Virgin Mary.
- Keep one hour of silence.
- Do not buy or sell in Sunday (which is also a commandment).
- Give food to the hungry.
- Give water to the thirsty.
- Visit the sick, and confort them.

IMPORTANT NOTES

☐ _____
☐ _____
☐ _____
☐ _____
☐ _____
☐ _____
☐ _____
☐ _____
☐ _____

YOUR SOUL'S GROWTH PLANNER

LONG LIVE CHRIST THE KING!

VIVA
CRISTO
REY.ORG

DATE: MONTH   DAY   YEAR

GOALS OF THE DAY

PRAYING THE ROSARY OF 15 DECADES................... ☐

READING THE HOLY BIBLE (15 MINUTES)............... ☐

DAILY SACRIFICES... ☐

☐ _____   ☐ _____
☐ _____   ☐ _____
☐ _____   ☐ _____
☐ _____   ☐ _____
☐ _____   ☐ _____
☐ _____   ☐ _____
☐ _____   ☐ _____
☐ _____   ☐ _____
☐ _____   ☐ _____

SUGGESTIONS

If you don't know how to pray the Holy Rosary, you can get our book "Rosary for beginners" in the following link: www.vcrey.com/rosary-book

Some sacrifices that you can do include:

- Not drinking water or liquids during a meal.
- Abstain from meat on Fridays (which is also required by Holy Mother Church).
- Not eating candy or dessert during one day.
- Take a cold shower.
- Not eating meat in saturdays in honor of the Blessed Virgin Mary.
- Keep one hour of silence.
- Do not buy or sell in Sunday (which is also a commandment).
- Give food to the hungry.
- Give water to the thirsty.
- Visit the sick, and confort them.

IMPORTANT NOTES

☐ _____
☐ _____
☐ _____
☐ _____
☐ _____
☐ _____
☐ _____
☐ _____
☐ _____

YOUR SOUL'S GROWTH PLANNER

LONG LIVE CHRIST THE KING!

VIVA CRISTO REY.ORG

DATE: MONTH   DAY   YEAR

GOALS OF THE DAY

PRAYING THE ROSARY OF 15 DECADES.................... ☐

READING THE HOLY BIBLE (15 MINUTES)................ ☐

DAILY SACRIFICES... ☐

☐ _____   ☐ _____

☐ _____   ☐ _____

☐ _____   ☐ _____

☐ _____   ☐ _____

☐ _____   ☐ _____

☐ _____   ☐ _____

☐ _____   ☐ _____

☐ _____   ☐ _____

☐ _____   ☐ _____

SUGGESTIONS

If you don't know how to pray the Holy Rosary, you can get our book "Rosary for beginners" in the following link: www.vcrey.com/rosary-book

Some sacrifices that you can do include:

- Not drinking water or liquids during a meal.
- Abstain from meat on Fridays (which is also required by Holy Mother Church).
- Not eating candy or dessert during one day.
- Take a cold shower.
- Not eating meat in saturdays in honor of the Blessed Virgin Mary.
- Keep one hour of silence.
- Do not buy or sell in Sunday (which is also a commandment).
- Give food to the hungry.
- Give water to the thirsty.
- Visit the sick, and confort them.

IMPORTANT NOTES

☐ _____

☐ _____

☐ _____

☐ _____

☐ _____

☐ _____

☐ _____

☐ _____

☐ _____

YOUR SOUL'S GROWTH PLANNER

LONG LIVE CHRIST THE KING!

VIVA
CRISTO
REY.ORG

DATE: MONTH   DAY   YEAR

GOALS OF THE DAY

PRAYING THE ROSARY OF 15 DECADES.................. ☐

READING THE HOLY BIBLE (15 MINUTES)............... ☐

DAILY SACRIFICES.. ☐

☐ _____   ☐ _____
☐ _____   ☐ _____
☐ _____   ☐ _____

☐ _____   ☐ _____
☐ _____   ☐ _____
☐ _____   ☐ _____

☐ _____   ☐ _____
☐ _____   ☐ _____

SUGGESTIONS

If you don't know how to pray the Holy Rosary, you can get our book "Rosary for beginners" in the following link: www.vcrey.com/rosary-book

Some sacrifices that you can do include:

- Not drinking water or liquids during a meal.
- Abstain from meat on Fridays (which is also required by Holy Mother Church).
- Not eating candy or dessert during one day.
- Take a cold shower.
- Not eating meat in saturdays in honor of the Blessed Virgin Mary.
- Keep one hour of silence.
- Do not buy or sell in Sunday (which is also a commandment).
- Give food to the hungry.
- Give water to the thirsty.
- Visit the sick, and confort them.

IMPORTANT NOTES

☐ _____
☐ _____
☐ _____
☐ _____
☐ _____
☐ _____
☐ _____
☐ _____
☐ _____

YOUR SOUL'S GROWTH PLANNER

LONG LIVE CHRIST THE KING!

VIVA
CRISTO
REY.ORG

DATE: MONTH   DAY   YEAR

GOALS OF THE DAY

PRAYING THE ROSARY OF 15 DECADES................... ☐

READING THE HOLY BIBLE (15 MINUTES)................ ☐

DAILY SACRIFICES.. ☐

☐ _____   ☐ _____

☐ _____   ☐ _____

☐ _____   ☐ _____

☐ _____   ☐ _____

☐ _____   ☐ _____

☐ _____   ☐ _____

☐ _____   ☐ _____

☐ _____   ☐ _____

☐ _____   ☐ _____

SUGGESTIONS

If you don't know how to pray the Holy Rosary, you can get our book "Rosary for beginners" in the following link: www.vcrey.com/rosary-book

Some sacrifices that you can do include:

- Not drinking water or liquids during a meal.
- Abstain from meat on Fridays (which is also required by Holy Mother Church).
- Not eating candy or dessert during one day.
- Take a cold shower.
- Not eating meat in saturdays in honor of the Blessed Virgin Mary.
- Keep one hour of silence.
- Do not buy or sell in Sunday (which is also a commandment).
- Give food to the hungry.
- Give water to the thirsty.
- Visit the sick, and confort them.

IMPORTANT NOTES

☐ _____

☐ _____

☐ _____

☐ _____

☐ _____

☐ _____

☐ _____

☐ _____

☐ _____

YOUR SOUL'S GROWTH PLANNER

LONG LIVE CHRIST THE KING!

VIVA CRISTO REY.ORG

DATE: MONTH   DAY   YEAR

GOALS OF THE DAY

PRAYING THE ROSARY OF 15 DECADES................... ☐

READING THE HOLY BIBLE (15 MINUTES)............... ☐

DAILY SACRIFICES... ☐

☐ _____   ☐ _____
☐ _____   ☐ _____
☐ _____   ☐ _____

☐ _____   ☐ _____
☐ _____   ☐ _____
☐ _____   ☐ _____
☐ _____   ☐ _____

☐ _____   ☐ _____
☐ _____   ☐ _____

SUGGESTIONS

If you don't know how to pray the Holy Rosary, you can get our book "Rosary for beginners" in the following link: www.vcrey.com/rosary-book

Some sacrifices that you can do include:

- Not drinking water or liquids during a meal.
- Abstain from meat on Fridays (which is also required by Holy Mother Church).
- Not eating candy or dessert during one day.
- Take a cold shower.
- Not eating meat in saturdays in honor of the Blessed Virgin Mary.
- Keep one hour of silence.
- Do not buy or sell in Sunday (which is also a commandment).
- Give food to the hungry.
- Give water to the thirsty.
- Visit the sick, and confort them.

IMPORTANT NOTES

☐ _____
☐ _____
☐ _____
☐ _____
☐ _____
☐ _____
☐ _____
☐ _____
☐ _____

YOUR SOUL'S GROWTH PLANNER

LONG LIVE CHRIST THE KING!

VIVA
CRISTO
REY.ORG

DATE: MONTH   DAY   YEAR

GOALS OF THE DAY

PRAYING THE ROSARY OF 15 DECADES.................. ☐

READING THE HOLY BIBLE (15 MINUTES)............... ☐

DAILY SACRIFICES... ☐

☐ _____   ☐ _____
☐ _____   ☐ _____
☐ _____   ☐ _____
☐ _____   ☐ _____
☐ _____   ☐ _____
☐ _____   ☐ _____
☐ _____   ☐ _____
☐ _____   ☐ _____
☐ _____   ☐ _____

SUGGESTIONS

If you don't know how to pray the Holy Rosary, you can get our book "Rosary for beginners" in the following link: www.vcrey.com/rosary-book

Some sacrifices that you can do include:

- Not drinking water or liquids during a meal.
- Abstain from meat on Fridays (which is also required by Holy Mother Church).
- Not eating candy or dessert during one day.
- Take a cold shower.
- Not eating meat in saturdays in honor of the Blessed Virgin Mary.
- Keep one hour of silence.
- Do not buy or sell in Sunday (which is also a commandment).
- Give food to the hungry.
- Give water to the thirsty.
- Visit the sick, and confort them.

IMPORTANT NOTES

☐ _____
☐ _____
☐ _____
☐ _____
☐ _____
☐ _____
☐ _____
☐ _____
☐ _____

YOUR SOUL'S GROWTH PLANNER

LONG LIVE CHRIST THE KING!

VIVA
CRISTO
REY.ORG

DATE: MONTH   DAY   YEAR

GOALS OF THE DAY

PRAYING THE ROSARY OF 15 DECADES.................... ☐

READING THE HOLY BIBLE (15 MINUTES)................ ☐

DAILY SACRIFICES... ☐

☐ _____   ☐ _____

☐ _____   ☐ _____

☐ _____   ☐ _____

☐ _____   ☐ _____

☐ _____   ☐ _____

☐ _____   ☐ _____

☐ _____   ☐ _____

☐ _____   ☐ _____

☐ _____

SUGGESTIONS

If you don't know how to pray the Holy Rosary, you can get our book "Rosary for beginners" in the following link: www.vcrey.com/rosary-book

Some sacrifices that you can do include:

- Not drinking water or liquids during a meal.
- Abstain from meat on Fridays (which is also required by Holy Mother Church).
- Not eating candy or dessert during one day.
- Take a cold shower.
- Not eating meat in saturdays in honor of the Blessed Virgin Mary.
- Keep one hour of silence.
- Do not buy or sell in Sunday (which is also a commandment).
- Give food to the hungry.
- Give water to the thirsty.
- Visit the sick, and confort them.

IMPORTANT NOTES

☐ _____

☐ _____

☐ _____

☐ _____

☐ _____

☐ _____

☐ _____

☐ _____

☐ _____

YOUR SOUL'S GROWTH PLANNER

LONG LIVE CHRIST THE KING!

VIVA
CRISTO
REY.ORG

DATE: MONTH   DAY   YEAR

GOALS OF THE DAY

PRAYING THE ROSARY OF 15 DECADES................... ☐

READING THE HOLY BIBLE (15 MINUTES)............... ☐

DAILY SACRIFICES... ☐

☐ _____   ☐ _____
☐ _____   ☐ _____
☐ _____   ☐ _____
☐ _____   ☐ _____
☐ _____   ☐ _____
☐ _____   ☐ _____
☐ _____   ☐ _____
☐ _____   ☐ _____
☐ _____   ☐ _____

SUGGESTIONS

If you don't know how to pray the Holy Rosary, you can get our book "Rosary for beginners" in the following link: www.vcrey.com/rosary-book

Some sacrifices that you can do include:

- Not drinking water or liquids during a meal.
- Abstain from meat on Fridays (which is also required by Holy Mother Church).
- Not eating candy or dessert during one day.
- Take a cold shower.
- Not eating meat in saturdays in honor of the Blessed Virgin Mary.
- Keep one hour of silence.
- Do not buy or sell in Sunday (which is also a commandment).
- Give food to the hungry.
- Give water to the thirsty.
- Visit the sick, and confort them.

IMPORTANT NOTES

☐ _____
☐ _____
☐ _____
☐ _____
☐ _____
☐ _____
☐ _____
☐ _____
☐ _____

YOUR SOUL'S GROWTH PLANNER

LONG LIVE CHRIST THE KING!

VIVA
CRISTO
REY.ORG

DATE: MONTH   DAY   YEAR

GOALS OF THE DAY

PRAYING THE ROSARY OF 15 DECADES.................. ☐

READING THE HOLY BIBLE (15 MINUTES)............... ☐

DAILY SACRIFICES...................................... ☐

☐ _____   ☐ _____
☐ _____   ☐ _____
☐ _____   ☐ _____

☐ _____   ☐ _____
☐ _____   ☐ _____
☐ _____   ☐ _____

☐ _____   ☐ _____
☐ _____   ☐ _____
☐ _____   ☐ _____

SUGGESTIONS

If you don't know how to pray the Holy Rosary, you can get our book "Rosary for beginners" in the following link: www.vcrey.com/rosary-book

Some sacrifices that you can do include:

- Not drinking water or liquids during a meal.
- Abstain from meat on Fridays (which is also required by Holy Mother Church).
- Not eating candy or dessert during one day.
- Take a cold shower.
- Not eating meat in saturdays in honor of the Blessed Virgin Mary.
- Keep one hour of silence.
- Do not buy or sell in Sunday (which is also a commandment).
- Give food to the hungry.
- Give water to the thirsty.
- Visit the sick, and confort them.

IMPORTANT NOTES

☐ _____
☐ _____
☐ _____
☐ _____
☐ _____
☐ _____
☐ _____
☐ _____
☐ _____

YOUR SOUL'S GROWTH PLANNER

LONG LIVE CHRIST THE KING!

VIVA CRISTO REY.ORG

DATE: MONTH   DAY   YEAR

GOALS OF THE DAY

PRAYING THE ROSARY OF 15 DECADES................... ☐

READING THE HOLY BIBLE (15 MINUTES)................ ☐

DAILY SACRIFICES... ☐

☐ _____   ☐ _____
☐ _____   ☐ _____
☐ _____   ☐ _____

☐ _____   ☐ _____
☐ _____   ☐ _____
☐ _____   ☐ _____
☐ _____   ☐ _____

☐ _____   ☐ _____
☐ _____   ☐ _____

SUGGESTIONS

If you don't know how to pray the Holy Rosary, you can get our book "Rosary for beginners" in the following link: www.vcrey.com/rosary-book

Some sacrifices that you can do include:

- Not drinking water or liquids during a meal.
- Abstain from meat on Fridays (which is also required by Holy Mother Church).
- Not eating candy or dessert during one day.
- Take a cold shower.
- Not eating meat in saturdays in honor of the Blessed Virgin Mary.
- Keep one hour of silence.
- Do not buy or sell in Sunday (which is also a commandment).
- Give food to the hungry.
- Give water to the thirsty.
- Visit the sick, and confort them.

IMPORTANT NOTES

☐ _____
☐ _____
☐ _____
☐ _____
☐ _____
☐ _____
☐ _____
☐ _____
☐ _____

YOUR SOUL'S GROWTH PLANNER

LONG LIVE CHRIST THE KING!

VIVA CRISTO REY.ORG

DATE: MONTH   DAY   YEAR

GOALS OF THE DAY

PRAYING THE ROSARY OF 15 DECADES.................... ☐

READING THE HOLY BIBLE (15 MINUTES)............... ☐

DAILY SACRIFICES... ☐

☐ _____   ☐ _____
☐ _____   ☐ _____
☐ _____   ☐ _____
☐ _____   ☐ _____
☐ _____   ☐ _____
☐ _____   ☐ _____
☐ _____   ☐ _____
☐ _____   ☐ _____
☐ _____   ☐ _____

SUGGESTIONS

If you don't know how to pray the Holy Rosary, you can get our book "Rosary for beginners" in the following link: www.vcrey.com/rosary-book

Some sacrifices that you can do include:

- Not drinking water or liquids during a meal.
- Abstain from meat on Fridays (which is also required by Holy Mother Church).
- Not eating candy or dessert during one day.
- Take a cold shower.
- Not eating meat in saturdays in honor of the Blessed Virgin Mary.
- Keep one hour of silence.
- Do not buy or sell in Sunday (which is also a commandment).
- Give food to the hungry.
- Give water to the thirsty.
- Visit the sick, and confort them.

IMPORTANT NOTES

☐ _____
☐ _____
☐ _____
☐ _____
☐ _____
☐ _____
☐ _____
☐ _____
☐ _____

YOUR SOUL'S GROWTH PLANNER

LONG LIVE CHRIST THE KING!

VIVA
CRISTO
REY.ORG

DATE: MONTH   DAY   YEAR

GOALS OF THE DAY

PRAYING THE ROSARY OF 15 DECADES.................... ☐

READING THE HOLY BIBLE (15 MINUTES)................ ☐

DAILY SACRIFICES... ☐

☐ _____   ☐ _____
☐ _____   ☐ _____
☐ _____   ☐ _____
☐ _____   ☐ _____
☐ _____   ☐ _____
☐ _____   ☐ _____
☐ _____   ☐ _____
☐ _____   ☐ _____
☐ _____   ☐ _____

SUGGESTIONS

If you don't know how to pray the Holy Rosary, you can get our book "Rosary for beginners" in the following link: www.vcrey.com/rosary-book

Some sacrifices that you can do include:

- Not drinking water or liquids during a meal.
- Abstain from meat on Fridays (which is also required by Holy Mother Church).
- Not eating candy or dessert during one day.
- Take a cold shower.
- Not eating meat in saturdays in honor of the Blessed Virgin Mary.
- Keep one hour of silence.
- Do not buy or sell in Sunday (which is also a commandment).
- Give food to the hungry.
- Give water to the thirsty.
- Visit the sick, and confort them.

IMPORTANT NOTES

☐ _____
☐ _____
☐ _____
☐ _____
☐ _____
☐ _____
☐ _____
☐ _____
☐ _____

YOUR SOUL'S GROWTH PLANNER

LONG LIVE CHRIST THE KING!

DATE: MONTH   DAY   YEAR

GOALS OF THE DAY

PRAYING THE ROSARY OF 15 DECADES.................... ☐

READING THE HOLY BIBLE (15 MINUTES)................ ☐

DAILY SACRIFICES.. ☐

☐ _____   ☐ _____

☐ _____   ☐ _____

☐ _____   ☐ _____

☐ _____   ☐ _____

☐ _____   ☐ _____

☐ _____   ☐ _____

☐ _____   ☐ _____

☐ _____   ☐ _____

☐ _____   ☐ _____

SUGGESTIONS

If you don't know how to pray the Holy Rosary, you can get our book "Rosary for beginners" in the following link: www.vcrey.com/rosary-book

Some sacrifices that you can do include:

- Not drinking water or liquids during a meal.
- Abstain from meat on Fridays (which is also required by Holy Mother Church).
- Not eating candy or dessert during one day.
- Take a cold shower.
- Not eating meat in saturdays in honor of the Blessed Virgin Mary.
- Keep one hour of silence.
- Do not buy or sell in Sunday (which is also a commandment).
- Give food to the hungry.
- Give water to the thirsty.
- Visit the sick, and confort them.

IMPORTANT NOTES

☐ _____

☐ _____

☐ _____

☐ _____

☐ _____

☐ _____

☐ _____

☐ _____

☐ _____

YOUR SOUL'S GROWTH PLANNER

LONG LIVE CHRIST THE KING!

VIVA
CRISTO
REY.ORG

DATE: MONTH   DAY   YEAR

GOALS OF THE DAY

PRAYING THE ROSARY OF 15 DECADES................... ☐

READING THE HOLY BIBLE (15 MINUTES)................ ☐

DAILY SACRIFICES.. ☐

☐ _____   ☐ _____
☐ _____   ☐ _____
☐ _____   ☐ _____
☐ _____   ☐ _____
☐ _____   ☐ _____
☐ _____   ☐ _____
☐ _____   ☐ _____
☐ _____   ☐ _____
☐ _____   ☐ _____

SUGGESTIONS

If you don't know how to pray the Holy Rosary, you can get our book "Rosary for beginners" in the following link: www.vcrey.com/rosary-book

Some sacrifices that you can do include:

- Not drinking water or liquids during a meal.
- Abstain from meat on Fridays (which is also required by Holy Mother Church).
- Not eating candy or dessert during one day.
- Take a cold shower.
- Not eating meat in saturdays in honor of the Blessed Virgin Mary.
- Keep one hour of silence.
- Do not buy or sell in Sunday (which is also a commandment).
- Give food to the hungry.
- Give water to the thirsty.
- Visit the sick, and confort them.

IMPORTANT NOTES

☐ _____
☐ _____
☐ _____
☐ _____
☐ _____
☐ _____
☐ _____
☐ _____
☐ _____

YOUR SOUL'S GROWTH PLANNER

LONG LIVE CHRIST THE KING!

VIVA
CRISTO
REY.ORG

DATE: MONTH   DAY   YEAR

GOALS OF THE DAY

PRAYING THE ROSARY OF 15 DECADES................... ☐

READING THE HOLY BIBLE (15 MINUTES)............... ☐

DAILY SACRIFICES.. ☐

☐ _____   ☐ _____
☐ _____   ☐ _____
☐ _____   ☐ _____

☐ _____   ☐ _____
☐ _____   ☐ _____
☐ _____   ☐ _____
☐ _____   ☐ _____

☐ _____   ☐ _____
☐ _____   ☐ _____

SUGGESTIONS

If you don't know how to pray the Holy Rosary, you can get our book "Rosary for beginners" in the following link: www.vcrey.com/rosary-book

Some sacrifices that you can do include:

- Not drinking water or liquids during a meal.
- Abstain from meat on Fridays (which is also required by Holy Mother Church).
- Not eating candy or dessert during one day.
- Take a cold shower.
- Not eating meat in saturdays in honor of the Blessed Virgin Mary.
- Keep one hour of silence.
- Do not buy or sell in Sunday (which is also a commandment).
- Give food to the hungry.
- Give water to the thirsty.
- Visit the sick, and confort them.

IMPORTANT NOTES

☐ _____
☐ _____
☐ _____
☐ _____
☐ _____
☐ _____
☐ _____
☐ _____
☐ _____

YOUR SOUL'S GROWTH PLANNER

LONG LIVE CHRIST THE KING!

VIVA
CRISTO
REY.ORG

DATE: MONTH   DAY   YEAR

GOALS OF THE DAY

PRAYING THE ROSARY OF 15 DECADES................... ☐

READING THE HOLY BIBLE (15 MINUTES)............... ☐

DAILY SACRIFICES.. ☐

☐ _____   ☐ _____
☐ _____   ☐ _____
☐ _____   ☐ _____
☐ _____   ☐ _____
☐ _____   ☐ _____
☐ _____   ☐ _____
☐ _____   ☐ _____
☐ _____   ☐ _____
☐ _____   ☐ _____

SUGGESTIONS

If you don't know how to pray the Holy Rosary, you can get our book "Rosary for beginners" in the following link: www.vcrey.com/rosary-book

Some sacrifices that you can do include:

- Not drinking water or liquids during a meal.
- Abstain from meat on Fridays (which is also required by Holy Mother Church).
- Not eating candy or dessert during one day.
- Take a cold shower.
- Not eating meat in saturdays in honor of the Blessed Virgin Mary.
- Keep one hour of silence.
- Do not buy or sell in Sunday (which is also a commandment).
- Give food to the hungry.
- Give water to the thirsty.
- Visit the sick, and confort them.

IMPORTANT NOTES

☐ _____
☐ _____
☐ _____
☐ _____
☐ _____
☐ _____
☐ _____
☐ _____
☐ _____

YOUR SOUL'S GROWTH PLANNER

LONG LIVE CHRIST THE KING!

VIVA CRISTO REY.ORG

DATE: MONTH   DAY   YEAR

GOALS OF THE DAY

PRAYING THE ROSARY OF 15 DECADES................... ☐

READING THE HOLY BIBLE (15 MINUTES)................ ☐

DAILY SACRIFICES... ☐

☐ _____ ☐ _____
☐ _____ ☐ _____
☐ _____ ☐ _____
☐ _____ ☐ _____
☐ _____ ☐ _____
☐ _____ ☐ _____
☐ _____ ☐ _____
☐ _____ ☐ _____
☐ _____ ☐ _____

SUGGESTIONS

If you don't know how to pray the Holy Rosary, you can get our book "Rosary for beginners" in the following link: www.vcrey.com/rosary-book

Some sacrifices that you can do include:

- Not drinking water or liquids during a meal.
- Abstain from meat on Fridays (which is also required by Holy Mother Church).
- Not eating candy or dessert during one day.
- Take a cold shower.
- Not eating meat in saturdays in honor of the Blessed Virgin Mary.
- Keep one hour of silence.
- Do not buy or sell in Sunday (which is also a commandment).
- Give food to the hungry.
- Give water to the thirsty.
- Visit the sick, and confort them.

IMPORTANT NOTES

☐ _____
☐ _____
☐ _____
☐ _____
☐ _____
☐ _____
☐ _____
☐ _____
☐ _____

YOUR SOUL'S GROWTH PLANNER

LONG LIVE CHRIST THE KING!

DATE: MONTH   DAY   YEAR

GOALS OF THE DAY

PRAYING THE ROSARY OF 15 DECADES................... ☐

READING THE HOLY BIBLE (15 MINUTES)............... ☐

DAILY SACRIFICES.. ☐

☐ _____   ☐ _____

☐ _____   ☐ _____

☐ _____   ☐ _____

☐ _____   ☐ _____

☐ _____   ☐ _____

☐ _____   ☐ _____

☐ _____   ☐ _____

☐ _____   ☐ _____

☐ _____   ☐ _____

SUGGESTIONS

If you don't know how to pray the Holy Rosary, you can get our book "Rosary for beginners" in the following link: www.vcrey.com/rosary-book

Some sacrifices that you can do include:

- Not drinking water or liquids during a meal.
- Abstain from meat on Fridays (which is also required by Holy Mother Church).
- Not eating candy or dessert during one day.
- Take a cold shower.
- Not eating meat in saturdays in honor of the Blessed Virgin Mary.
- Keep one hour of silence.
- Do not buy or sell in Sunday (which is also a commandment).
- Give food to the hungry.
- Give water to the thirsty.
- Visit the sick, and confort them.

IMPORTANT NOTES

☐ _____

☐ _____

☐ _____

☐ _____

☐ _____

☐ _____

☐ _____

☐ _____

☐ _____

YOUR SOUL'S GROWTH PLANNER

LONG LIVE CHRIST THE KING!

VIVA
CRISTO
REY.ORG

DATE: MONTH   DAY   YEAR

GOALS OF THE DAY

PRAYING THE ROSARY OF 15 DECADES................... ☐

READING THE HOLY BIBLE (15 MINUTES)............... ☐

DAILY SACRIFICES... ☐

☐ _____   ☐ _____
☐ _____   ☐ _____
☐ _____   ☐ _____
☐ _____   ☐ _____
☐ _____   ☐ _____
☐ _____   ☐ _____
☐ _____   ☐ _____
☐ _____   ☐ _____
☐ _____   ☐ _____

SUGGESTIONS

If you don't know how to pray the Holy Rosary, you can get our book "Rosary for beginners" in the following link: www.vcrey.com/rosary-book

Some sacrifices that you can do include:

- Not drinking water or liquids during a meal.
- Abstain from meat on Fridays (which is also required by Holy Mother Church).
- Not eating candy or dessert during one day.
- Take a cold shower.
- Not eating meat in saturdays in honor of the Blessed Virgin Mary.
- Keep one hour of silence.
- Do not buy or sell in Sunday (which is also a commandment).
- Give food to the hungry.
- Give water to the thirsty.
- Visit the sick, and confort them.

IMPORTANT NOTES

☐ _____
☐ _____
☐ _____
☐ _____
☐ _____
☐ _____
☐ _____
☐ _____
☐ _____

YOUR SOUL'S GROWTH PLANNER

LONG LIVE CHRIST THE KING!

VIVA CRISTO REY.ORG

DATE: MONTH   DAY   YEAR

GOALS OF THE DAY

PRAYING THE ROSARY OF 15 DECADES.................... ☐

READING THE HOLY BIBLE (15 MINUTES)............... ☐

DAILY SACRIFICES.. ☐

☐ _____   ☐ _____

☐ _____   ☐ _____

☐ _____   ☐ _____

☐ _____   ☐ _____

☐ _____   ☐ _____

☐ _____   ☐ _____

☐ _____   ☐ _____

☐ _____   ☐ _____

☐ _____   ☐ _____

SUGGESTIONS

If you don't know how to pray the Holy Rosary, you can get our book "Rosary for beginners" in the following link: www.vcrey.com/rosary-book

Some sacrifices that you can do include:

- Not drinking water or liquids during a meal.
- Abstain from meat on Fridays (which is also required by Holy Mother Church).
- Not eating candy or dessert during one day.
- Take a cold shower.
- Not eating meat in saturdays in honor of the Blessed Virgin Mary.
- Keep one hour of silence.
- Do not buy or sell in Sunday (which is also a commandment).
- Give food to the hungry.
- Give water to the thirsty.
- Visit the sick, and confort them.

IMPORTANT NOTES

☐ _____

☐ _____

☐ _____

☐ _____

☐ _____

☐ _____

☐ _____

☐ _____

☐ _____

YOUR SOUL'S GROWTH PLANNER

LONG LIVE CHRIST THE KING!

DATE: MONTH   DAY   YEAR

GOALS OF THE DAY

PRAYING THE ROSARY OF 15 DECADES.................. ☐

READING THE HOLY BIBLE (15 MINUTES)............... ☐

DAILY SACRIFICES... ☐

☐ _____   ☐ _____
☐ _____   ☐ _____
☐ _____   ☐ _____
☐ _____   ☐ _____
☐ _____   ☐ _____
☐ _____   ☐ _____
☐ _____   ☐ _____
☐ _____   ☐ _____
☐ _____   ☐ _____

SUGGESTIONS

If you don't know how to pray the Holy Rosary, you can get our book "Rosary for beginners" in the following link: www.vcrey.com/rosary-book

Some sacrifices that you can do include:

- Not drinking water or liquids during a meal.
- Abstain from meat on Fridays (which is also required by Holy Mother Church).
- Not eating candy or dessert during one day.
- Take a cold shower.
- Not eating meat in saturdays in honor of the Blessed Virgin Mary.
- Keep one hour of silence.
- Do not buy or sell in Sunday (which is also a commandment).
- Give food to the hungry.
- Give water to the thirsty.
- Visit the sick, and confort them.

IMPORTANT NOTES

☐ _____
☐ _____
☐ _____
☐ _____
☐ _____
☐ _____
☐ _____
☐ _____
☐ _____

YOUR SOUL'S GROWTH PLANNER

LONG LIVE CHRIST THE KING!

VIVA
CRISTO
REY.ORG

DATE: MONTH   DAY   YEAR

GOALS OF THE DAY

PRAYING THE ROSARY OF 15 DECADES................... ☐

READING THE HOLY BIBLE (15 MINUTES)............... ☐

DAILY SACRIFICES... ☐

☐ _____ ☐ _____
☐ _____ ☐ _____
☐ _____ ☐ _____
☐ _____ ☐ _____
☐ _____ ☐ _____
☐ _____ ☐ _____
☐ _____ ☐ _____
☐ _____ ☐ _____
☐ _____ ☐ _____

SUGGESTIONS

If you don't know how to pray the Holy Rosary, you can get our book "Rosary for beginners" in the following link: www.vcrey.com/rosary-book

Some sacrifices that you can do include:

- Not drinking water or liquids during a meal.
- Abstain from meat on Fridays (which is also required by Holy Mother Church).
- Not eating candy or dessert during one day.
- Take a cold shower.
- Not eating meat in saturdays in honor of the Blessed Virgin Mary.
- Keep one hour of silence.
- Do not buy or sell in Sunday (which is also a commandment).
- Give food to the hungry.
- Give water to the thirsty.
- Visit the sick, and confort them.

IMPORTANT NOTES

☐ _____
☐ _____
☐ _____
☐ _____
☐ _____
☐ _____
☐ _____
☐ _____
☐ _____

YOUR SOUL'S GROWTH PLANNER

LONG LIVE CHRIST THE KING!

VIVA
CRISTO
REY.ORG

DATE: MONTH   DAY   YEAR

GOALS OF THE DAY

PRAYING THE ROSARY OF 15 DECADES................... ☐

READING THE HOLY BIBLE (15 MINUTES).............. ☐

DAILY SACRIFICES... ☐

☐ _____   ☐ _____
☐ _____   ☐ _____
☐ _____   ☐ _____

☐ _____   ☐ _____
☐ _____   ☐ _____
☐ _____   ☐ _____

☐ _____   ☐ _____

☐ _____   ☐ _____
☐ _____   ☐ _____

SUGGESTIONS

If you don't know how to pray the Holy Rosary, you can get our book "Rosary for beginners" in the following link: www.vcrey.com/rosary-book

Some sacrifices that you can do include:

- Not drinking water or liquids during a meal.
- Abstain from meat on Fridays (which is also required by Holy Mother Church).
- Not eating candy or dessert during one day.
- Take a cold shower.
- Not eating meat in saturdays in honor of the Blessed Virgin Mary.
- Keep one hour of silence.
- Do not buy or sell in Sunday (which is also a commandment).
- Give food to the hungry.
- Give water to the thirsty.
- Visit the sick, and confort them.

IMPORTANT NOTES

☐ _____
☐ _____
☐ _____
☐ _____
☐ _____
☐ _____
☐ _____
☐ _____
☐ _____

YOUR SOUL'S GROWTH PLANNER

LONG LIVE CHRIST THE KING!

VIVA
CRISTO
REY.ORG

DATE: MONTH   DAY   YEAR

GOALS OF THE DAY

PRAYING THE ROSARY OF 15 DECADES................... ☐

READING THE HOLY BIBLE (15 MINUTES)................ ☐

DAILY SACRIFICES... ☐

☐ _____   ☐ _____
☐ _____   ☐ _____
☐ _____   ☐ _____
☐ _____   ☐ _____
☐ _____   ☐ _____
☐ _____   ☐ _____
☐ _____   ☐ _____
☐ _____   ☐ _____
☐ _____   ☐ _____

SUGGESTIONS

If you don't know how to pray the Holy Rosary, you can get our book "Rosary for beginners" in the following link: www.vcrey.com/rosary-book

Some sacrifices that you can do include:

- Not drinking water or liquids during a meal.
- Abstain from meat on Fridays (which is also required by Holy Mother Church).
- Not eating candy or dessert during one day.
- Take a cold shower.
- Not eating meat in saturdays in honor of the Blessed Virgin Mary.
- Keep one hour of silence.
- Do not buy or sell in Sunday (which is also a commandment).
- Give food to the hungry.
- Give water to the thirsty.
- Visit the sick, and confort them.

IMPORTANT NOTES

☐ _____
☐ _____
☐ _____
☐ _____
☐ _____
☐ _____
☐ _____
☐ _____
☐ _____

YOUR SOUL'S GROWTH PLANNER

LONG LIVE CHRIST THE KING!

VIVA
CRISTO
REY.ORG

DATE: MONTH   DAY   YEAR

GOALS OF THE DAY

PRAYING THE ROSARY OF 15 DECADES.................. ☐

READING THE HOLY BIBLE (15 MINUTES)............... ☐

DAILY SACRIFICES... ☐

☐ _____ ☐ _____
☐ _____ ☐ _____
☐ _____ ☐ _____
☐ _____ ☐ _____
☐ _____ ☐ _____
☐ _____ ☐ _____
☐ _____ ☐ _____
☐ _____ ☐ _____
☐ _____ ☐ _____

SUGGESTIONS

If you don't know how to pray the Holy Rosary, you can get our book "Rosary for beginners" in the following link: www.vcrey.com/rosary-book

Some sacrifices that you can do include:

- Not drinking water or liquids during a meal.
- Abstain from meat on Fridays (which is also required by Holy Mother Church).
- Not eating candy or dessert during one day.
- Take a cold shower.
- Not eating meat in saturdays in honor of the Blessed Virgin Mary.
- Keep one hour of silence.
- Do not buy or sell in Sunday (which is also a commandment).
- Give food to the hungry.
- Give water to the thirsty.
- Visit the sick, and confort them.

IMPORTANT NOTES

☐ _____
☐ _____
☐ _____
☐ _____
☐ _____
☐ _____
☐ _____
☐ _____
☐ _____

YOUR SOUL'S GROWTH PLANNER

LONG LIVE CHRIST THE KING!

VIVA
CRISTO
REY.ORG

DATE: MONTH   DAY   YEAR

GOALS OF THE DAY

PRAYING THE ROSARY OF 15 DECADES.................. ☐

READING THE HOLY BIBLE (15 MINUTES)............... ☐

DAILY SACRIFICES.. ☐

☐ _____   ☐ _____
☐ _____   ☐ _____
☐ _____   ☐ _____
☐ _____   ☐ _____
☐ _____   ☐ _____
☐ _____
☐ _____   ☐ _____
☐ _____   ☐ _____
☐ _____   ☐ _____

IMPORTANT NOTES

☐ _____
☐ _____
☐ _____
☐ _____
☐ _____
☐ _____
☐ _____
☐ _____
☐ _____

YOUR SOUL'S GROWTH PLANNER

LONG LIVE CHRIST THE KING!

VIVA CRISTO REY.ORG

DATE: MONTH   DAY   YEAR

GOALS OF THE DAY

PRAYING THE ROSARY OF 15 DECADES.................. ☐

READING THE HOLY BIBLE (15 MINUTES)................ ☐

DAILY SACRIFICES... ☐

☐ _____   ☐ _____
☐ _____   ☐ _____
☐ _____   ☐ _____
☐ _____   ☐ _____
☐ _____   ☐ _____
☐ _____   ☐ _____
☐ _____   ☐ _____
☐ _____   ☐ _____
☐ _____   ☐ _____

SUGGESTIONS

If you don't know how to pray the Holy Rosary, you can get our book "Rosary for beginners" in the following link: www.vcrey.com/rosary-book

Some sacrifices that you can do include:

- Not drinking water or liquids during a meal.
- Abstain from meat on Fridays (which is also required by Holy Mother Church).
- Not eating candy or dessert during one day.
- Take a cold shower.
- Not eating meat in saturdays in honor of the Blessed Virgin Mary.
- Keep one hour of silence.
- Do not buy or sell in Sunday (which is also a commandment).
- Give food to the hungry.
- Give water to the thirsty.
- Visit the sick, and confort them.

IMPORTANT NOTES

☐ _____
☐ _____
☐ _____
☐ _____
☐ _____
☐ _____
☐ _____
☐ _____
☐ _____

YOUR SOUL'S GROWTH PLANNER

LONG LIVE CHRIST THE KING!

VIVA
CRISTO
REY.ORG

DATE: MONTH   DAY   YEAR

GOALS OF THE DAY

PRAYING THE ROSARY OF 15 DECADES.................. ☐

READING THE HOLY BIBLE (15 MINUTES)............... ☐

DAILY SACRIFICES... ☐

☐ _____   ☐ _____
☐ _____   ☐ _____
☐ _____   ☐ _____
☐ _____   ☐ _____
☐ _____   ☐ _____
☐ _____   ☐ _____
☐ _____   ☐ _____
☐ _____   ☐ _____
☐ _____   ☐ _____

SUGGESTIONS

If you don't know how to pray the Holy Rosary, you can get our book "Rosary for beginners" in the following link: www.vcrey.com/rosary-book

Some sacrifices that you can do include:

- Not drinking water or liquids during a meal.
- Abstain from meat on Fridays (which is also required by Holy Mother Church).
- Not eating candy or dessert during one day.
- Take a cold shower.
- Not eating meat in saturdays in honor of the Blessed Virgin Mary.
- Keep one hour of silence.
- Do not buy or sell in Sunday (which is also a commandment).
- Give food to the hungry.
- Give water to the thirsty.
- Visit the sick, and confort them.

IMPORTANT NOTES

☐ _____
☐ _____
☐ _____
☐ _____
☐ _____
☐ _____
☐ _____
☐ _____
☐ _____

YOUR SOUL'S GROWTH PLANNER

LONG LIVE CHRIST THE KING!

VIVA
CRISTO
REY.ORG

DATE: MONTH   DAY   YEAR

GOALS OF THE DAY

PRAYING THE ROSARY OF 15 DECADES................... ☐

READING THE HOLY BIBLE (15 MINUTES)................ ☐

DAILY SACRIFICES....................................... ☐

☐ _____   ☐ _____
☐ _____   ☐ _____
☐ _____   ☐ _____
☐ _____   ☐ _____
☐ _____   ☐ _____
☐ _____   ☐ _____
☐ _____   ☐ _____
☐ _____   ☐ _____
☐ _____   ☐ _____

SUGGESTIONS

If you don't know how to pray the Holy Rosary, you can get our book "Rosary for beginners" in the following link: www.vcrey.com/rosary-book

Some sacrifices that you can do include:

- Not drinking water or liquids during a meal.
- Abstain from meat on Fridays (which is also required by Holy Mother Church).
- Not eating candy or dessert during one day.
- Take a cold shower.
- Not eating meat in saturdays in honor of the Blessed Virgin Mary.
- Keep one hour of silence.
- Do not buy or sell in Sunday (which is also a commandment).
- Give food to the hungry.
- Give water to the thirsty.
- Visit the sick, and confort them.

IMPORTANT NOTES

☐ _____
☐ _____
☐ _____
☐ _____
☐ _____
☐ _____
☐ _____
☐ _____
☐ _____

YOUR SOUL'S GROWTH PLANNER

LONG LIVE CHRIST THE KING!

VIVA
CRISTO
REY.ORG

DATE: MONTH   DAY   YEAR

GOALS OF THE DAY

PRAYING THE ROSARY OF 15 DECADES................... ☐

READING THE HOLY BIBLE (15 MINUTES)................ ☐

DAILY SACRIFICES... ☐

☐ _____   ☐ _____

☐ _____   ☐ _____

☐ _____   ☐ _____

☐ _____   ☐ _____

☐ _____   ☐ _____

☐ _____   ☐ _____

☐ _____   ☐ _____

☐ _____   ☐ _____

☐ _____   ☐ _____

SUGGESTIONS

If you don't know how to pray the Holy Rosary, you can get our book "Rosary for beginners" in the following link: www.vcrey.com/rosary-book

Some sacrifices that you can do include:

- Not drinking water or liquids during a meal.
- Abstain from meat on Fridays (which is also required by Holy Mother Church).
- Not eating candy or dessert during one day.
- Take a cold shower.
- Not eating meat in saturdays in honor of the Blessed Virgin Mary.
- Keep one hour of silence.
- Do not buy or sell in Sunday (which is also a commandment).
- Give food to the hungry.
- Give water to the thirsty.
- Visit the sick, and confort them.

IMPORTANT NOTES

☐ _____

☐ _____

☐ _____

☐ _____

☐ _____

☐ _____

☐ _____

☐ _____

☐ _____

YOUR SOUL'S GROWTH PLANNER

LONG LIVE CHRIST THE KING!

VIVA
CRISTO
REY.ORG

DATE: MONTH   DAY   YEAR

GOALS OF THE DAY

PRAYING THE ROSARY OF 15 DECADES.................. ☐

READING THE HOLY BIBLE (15 MINUTES)............... ☐

DAILY SACRIFICES.. ☐

☐ _____   ☐ _____
☐ _____   ☐ _____
☐ _____   ☐ _____
☐ _____   ☐ _____
☐ _____   ☐ _____
☐ _____   ☐ _____
☐ _____   ☐ _____
☐ _____   ☐ _____
☐ _____   ☐ _____

SUGGESTIONS

If you don't know how to pray the Holy Rosary, you can get our book "Rosary for beginners" in the following link: www.vcrey.com/rosary-book

Some sacrifices that you can do include:

- Not drinking water or liquids during a meal.
- Abstain from meat on Fridays (which is also required by Holy Mother Church).
- Not eating candy or dessert during one day.
- Take a cold shower.
- Not eating meat in saturdays in honor of the Blessed Virgin Mary.
- Keep one hour of silence.
- Do not buy or sell in Sunday (which is also a commandment).
- Give food to the hungry.
- Give water to the thirsty.
- Visit the sick, and confort them.

IMPORTANT NOTES

☐ _____
☐ _____
☐ _____
☐ _____
☐ _____
☐ _____
☐ _____
☐ _____
☐ _____

YOUR SOUL'S GROWTH PLANNER

VIVA
CRISTO
REY.ORG

LONG LIVE CHRIST THE KING!

DATE: MONTH   DAY   YEAR

GOALS OF THE DAY

PRAYING THE ROSARY OF 15 DECADES................... ☐

READING THE HOLY BIBLE (15 MINUTES)............... ☐

DAILY SACRIFICES... ☐

☐ _____ ☐ _____

☐ _____ ☐ _____

☐ _____ ☐ _____

☐ _____ ☐ _____

☐ _____ ☐ _____

☐ _____ ☐ _____

☐ _____ ☐ _____

☐ _____ ☐ _____

☐ _____ ☐ _____

SUGGESTIONS

If you don't know how to pray the Holy Rosary, you can get our book "Rosary for beginners" in the following link: www.vcrey.com/rosary-book

Some sacrifices that you can do include:

- Not drinking water or liquids during a meal.
- Abstain from meat on Fridays (which is also required by Holy Mother Church).
- Not eating candy or dessert during one day.
- Take a cold shower.
- Not eating meat in saturdays in honor of the Blessed Virgin Mary.
- Keep one hour of silence.
- Do not buy or sell in Sunday (which is also a commandment).
- Give food to the hungry.
- Give water to the thirsty.
- Visit the sick, and confort them.

IMPORTANT NOTES

☐ _____

☐ _____

☐ _____

☐ _____

☐ _____

☐ _____

☐ _____

☐ _____

☐ _____

YOUR SOUL'S GROWTH PLANNER

LONG LIVE CHRIST THE KING!

DATE: MONTH   DAY   YEAR

GOALS OF THE DAY

PRAYING THE ROSARY OF 15 DECADES.................. ☐

READING THE HOLY BIBLE (15 MINUTES)............... ☐

DAILY SACRIFICES... ☐

☐ _____   ☐ _____

☐ _____   ☐ _____

☐ _____   ☐ _____

☐ _____   ☐ _____

☐ _____   ☐ _____

☐ _____   ☐ _____

☐ _____   ☐ _____

☐ _____   ☐ _____

☐ _____   ☐ _____

SUGGESTIONS

If you don't know how to pray the Holy Rosary, you can get our book "Rosary for beginners" in the following link: www.vcrey.com/rosary-book

Some sacrifices that you can do include:

- Not drinking water or liquids during a meal.
- Abstain from meat on Fridays (which is also required by Holy Mother Church).
- Not eating candy or dessert during one day.
- Take a cold shower.
- Not eating meat in saturdays in honor of the Blessed Virgin Mary.
- Keep one hour of silence.
- Do not buy or sell in Sunday (which is also a commandment).
- Give food to the hungry.
- Give water to the thirsty.
- Visit the sick, and confort them.

IMPORTANT NOTES

☐ _____

☐ _____

☐ _____

☐ _____

☐ _____

☐ _____

☐ _____

☐ _____

☐ _____

YOUR SOUL'S GROWTH PLANNER

LONG LIVE CHRIST THE KING!

VIVA CRISTO REY.ORG

DATE: MONTH   DAY   YEAR

GOALS OF THE DAY

PRAYING THE ROSARY OF 15 DECADES................... ☐

READING THE HOLY BIBLE (15 MINUTES)................ ☐

DAILY SACRIFICES.. ☐

☐ _____   ☐ _____
☐ _____   ☐ _____
☐ _____   ☐ _____
☐ _____   ☐ _____
☐ _____   ☐ _____
☐ _____   ☐ _____
☐ _____   ☐ _____
☐ _____   ☐ _____
☐ _____   ☐ _____

SUGGESTIONS

If you don't know how to pray the Holy Rosary, you can get our book "Rosary for beginners" in the following link: www.vcrey.com/rosary-book

Some sacrifices that you can do include:

- Not drinking water or liquids during a meal.
- Abstain from meat on Fridays (which is also required by Holy Mother Church).
- Not eating candy or dessert during one day.
- Take a cold shower.
- Not eating meat in saturdays in honor of the Blessed Virgin Mary.
- Keep one hour of silence.
- Do not buy or sell in Sunday (which is also a commandment).
- Give food to the hungry.
- Give water to the thirsty.
- Visit the sick, and confort them.

IMPORTANT NOTES

☐ _____
☐ _____
☐ _____
☐ _____
☐ _____
☐ _____
☐ _____
☐ _____
☐ _____

YOUR SOUL'S GROWTH PLANNER

LONG LIVE CHRIST THE KING!

VIVA CRISTO REY.ORG

DATE: MONTH   DAY   YEAR

GOALS OF THE DAY

PRAYING THE ROSARY OF 15 DECADES................... ☐

READING THE HOLY BIBLE (15 MINUTES)............... ☐

DAILY SACRIFICES... ☐

☐ _____   ☐ _____
☐ _____   ☐ _____
☐ _____   ☐ _____
☐ _____   ☐ _____
☐ _____   ☐ _____
☐ _____   ☐ _____
☐ _____   ☐ _____
☐ _____   ☐ _____
☐ _____   ☐ _____

SUGGESTIONS

If you don't know how to pray the Holy Rosary, you can get our book "Rosary for beginners" in the following link: www.vcrey.com/rosary-book

Some sacrifices that you can do include:

- Not drinking water or liquids during a meal.
- Abstain from meat on Fridays (which is also required by Holy Mother Church).
- Not eating candy or dessert during one day.
- Take a cold shower.
- Not eating meat in saturdays in honor of the Blessed Virgin Mary.
- Keep one hour of silence.
- Do not buy or sell in Sunday (which is also a commandment).
- Give food to the hungry.
- Give water to the thirsty.
- Visit the sick, and confort them.

IMPORTANT NOTES

☐ _____
☐ _____
☐ _____
☐ _____
☐ _____
☐ _____
☐ _____
☐ _____
☐ _____

YOUR SOUL'S GROWTH PLANNER

LONG LIVE CHRIST THE KING!

VIVA CRISTO REY.ORG

DATE: MONTH   DAY   YEAR

GOALS OF THE DAY

PRAYING THE ROSARY OF 15 DECADES................... ☐

READING THE HOLY BIBLE (15 MINUTES)................ ☐

DAILY SACRIFICES... ☐

☐ _____   ☐ _____
☐ _____   ☐ _____
☐ _____   ☐ _____
☐ _____   ☐ _____
☐ _____   ☐ _____
☐ _____   ☐ _____
☐ _____   ☐ _____
☐ _____   ☐ _____
☐ _____   ☐ _____

SUGGESTIONS

If you don't know how to pray the Holy Rosary, you can get our book "Rosary for beginners" in the following link: www.vcrey.com/rosary-book

Some sacrifices that you can do include:

- Not drinking water or liquids during a meal.
- Abstain from meat on Fridays (which is also required by Holy Mother Church).
- Not eating candy or dessert during one day.
- Take a cold shower.
- Not eating meat in saturdays in honor of the Blessed Virgin Mary.
- Keep one hour of silence.
- Do not buy or sell in Sunday (which is also a commandment).
- Give food to the hungry.
- Give water to the thirsty.
- Visit the sick, and confort them.

IMPORTANT NOTES

☐ _____
☐ _____
☐ _____
☐ _____
☐ _____
☐ _____
☐ _____
☐ _____
☐ _____

YOUR SOUL'S GROWTH PLANNER

LONG LIVE CHRIST THE KING!

VIVA
CRISTO
REY.ORG

DATE: MONTH   DAY   YEAR

GOALS OF THE DAY

PRAYING THE ROSARY OF 15 DECADES................... ☐

READING THE HOLY BIBLE (15 MINUTES)............... ☐

DAILY SACRIFICES... ☐

☐ _____ ☐ _____
☐ _____ ☐ _____
☐ _____ ☐ _____
☐ _____ ☐ _____
☐ _____ ☐ _____
☐ _____ ☐ _____
☐ _____ ☐ _____
☐ _____ ☐ _____
☐ _____ ☐ _____

SUGGESTIONS

If you don't know how to pray the Holy Rosary, you can get our book "Rosary for beginners" in the following link: www.vcrey.com/rosary-book

Some sacrifices that you can do include:

- Not drinking water or liquids during a meal.
- Abstain from meat on Fridays (which is also required by Holy Mother Church).
- Not eating candy or dessert during one day.
- Take a cold shower.
- Not eating meat in saturdays in honor of the Blessed Virgin Mary.
- Keep one hour of silence.
- Do not buy or sell in Sunday (which is also a commandment).
- Give food to the hungry.
- Give water to the thirsty.
- Visit the sick, and confort them.

IMPORTANT NOTES

☐ _____
☐ _____
☐ _____
☐ _____
☐ _____
☐ _____
☐ _____
☐ _____
☐ _____

YOUR SOUL'S GROWTH PLANNER

LONG LIVE CHRIST THE KING!

VIVA CRISTO REY.ORG

DATE: MONTH   DAY   YEAR

GOALS OF THE DAY

PRAYING THE ROSARY OF 15 DECADES.................. ☐

READING THE HOLY BIBLE (15 MINUTES)............... ☐

DAILY SACRIFICES... ☐

☐ _____   ☐ _____
☐ _____   ☐ _____
☐ _____   ☐ _____
☐ _____   ☐ _____
☐ _____   ☐ _____
☐ _____   ☐ _____
☐ _____   ☐ _____
☐ _____   ☐ _____
☐ _____   ☐ _____

SUGGESTIONS

If you don't know how to pray the Holy Rosary, you can get our book "Rosary for beginners" in the following link: www.vcrey.com/rosary-book

Some sacrifices that you can do include:

- Not drinking water or liquids during a meal.
- Abstain from meat on Fridays (which is also required by Holy Mother Church).
- Not eating candy or dessert during one day.
- Take a cold shower.
- Not eating meat in saturdays in honor of the Blessed Virgin Mary.
- Keep one hour of silence.
- Do not buy or sell in Sunday (which is also a commandment).
- Give food to the hungry.
- Give water to the thirsty.
- Visit the sick, and confort them.

IMPORTANT NOTES

☐ _____
☐ _____
☐ _____
☐ _____
☐ _____
☐ _____
☐ _____
☐ _____
☐ _____

YOUR SOUL'S GROWTH PLANNER

LONG LIVE CHRIST THE KING!

VIVA
CRISTO
REY.ORG

DATE: MONTH   DAY   YEAR

GOALS OF THE DAY

PRAYING THE ROSARY OF 15 DECADES.................. ☐

READING THE HOLY BIBLE (15 MINUTES)............... ☐

DAILY SACRIFICES.. ☐

☐ _____   ☐ _____
☐ _____   ☐ _____
☐ _____   ☐ _____
☐ _____   ☐ _____
☐ _____   ☐ _____
☐ _____   ☐ _____
☐ _____   ☐ _____
☐ _____   ☐ _____
☐ _____   ☐ _____

SUGGESTIONS

If you don't know how to pray the Holy Rosary, you can get our book "Rosary for beginners" in the following link: www.vcrey.com/rosary-book

Some sacrifices that you can do include:

- Not drinking water or liquids during a meal.
- Abstain from meat on Fridays (which is also required by Holy Mother Church).
- Not eating candy or dessert during one day.
- Take a cold shower.
- Not eating meat in saturdays in honor of the Blessed Virgin Mary.
- Keep one hour of silence.
- Do not buy or sell in Sunday (which is also a commandment).
- Give food to the hungry.
- Give water to the thirsty.
- Visit the sick, and confort them.

IMPORTANT NOTES

☐ _____
☐ _____
☐ _____
☐ _____
☐ _____
☐ _____
☐ _____
☐ _____
☐ _____

YOUR SOUL'S GROWTH PLANNER

LONG LIVE CHRIST THE KING!

VIVA CRISTO REY.ORG

DATE: MONTH   DAY   YEAR

GOALS OF THE DAY

PRAYING THE ROSARY OF 15 DECADES................... ☐

READING THE HOLY BIBLE (15 MINUTES)............... ☐

DAILY SACRIFICES... ☐

☐ _____   ☐ _____

☐ _____   ☐ _____

☐ _____   ☐ _____

☐ _____   ☐ _____

☐ _____   ☐ _____

☐ _____   ☐ _____

☐ _____   ☐ _____

☐ _____   ☐ _____

☐ _____   ☐ _____

SUGGESTIONS

If you don't know how to pray the Holy Rosary, you can get our book "Rosary for beginners" in the following link: www.vcrey.com/rosary-book

Some sacrifices that you can do include:

- Not drinking water or liquids during a meal.
- Abstain from meat on Fridays (which is also required by Holy Mother Church).
- Not eating candy or dessert during one day.
- Take a cold shower.
- Not eating meat in saturdays in honor of the Blessed Virgin Mary.
- Keep one hour of silence.
- Do not buy or sell in Sunday (which is also a commandment).
- Give food to the hungry.
- Give water to the thirsty.
- Visit the sick, and confort them.

IMPORTANT NOTES

☐ _____

☐ _____

☐ _____

☐ _____

☐ _____

☐ _____

☐ _____

☐ _____

☐ _____

YOUR SOUL'S GROWTH PLANNER

LONG LIVE CHRIST THE KING!

VIVA CRISTO REY.ORG

DATE: MONTH   DAY   YEAR

GOALS OF THE DAY

PRAYING THE ROSARY OF 15 DECADES................... ☐

READING THE HOLY BIBLE (15 MINUTES)............... ☐

DAILY SACRIFICES... ☐

☐ _____   ☐ _____
☐ _____   ☐ _____
☐ _____   ☐ _____
☐ _____   ☐ _____
☐ _____   ☐ _____
☐ _____   ☐ _____
☐ _____   ☐ _____
☐ _____   ☐ _____
☐ _____   ☐ _____

SUGGESTIONS

If you don't know how to pray the Holy Rosary, you can get our book "Rosary for beginners" in the following link: www.vcrey.com/rosary-book

Some sacrifices that you can do include:

- Not drinking water or liquids during a meal.
- Abstain from meat on Fridays (which is also required by Holy Mother Church).
- Not eating candy or dessert during one day.
- Take a cold shower.
- Not eating meat in saturdays in honor of the Blessed Virgin Mary.
- Keep one hour of silence.
- Do not buy or sell in Sunday (which is also a commandment).
- Give food to the hungry.
- Give water to the thirsty.
- Visit the sick, and confort them.

IMPORTANT NOTES

☐ _____
☐ _____
☐ _____
☐ _____
☐ _____
☐ _____
☐ _____
☐ _____
☐ _____

YOUR SOUL'S GROWTH PLANNER

LONG LIVE CHRIST THE KING!

VIVA CRISTO REY.ORG

DATE: MONTH   DAY   YEAR

GOALS OF THE DAY

PRAYING THE ROSARY OF 15 DECADES................... ☐

READING THE HOLY BIBLE (15 MINUTES)................ ☐

DAILY SACRIFICES... ☐

☐ _____ ☐ _____
☐ _____ ☐ _____
☐ _____ ☐ _____
☐ _____ ☐ _____
☐ _____ ☐ _____
☐ _____ ☐ _____
☐ _____ ☐ _____
☐ _____ ☐ _____
☐ _____ ☐ _____

SUGGESTIONS

If you don't know how to pray the Holy Rosary, you can get our book "Rosary for beginners" in the following link: www.vcrey.com/rosary-book

Some sacrifices that you can do include:

- Not drinking water or liquids during a meal.
- Abstain from meat on Fridays (which is also required by Holy Mother Church).
- Not eating candy or dessert during one day.
- Take a cold shower.
- Not eating meat in saturdays in honor of the Blessed Virgin Mary.
- Keep one hour of silence.
- Do not buy or sell in Sunday (which is also a commandment).
- Give food to the hungry.
- Give water to the thirsty.
- Visit the sick, and confort them.

IMPORTANT NOTES

☐ _____
☐ _____
☐ _____
☐ _____
☐ _____
☐ _____
☐ _____
☐ _____
☐ _____

YOUR SOUL'S GROWTH PLANNER

LONG LIVE CHRIST THE KING!

VIVA CRISTO REY.ORG

DATE: MONTH   DAY   YEAR

GOALS OF THE DAY

PRAYING THE ROSARY OF 15 DECADES................... ☐

READING THE HOLY BIBLE (15 MINUTES)................ ☐

DAILY SACRIFICES.. ☐

☐ _____   ☐ _____

☐ _____   ☐ _____

☐ _____   ☐ _____

☐ _____   ☐ _____

☐ _____   ☐ _____

☐ _____   ☐ _____

☐ _____   ☐ _____

☐ _____   ☐ _____

☐ _____   ☐ _____

SUGGESTIONS

If you don't know how to pray the Holy Rosary, you can get our book "Rosary for beginners" in the following link: www.vcrey.com/rosary-book

Some sacrifices that you can do include:

- Not drinking water or liquids during a meal.
- Abstain from meat on Fridays (which is also required by Holy Mother Church).
- Not eating candy or dessert during one day.
- Take a cold shower.
- Not eating meat in saturdays in honor of the Blessed Virgin Mary.
- Keep one hour of silence.
- Do not buy or sell in Sunday (which is also a commandment).
- Give food to the hungry.
- Give water to the thirsty.
- Visit the sick, and confort them.

IMPORTANT NOTES

☐ _____

☐ _____

☐ _____

☐ _____

☐ _____

☐ _____

☐ _____

☐ _____

☐ _____

YOUR SOUL'S GROWTH PLANNER

LONG LIVE CHRIST THE KING!

VIVA CRISTO REY.ORG

DATE: MONTH   DAY   YEAR

GOALS OF THE DAY

PRAYING THE ROSARY OF 15 DECADES................... ☐

READING THE HOLY BIBLE (15 MINUTES)................ ☐

DAILY SACRIFICES... ☐

☐ _____   ☐ _____
☐ _____   ☐ _____
☐ _____   ☐ _____
☐ _____   ☐ _____
☐ _____   ☐ _____
☐ _____   ☐ _____
☐ _____   ☐ _____
☐ _____   ☐ _____
☐ _____   ☐ _____

SUGGESTIONS

If you don't know how to pray the Holy Rosary, you can get our book "Rosary for beginners" in the following link: www.vcrey.com/rosary-book

Some sacrifices that you can do include:

- Not drinking water or liquids during a meal.
- Abstain from meat on Fridays (which is also required by Holy Mother Church).
- Not eating candy or dessert during one day.
- Take a cold shower.
- Not eating meat in saturdays in honor of the Blessed Virgin Mary.
- Keep one hour of silence.
- Do not buy or sell in Sunday (which is also a commandment).
- Give food to the hungry.
- Give water to the thirsty.
- Visit the sick, and confort them.

IMPORTANT NOTES

☐ _____
☐ _____
☐ _____
☐ _____
☐ _____
☐ _____
☐ _____
☐ _____
☐ _____

YOUR SOUL'S GROWTH PLANNER

LONG LIVE CHRIST THE KING!

VIVA
CRISTO
REY.ORG

DATE: MONTH   DAY   YEAR

GOALS OF THE DAY

PRAYING THE ROSARY OF 15 DECADES................... ☐

READING THE HOLY BIBLE (15 MINUTES)................ ☐

DAILY SACRIFICES... ☐

☐ _____   ☐ _____
☐ _____   ☐ _____
☐ _____   ☐ _____
☐ _____   ☐ _____
☐ _____   ☐ _____
☐ _____   ☐ _____
☐ _____   ☐ _____
☐ _____   ☐ _____
☐ _____   ☐ _____

SUGGESTIONS

If you don't know how to pray the Holy Rosary, you can get our book "Rosary for beginners" in the following link: www.vcrey.com/rosary-book

Some sacrifices that you can do include:

- Not drinking water or liquids during a meal.
- Abstain from meat on Fridays (which is also required by Holy Mother Church).
- Not eating candy or dessert during one day.
- Take a cold shower.
- Not eating meat in saturdays in honor of the Blessed Virgin Mary.
- Keep one hour of silence.
- Do not buy or sell in Sunday (which is also a commandment).
- Give food to the hungry.
- Give water to the thirsty.
- Visit the sick, and confort them.

IMPORTANT NOTES

☐ _____
☐ _____
☐ _____
☐ _____
☐ _____
☐ _____
☐ _____
☐ _____
☐ _____

YOUR SOUL'S GROWTH PLANNER

LONG LIVE CHRIST THE KING!

VIVA
CRISTO
REY.ORG

DATE: MONTH   DAY   YEAR

GOALS OF THE DAY

PRAYING THE ROSARY OF 15 DECADES.................. ☐

READING THE HOLY BIBLE (15 MINUTES)............... ☐

DAILY SACRIFICES.. ☐

☐ _____   ☐ _____
☐ _____   ☐ _____
☐ _____   ☐ _____
☐ _____   ☐ _____
☐ _____   ☐ _____
☐ _____   ☐ _____
☐ _____   ☐ _____
☐ _____   ☐ _____
☐ _____   ☐ _____

SUGGESTIONS

If you don't know how to pray the Holy Rosary, you can get our book "Rosary for beginners" in the following link: www.vcrey.com/rosary-book

Some sacrifices that you can do include:

- Not drinking water or liquids during a meal.
- Abstain from meat on Fridays (which is also required by Holy Mother Church).
- Not eating candy or dessert during one day.
- Take a cold shower.
- Not eating meat in saturdays in honor of the Blessed Virgin Mary.
- Keep one hour of silence.
- Do not buy or sell in Sunday (which is also a commandment).
- Give food to the hungry.
- Give water to the thirsty.
- Visit the sick, and confort them.

IMPORTANT NOTES

☐ _____
☐ _____
☐ _____
☐ _____
☐ _____
☐ _____
☐ _____
☐ _____
☐ _____

YOUR SOUL'S GROWTH PLANNER

LONG LIVE CHRIST THE KING!

VIVA CRISTO REY.ORG

DATE: MONTH   DAY   YEAR

GOALS OF THE DAY

PRAYING THE ROSARY OF 15 DECADES................... ☐

READING THE HOLY BIBLE (15 MINUTES)............... ☐

DAILY SACRIFICES... ☐

☐ _____   ☐ _____
☐ _____   ☐ _____
☐ _____   ☐ _____
☐ _____   ☐ _____
☐ _____   ☐ _____
☐ _____   ☐ _____
☐ _____   ☐ _____
☐ _____   ☐ _____
☐ _____   ☐ _____

SUGGESTIONS

If you don't know how to pray the Holy Rosary, you can get our book "Rosary for beginners" in the following link: www.vcrey.com/rosary-book

Some sacrifices that you can do include:

- Not drinking water or liquids during a meal.
- Abstain from meat on Fridays (which is also required by Holy Mother Church).
- Not eating candy or dessert during one day.
- Take a cold shower.
- Not eating meat in saturdays in honor of the Blessed Virgin Mary.
- Keep one hour of silence.
- Do not buy or sell in Sunday (which is also a commandment).
- Give food to the hungry.
- Give water to the thirsty.
- Visit the sick, and confort them.

IMPORTANT NOTES

☐ _____
☐ _____
☐ _____
☐ _____
☐ _____
☐ _____
☐ _____
☐ _____
☐ _____

YOUR SOUL'S GROWTH PLANNER

LONG LIVE CHRIST THE KING!

VIVA CRISTO REY.ORG

DATE: MONTH   DAY   YEAR

GOALS OF THE DAY

PRAYING THE ROSARY OF 15 DECADES................... ☐

READING THE HOLY BIBLE (15 MINUTES)................ ☐

DAILY SACRIFICES.. ☐

☐ _____   ☐ _____
☐ _____   ☐ _____
☐ _____   ☐ _____
☐ _____   ☐ _____
☐ _____   ☐ _____
☐ _____   ☐ _____
☐ _____   ☐ _____
☐ _____   ☐ _____
☐ _____   ☐ _____

SUGGESTIONS

If you don't know how to pray the Holy Rosary, you can get our book "Rosary for beginners" in the following link: www.vcrey.com/rosary-book

Some sacrifices that you can do include:

- Not drinking water or liquids during a meal.
- Abstain from meat on Fridays (which is also required by Holy Mother Church).
- Not eating candy or dessert during one day.
- Take a cold shower.
- Not eating meat in saturdays in honor of the Blessed Virgin Mary.
- Keep one hour of silence.
- Do not buy or sell in Sunday (which is also a commandment).
- Give food to the hungry.
- Give water to the thirsty.
- Visit the sick, and confort them.

IMPORTANT NOTES

☐ _____
☐ _____
☐ _____
☐ _____
☐ _____
☐ _____
☐ _____
☐ _____
☐ _____

YOUR SOUL'S GROWTH PLANNER

LONG LIVE CHRIST THE KING!

VIVA
CRISTO
REY.ORG

DATE: MONTH   DAY   YEAR

GOALS OF THE DAY

PRAYING THE ROSARY OF 15 DECADES................... ☐

READING THE HOLY BIBLE (15 MINUTES)............... ☐

DAILY SACRIFICES... ☐

☐ _____   ☐ _____
☐ _____   ☐ _____
☐ _____   ☐ _____
☐ _____   ☐ _____
☐ _____   ☐ _____
☐ _____   ☐ _____
☐ _____   ☐ _____
☐ _____   ☐ _____
☐ _____   ☐ _____

SUGGESTIONS

If you don't know how to pray the Holy Rosary, you can get our book "Rosary for beginners" in the following link: www.vcrey.com/rosary-book

Some sacrifices that you can do include:

- Not drinking water or liquids during a meal.
- Abstain from meat on Fridays (which is also required by Holy Mother Church).
- Not eating candy or dessert during one day.
- Take a cold shower.
- Not eating meat in saturdays in honor of the Blessed Virgin Mary.
- Keep one hour of silence.
- Do not buy or sell in Sunday (which is also a commandment).
- Give food to the hungry.
- Give water to the thirsty.
- Visit the sick, and confort them.

IMPORTANT NOTES

☐ _____
☐ _____
☐ _____
☐ _____
☐ _____
☐ _____
☐ _____
☐ _____
☐ _____

YOUR SOUL'S GROWTH PLANNER

LONG LIVE CHRIST THE KING!

VIVA CRISTO REY.ORG

DATE: MONTH   DAY   YEAR

GOALS OF THE DAY

PRAYING THE ROSARY OF 15 DECADES................... ☐

READING THE HOLY BIBLE (15 MINUTES)............... ☐

DAILY SACRIFICES.. ☐

☐ _____   ☐ _____

☐ _____   ☐ _____

☐ _____   ☐ _____

☐ _____   ☐ _____

☐ _____   ☐ _____

☐ _____   ☐ _____

☐ _____   ☐ _____

☐ _____   ☐ _____

☐ _____   ☐ _____

SUGGESTIONS

If you don't know how to pray the Holy Rosary, you can get our book "Rosary for beginners" in the following link: www.vcrey.com/rosary-book

Some sacrifices that you can do include:

- Not drinking water or liquids during a meal.
- Abstain from meat on Fridays (which is also required by Holy Mother Church).
- Not eating candy or dessert during one day.
- Take a cold shower.
- Not eating meat in saturdays in honor of the Blessed Virgin Mary.
- Keep one hour of silence.
- Do not buy or sell in Sunday (which is also a commandment).
- Give food to the hungry.
- Give water to the thirsty.
- Visit the sick, and confort them.

IMPORTANT NOTES

☐ _____

☐ _____

☐ _____

☐ _____

☐ _____

☐ _____

☐ _____

☐ _____

☐ _____

YOUR SOUL'S GROWTH PLANNER

LONG LIVE CHRIST THE KING!

VIVA
CRISTO
REY.ORG

DATE: MONTH   DAY   YEAR

GOALS OF THE DAY

PRAYING THE ROSARY OF 15 DECADES.................. ☐

READING THE HOLY BIBLE (15 MINUTES)............... ☐

DAILY SACRIFICES... ☐

☐ _____   ☐ _____
☐ _____   ☐ _____
☐ _____   ☐ _____
☐ _____   ☐ _____
☐ _____   ☐ _____
☐ _____   ☐ _____
☐ _____   ☐ _____
☐ _____   ☐ _____
☐ _____   ☐ _____

SUGGESTIONS

If you don't know how to pray the Holy Rosary, you can get our book "Rosary for beginners" in the following link: www.vcrey.com/rosary-book

Some sacrifices that you can do include:

- Not drinking water or liquids during a meal.
- Abstain from meat on Fridays (which is also required by Holy Mother Church).
- Not eating candy or dessert during one day.
- Take a cold shower.
- Not eating meat in saturdays in honor of the Blessed Virgin Mary.
- Keep one hour of silence.
- Do not buy or sell in Sunday (which is also a commandment).
- Give food to the hungry.
- Give water to the thirsty.
- Visit the sick, and confort them.

IMPORTANT NOTES

☐ _____
☐ _____
☐ _____
☐ _____
☐ _____
☐ _____
☐ _____
☐ _____
☐ _____

YOUR SOUL'S GROWTH PLANNER

LONG LIVE CHRIST THE KING!

VIVA
CRISTO
REY.ORG

DATE: MONTH   DAY   YEAR

GOALS OF THE DAY

PRAYING THE ROSARY OF 15 DECADES.................... ☐

READING THE HOLY BIBLE (15 MINUTES)................ ☐

DAILY SACRIFICES... ☐

☐ _____   ☐ _____
☐ _____   ☐ _____
☐ _____   ☐ _____
☐ _____   ☐ _____
☐ _____   ☐ _____
☐ _____   ☐ _____
☐ _____   ☐ _____
☐ _____   ☐ _____
☐ _____   ☐ _____

SUGGESTIONS

If you don't know how to pray the Holy Rosary, you can get our book "Rosary for beginners" in the following link: www.vcrey.com/rosary-book

Some sacrifices that you can do include:

- Not drinking water or liquids during a meal.
- Abstain from meat on Fridays (which is also required by Holy Mother Church).
- Not eating candy or dessert during one day.
- Take a cold shower.
- Not eating meat in saturdays in honor of the Blessed Virgin Mary.
- Keep one hour of silence.
- Do not buy or sell in Sunday (which is also a commandment).
- Give food to the hungry.
- Give water to the thirsty.
- Visit the sick, and confort them.

IMPORTANT NOTES

☐ _____
☐ _____
☐ _____
☐ _____
☐ _____
☐ _____
☐ _____
☐ _____
☐ _____

YOUR SOUL'S GROWTH PLANNER

LONG LIVE CHRIST THE KING!

VIVA
CRISTO
REY.ORG

DATE: MONTH   DAY   YEAR

GOALS OF THE DAY

PRAYING THE ROSARY OF 15 DECADES.................. ☐

READING THE HOLY BIBLE (15 MINUTES)............... ☐

DAILY SACRIFICES... ☐

☐ _____   ☐ _____

☐ _____   ☐ _____

☐ _____   ☐ _____

☐ _____   ☐ _____

☐ _____   ☐ _____

☐ _____   ☐ _____

☐ _____   ☐ _____

☐ _____   ☐ _____

☐ _____   ☐ _____

SUGGESTIONS

If you don't know how to pray the Holy Rosary, you can get our book "Rosary for beginners" in the following link: www.vcrey.com/rosary-book

Some sacrifices that you can do include:

- Not drinking water or liquids during a meal.
- Abstain from meat on Fridays (which is also required by Holy Mother Church).
- Not eating candy or dessert during one day.
- Take a cold shower.
- Not eating meat in saturdays in honor of the Blessed Virgin Mary.
- Keep one hour of silence.
- Do not buy or sell in Sunday (which is also a commandment).
- Give food to the hungry.
- Give water to the thirsty.
- Visit the sick, and confort them.

IMPORTANT NOTES

☐ _____

☐ _____

☐ _____

☐ _____

☐ _____

☐ _____

☐ _____

☐ _____

☐ _____

YOUR SOUL'S GROWTH PLANNER

VIVA CRISTO REY.ORG

LONG LIVE CHRIST THE KING!

DATE: MONTH   DAY   YEAR

GOALS OF THE DAY

PRAYING THE ROSARY OF 15 DECADES................... ☐

READING THE HOLY BIBLE (15 MINUTES)................ ☐

DAILY SACRIFICES... ☐

☐ _____ ☐ _____
☐ _____ ☐ _____
☐ _____ ☐ _____
☐ _____ ☐ _____
☐ _____ ☐ _____
☐ _____ ☐ _____
☐ _____ ☐ _____
☐ _____ ☐ _____
☐ _____ ☐ _____

SUGGESTIONS

If you don't know how to pray the Holy Rosary, you can get our book "Rosary for beginners" in the following link: www.vcrey.com/rosary-book

Some sacrifices that you can do include:

- Not drinking water or liquids during a meal.
- Abstain from meat on Fridays (which is also required by Holy Mother Church).
- Not eating candy or dessert during one day.
- Take a cold shower.
- Not eating meat in saturdays in honor of the Blessed Virgin Mary.
- Keep one hour of silence.
- Do not buy or sell in Sunday (which is also a commandment).
- Give food to the hungry.
- Give water to the thirsty.
- Visit the sick, and confort them.

IMPORTANT NOTES

☐ _____
☐ _____
☐ _____
☐ _____
☐ _____
☐ _____
☐ _____
☐ _____
☐ _____

YOUR SOUL'S GROWTH PLANNER

LONG LIVE CHRIST THE KING!

VIVA
CRISTO
REY.ORG

DATE: MONTH   DAY   YEAR

GOALS OF THE DAY

PRAYING THE ROSARY OF 15 DECADES.................. ☐

READING THE HOLY BIBLE (15 MINUTES)............... ☐

DAILY SACRIFICES... ☐

☐ _____   ☐ _____

☐ _____   ☐ _____

☐ _____   ☐ _____

☐ _____   ☐ _____

☐ _____   ☐ _____

☐ _____   ☐ _____

☐ _____   ☐ _____

☐ _____   ☐ _____

☐ _____   ☐ _____

SUGGESTIONS

If you don't know how to pray the Holy Rosary, you can get our book "Rosary for beginners" in the following link: www.vcrey.com/rosary-book

Some sacrifices that you can do include:

- Not drinking water or liquids during a meal.
- Abstain from meat on Fridays (which is also required by Holy Mother Church).
- Not eating candy or dessert during one day.
- Take a cold shower.
- Not eating meat in saturdays in honor of the Blessed Virgin Mary.
- Keep one hour of silence.
- Do not buy or sell in Sunday (which is also a commandment).
- Give food to the hungry.
- Give water to the thirsty.
- Visit the sick, and confort them.

IMPORTANT NOTES

☐ _____

☐ _____

☐ _____

☐ _____

☐ _____

☐ _____

☐ _____

☐ _____

☐ _____

YOUR SOUL'S GROWTH PLANNER

LONG LIVE CHRIST THE KING!

VIVA
CRISTO
REY.ORG

DATE: MONTH   DAY   YEAR

GOALS OF THE DAY

PRAYING THE ROSARY OF 15 DECADES................... ☐

READING THE HOLY BIBLE (15 MINUTES)............... ☐

DAILY SACRIFICES.. ☐

☐ _____   ☐ _____
☐ _____   ☐ _____
☐ _____   ☐ _____
☐ _____   ☐ _____
☐ _____   ☐ _____
☐ _____   ☐ _____
☐ _____   ☐ _____
☐ _____   ☐ _____
☐ _____   ☐ _____

SUGGESTIONS

If you don't know how to pray the Holy Rosary, you can get our book "Rosary for beginners" in the following link: www.vcrey.com/rosary-book

Some sacrifices that you can do include:

- Not drinking water or liquids during a meal.
- Abstain from meat on Fridays (which is also required by Holy Mother Church).
- Not eating candy or dessert during one day.
- Take a cold shower.
- Not eating meat in saturdays in honor of the Blessed Virgin Mary.
- Keep one hour of silence.
- Do not buy or sell in Sunday (which is also a commandment).
- Give food to the hungry.
- Give water to the thirsty.
- Visit the sick, and confort them.

IMPORTANT NOTES

☐ _____
☐ _____
☐ _____
☐ _____
☐ _____
☐ _____
☐ _____
☐ _____
☐ _____

YOUR SOUL'S GROWTH PLANNER

LONG LIVE CHRIST THE KING!

VIVA
CRISTO
REY.ORG

DATE: MONTH   DAY   YEAR

GOALS OF THE DAY

PRAYING THE ROSARY OF 15 DECADES................... ☐

READING THE HOLY BIBLE (15 MINUTES)............... ☐

DAILY SACRIFICES... ☐

☐ _____   ☐ _____
☐ _____   ☐ _____
☐ _____   ☐ _____
☐ _____   ☐ _____
☐ _____   ☐ _____
☐ _____   ☐ _____
☐ _____   ☐ _____
☐ _____   ☐ _____
☐ _____   ☐ _____

SUGGESTIONS

If you don't know how to pray the Holy Rosary, you can get our book "Rosary for beginners" in the following link: www.vcrey.com/rosary-book

Some sacrifices that you can do include:

- Not drinking water or liquids during a meal.
- Abstain from meat on Fridays (which is also required by Holy Mother Church).
- Not eating candy or dessert during one day.
- Take a cold shower.
- Not eating meat in saturdays in honor of the Blessed Virgin Mary.
- Keep one hour of silence.
- Do not buy or sell in Sunday (which is also a commandment).
- Give food to the hungry.
- Give water to the thirsty.
- Visit the sick, and confort them.

IMPORTANT NOTES

☐ _____
☐ _____
☐ _____
☐ _____
☐ _____
☐ _____
☐ _____
☐ _____
☐ _____

YOUR SOUL'S GROWTH PLANNER

LONG LIVE CHRIST THE KING!

VIVA CRISTO REY.ORG

DATE: MONTH   DAY   YEAR

GOALS OF THE DAY

PRAYING THE ROSARY OF 15 DECADES................... ☐

READING THE HOLY BIBLE (15 MINUTES)................ ☐

DAILY SACRIFICES... ☐

☐ _____   ☐ _____
☐ _____   ☐ _____
☐ _____   ☐ _____
☐ _____   ☐ _____
☐ _____   ☐ _____
☐ _____   ☐ _____
☐ _____   ☐ _____
☐ _____   ☐ _____
☐ _____   ☐ _____

SUGGESTIONS

If you don't know how to pray the Holy Rosary, you can get our book "Rosary for beginners" in the following link: www.vcrey.com/rosary-book

Some sacrifices that you can do include:

- Not drinking water or liquids during a meal.
- Abstain from meat on Fridays (which is also required by Holy Mother Church).
- Not eating candy or dessert during one day.
- Take a cold shower.
- Not eating meat in saturdays in honor of the Blessed Virgin Mary.
- Keep one hour of silence.
- Do not buy or sell in Sunday (which is also a commandment).
- Give food to the hungry.
- Give water to the thirsty.
- Visit the sick, and confort them.

IMPORTANT NOTES

☐ _____
☐ _____
☐ _____
☐ _____
☐ _____
☐ _____
☐ _____
☐ _____
☐ _____

YOUR SOUL'S GROWTH PLANNER

LONG LIVE CHRIST THE KING!

VIVA
CRISTO
REY.ORG

DATE: MONTH   DAY   YEAR

GOALS OF THE DAY

PRAYING THE ROSARY OF 15 DECADES................... ☐

READING THE HOLY BIBLE (15 MINUTES)............... ☐

DAILY SACRIFICES... ☐

☐ _____   ☐ _____
☐ _____   ☐ _____
☐ _____   ☐ _____

☐ _____   ☐ _____
☐ _____   ☐ _____
☐ _____   ☐ _____
☐ _____   ☐ _____
☐ _____   ☐ _____
☐ _____   ☐ _____

SUGGESTIONS

If you don't know how to pray the Holy Rosary, you can get our book "Rosary for beginners" in the following link: www.vcrey.com/rosary-book

Some sacrifices that you can do include:

- Not drinking water or liquids during a meal.
- Abstain from meat on Fridays (which is also required by Holy Mother Church).
- Not eating candy or dessert during one day.
- Take a cold shower.
- Not eating meat in saturdays in honor of the Blessed Virgin Mary.
- Keep one hour of silence.
- Do not buy or sell in Sunday (which is also a commandment).
- Give food to the hungry.
- Give water to the thirsty.
- Visit the sick, and confort them.

IMPORTANT NOTES

☐ _____
☐ _____
☐ _____
☐ _____
☐ _____
☐ _____
☐ _____
☐ _____
☐ _____

YOUR SOUL'S GROWTH PLANNER

LONG LIVE CHRIST THE KING!

VIVA CRISTO REY.ORG

DATE: MONTH   DAY   YEAR

GOALS OF THE DAY

PRAYING THE ROSARY OF 15 DECADES................... ☐

READING THE HOLY BIBLE (15 MINUTES)................ ☐

DAILY SACRIFICES.. ☐

☐ _____   ☐ _____

☐ _____   ☐ _____

☐ _____   ☐ _____

☐ _____   ☐ _____

☐ _____   ☐ _____

☐ _____   ☐ _____

☐ _____   ☐ _____

☐ _____   ☐ _____

☐ _____   ☐ _____

SUGGESTIONS

If you don't know how to pray the Holy Rosary, you can get our book "Rosary for beginners" in the following link: www.vcrey.com/rosary-book

Some sacrifices that you can do include:

- Not drinking water or liquids during a meal.
- Abstain from meat on Fridays (which is also required by Holy Mother Church).
- Not eating candy or dessert during one day.
- Take a cold shower.
- Not eating meat in saturdays in honor of the Blessed Virgin Mary.
- Keep one hour of silence.
- Do not buy or sell in Sunday (which is also a commandment).
- Give food to the hungry.
- Give water to the thirsty.
- Visit the sick, and confort them.

IMPORTANT NOTES

☐ _____

☐ _____

☐ _____

☐ _____

☐ _____

☐ _____

☐ _____

☐ _____

☐ _____

YOUR SOUL'S GROWTH PLANNER

LONG LIVE CHRIST THE KING!

VIVA CRISTO REY.ORG

DATE: MONTH   DAY   YEAR

GOALS OF THE DAY

PRAYING THE ROSARY OF 15 DECADES.................. ☐

READING THE HOLY BIBLE (15 MINUTES)............... ☐

DAILY SACRIFICES... ☐

☐ _____ ☐ _____
☐ _____ ☐ _____
☐ _____ ☐ _____

☐ _____ ☐ _____
☐ _____ ☐ _____
☐ _____ ☐ _____
☐ _____ ☐ _____

☐ _____ ☐ _____
☐ _____ ☐ _____

SUGGESTIONS

If you don't know how to pray the Holy Rosary, you can get our book "Rosary for beginners" in the following link: www.vcrey.com/rosary-book

Some sacrifices that you can do include:

- Not drinking water or liquids during a meal.
- Abstain from meat on Fridays (which is also required by Holy Mother Church).
- Not eating candy or dessert during one day.
- Take a cold shower.
- Not eating meat in saturdays in honor of the Blessed Virgin Mary.
- Keep one hour of silence.
- Do not buy or sell in Sunday (which is also a commandment).
- Give food to the hungry.
- Give water to the thirsty.
- Visit the sick, and confort them.

IMPORTANT NOTES

☐ _____
☐ _____
☐ _____
☐ _____
☐ _____
☐ _____
☐ _____
☐ _____
☐ _____

YOUR SOUL'S GROWTH PLANNER

LONG LIVE CHRIST THE KING!

VIVA
CRISTO
REY.ORG

DATE: MONTH   DAY   YEAR

GOALS OF THE DAY

PRAYING THE ROSARY OF 15 DECADES.................. ☐

READING THE HOLY BIBLE (15 MINUTES)............... ☐

DAILY SACRIFICES.. ☐

☐ _____   ☐ _____
☐ _____   ☐ _____
☐ _____   ☐ _____
☐ _____   ☐ _____
☐ _____   ☐ _____
☐ _____   ☐ _____
☐ _____   ☐ _____
☐ _____   ☐ _____
☐ _____   ☐ _____

SUGGESTIONS

If you don't know how to pray the Holy Rosary, you can get our book "Rosary for beginners" in the following link: www.vcrey.com/rosary-book

Some sacrifices that you can do include:

- Not drinking water or liquids during a meal.
- Abstain from meat on Fridays (which is also required by Holy Mother Church).
- Not eating candy or dessert during one day.
- Take a cold shower.
- Not eating meat in saturdays in honor of the Blessed Virgin Mary.
- Keep one hour of silence.
- Do not buy or sell in Sunday (which is also a commandment).
- Give food to the hungry.
- Give water to the thirsty.
- Visit the sick, and confort them.

IMPORTANT NOTES

☐ _____
☐ _____
☐ _____
☐ _____
☐ _____
☐ _____
☐ _____
☐ _____
☐ _____

YOUR SOUL'S GROWTH PLANNER

LONG LIVE CHRIST THE KING!

VIVA
CRISTO
REY.ORG

DATE: MONTH   DAY   YEAR

GOALS OF THE DAY

PRAYING THE ROSARY OF 15 DECADES.................... ☐

READING THE HOLY BIBLE (15 MINUTES)................ ☐

DAILY SACRIFICES... ☐

☐ _____   ☐ _____
☐ _____   ☐ _____
☐ _____   ☐ _____
☐ _____   ☐ _____
☐ _____   ☐ _____
☐ _____   ☐ _____
☐ _____   ☐ _____
☐ _____   ☐ _____
☐ _____   ☐ _____

SUGGESTIONS

If you don't know how to pray the Holy Rosary, you can get our book "Rosary for beginners" in the following link: www.vcrey.com/rosary-book

Some sacrifices that you can do include:

- Not drinking water or liquids during a meal.
- Abstain from meat on Fridays (which is also required by Holy Mother Church).
- Not eating candy or dessert during one day.
- Take a cold shower.
- Not eating meat in saturdays in honor of the Blessed Virgin Mary.
- Keep one hour of silence.
- Do not buy or sell in Sunday (which is also a commandment).
- Give food to the hungry.
- Give water to the thirsty.
- Visit the sick, and confort them.

IMPORTANT NOTES

☐ _____
☐ _____
☐ _____
☐ _____
☐ _____
☐ _____
☐ _____
☐ _____
☐ _____

YOUR SOUL'S GROWTH PLANNER

LONG LIVE CHRIST THE KING!

VIVA CRISTO REY.ORG

DATE: MONTH   DAY   YEAR

GOALS OF THE DAY

PRAYING THE ROSARY OF 15 DECADES................... ☐

READING THE HOLY BIBLE (15 MINUTES)................ ☐

DAILY SACRIFICES... ☐

☐ _____   ☐ _____
☐ _____   ☐ _____
☐ _____   ☐ _____
☐ _____   ☐ _____
☐ _____   ☐ _____
☐ _____   ☐ _____
☐ _____   ☐ _____
☐ _____   ☐ _____
☐ _____   ☐ _____

SUGGESTIONS

If you don't know how to pray the Holy Rosary, you can get our book "Rosary for beginners" in the following link: www.vcrey.com/rosary-book

Some sacrifices that you can do include:

- Not drinking water or liquids during a meal.
- Abstain from meat on Fridays (which is also required by Holy Mother Church).
- Not eating candy or dessert during one day.
- Take a cold shower.
- Not eating meat in saturdays in honor of the Blessed Virgin Mary.
- Keep one hour of silence.
- Do not buy or sell in Sunday (which is also a commandment).
- Give food to the hungry.
- Give water to the thirsty.
- Visit the sick, and confort them.

IMPORTANT NOTES

☐ _____
☐ _____
☐ _____
☐ _____
☐ _____
☐ _____
☐ _____
☐ _____
☐ _____

YOUR SOUL'S GROWTH PLANNER

LONG LIVE CHRIST THE KING!

VIVA
CRISTO
REY.ORG

DATE: MONTH   DAY   YEAR

GOALS OF THE DAY

PRAYING THE ROSARY OF 15 DECADES................... ☐

READING THE HOLY BIBLE (15 MINUTES)............... ☐

DAILY SACRIFICES.. ☐

☐ _____   ☐ _____
☐ _____   ☐ _____
☐ _____   ☐ _____

☐ _____   ☐ _____
☐ _____   ☐ _____
☐ _____   ☐ _____
☐ _____   ☐ _____

☐ _____   ☐ _____
☐ _____   ☐ _____

SUGGESTIONS

If you don't know how to pray the Holy Rosary, you can get our book "Rosary for beginners" in the following link: www.vcrey.com/rosary-book

Some sacrifices that you can do include:

- Not drinking water or liquids during a meal.
- Abstain from meat on Fridays (which is also required by Holy Mother Church).
- Not eating candy or dessert during one day.
- Take a cold shower.
- Not eating meat in saturdays in honor of the Blessed Virgin Mary.
- Keep one hour of silence.
- Do not buy or sell in Sunday (which is also a commandment).
- Give food to the hungry.
- Give water to the thirsty.
- Visit the sick, and confort them.

IMPORTANT NOTES

☐ _____
☐ _____
☐ _____
☐ _____
☐ _____
☐ _____
☐ _____
☐ _____
☐ _____

YOUR SOUL'S GROWTH PLANNER

LONG LIVE CHRIST THE KING!

VIVA CRISTO REY.ORG

DATE: MONTH   DAY   YEAR

GOALS OF THE DAY

PRAYING THE ROSARY OF 15 DECADES................... ☐

READING THE HOLY BIBLE (15 MINUTES)................ ☐

DAILY SACRIFICES... ☐

☐ _____   ☐ _____
☐ _____   ☐ _____
☐ _____   ☐ _____
☐ _____   ☐ _____
☐ _____   ☐ _____
☐ _____   ☐ _____
☐ _____   ☐ _____
☐ _____   ☐ _____
☐ _____   ☐ _____

SUGGESTIONS

If you don't know how to pray the Holy Rosary, you can get our book "Rosary for beginners" in the following link: www.vcrey.com/rosary-book

Some sacrifices that you can do include:

- Not drinking water or liquids during a meal.
- Abstain from meat on Fridays (which is also required by Holy Mother Church).
- Not eating candy or dessert during one day.
- Take a cold shower.
- Not eating meat in saturdays in honor of the Blessed Virgin Mary.
- Keep one hour of silence.
- Do not buy or sell in Sunday (which is also a commandment).
- Give food to the hungry.
- Give water to the thirsty.
- Visit the sick, and confort them.

IMPORTANT NOTES

☐ _____
☐ _____
☐ _____
☐ _____
☐ _____
☐ _____
☐ _____
☐ _____
☐ _____

YOUR SOUL'S GROWTH PLANNER

LONG LIVE CHRIST THE KING!

VIVA CRISTO REY.ORG

DATE: MONTH   DAY   YEAR

GOALS OF THE DAY

PRAYING THE ROSARY OF 15 DECADES................... ☐

READING THE HOLY BIBLE (15 MINUTES)............... ☐

DAILY SACRIFICES... ☐

☐ _____   ☐ _____
☐ _____   ☐ _____
☐ _____   ☐ _____
☐ _____   ☐ _____
☐ _____   ☐ _____
☐ _____   ☐ _____
☐ _____   ☐ _____
☐ _____   ☐ _____
☐ _____   ☐ _____

SUGGESTIONS

If you don't know how to pray the Holy Rosary, you can get our book "Rosary for beginners" in the following link: www.vcrey.com/rosary-book

Some sacrifices that you can do include:

- Not drinking water or liquids during a meal.
- Abstain from meat on Fridays (which is also required by Holy Mother Church).
- Not eating candy or dessert during one day.
- Take a cold shower.
- Not eating meat in saturdays in honor of the Blessed Virgin Mary.
- Keep one hour of silence.
- Do not buy or sell in Sunday (which is also a commandment).
- Give food to the hungry.
- Give water to the thirsty.
- Visit the sick, and confort them.

IMPORTANT NOTES

☐ _____
☐ _____
☐ _____
☐ _____
☐ _____
☐ _____
☐ _____
☐ _____
☐ _____

YOUR SOUL'S GROWTH PLANNER

LONG LIVE CHRIST THE KING!

VIVA
CRISTO
REY.ORG

DATE: MONTH   DAY   YEAR

GOALS OF THE DAY

PRAYING THE ROSARY OF 15 DECADES................... ☐

READING THE HOLY BIBLE (15 MINUTES)................ ☐

DAILY SACRIFICES.. ☐

☐ _____   ☐ _____
☐ _____   ☐ _____
☐ _____   ☐ _____
☐ _____   ☐ _____
☐ _____   ☐ _____
☐ _____   ☐ _____
☐ _____   ☐ _____
☐ _____   ☐ _____
☐ _____   ☐ _____

SUGGESTIONS

If you don't know how to pray the Holy Rosary, you can get our book "Rosary for beginners" in the following link: www.vcrey.com/rosary-book

Some sacrifices that you can do include:

- Not drinking water or liquids during a meal.
- Abstain from meat on Fridays (which is also required by Holy Mother Church).
- Not eating candy or dessert during one day.
- Take a cold shower.
- Not eating meat in saturdays in honor of the Blessed Virgin Mary.
- Keep one hour of silence.
- Do not buy or sell in Sunday (which is also a commandment).
- Give food to the hungry.
- Give water to the thirsty.
- Visit the sick, and confort them.

IMPORTANT NOTES

☐ _____
☐ _____
☐ _____
☐ _____
☐ _____
☐ _____
☐ _____
☐ _____
☐ _____

YOUR SOUL'S GROWTH PLANNER

LONG LIVE CHRIST THE KING!

VIVA CRISTO REY.ORG

DATE: MONTH   DAY   YEAR

GOALS OF THE DAY

PRAYING THE ROSARY OF 15 DECADES.................. ☐

READING THE HOLY BIBLE (15 MINUTES)............... ☐

DAILY SACRIFICES... ☐

☐ _____   ☐ _____
☐ _____   ☐ _____
☐ _____   ☐ _____

☐ _____   ☐ _____
☐ _____   ☐ _____
☐ _____   ☐ _____

☐ _____   ☐ _____

☐ _____   ☐ _____
☐ _____   ☐ _____

SUGGESTIONS

If you don't know how to pray the Holy Rosary, you can get our book "Rosary for beginners" in the following link: www.vcrey.com/rosary-book

Some sacrifices that you can do include:

- Not drinking water or liquids during a meal.
- Abstain from meat on Fridays (which is also required by Holy Mother Church).
- Not eating candy or dessert during one day.
- Take a cold shower.
- Not eating meat in saturdays in honor of the Blessed Virgin Mary.
- Keep one hour of silence.
- Do not buy or sell in Sunday (which is also a commandment).
- Give food to the hungry.
- Give water to the thirsty.
- Visit the sick, and confort them.

IMPORTANT NOTES

☐ _____
☐ _____
☐ _____
☐ _____
☐ _____
☐ _____
☐ _____
☐ _____
☐ _____

YOUR SOUL'S GROWTH PLANNER

LONG LIVE CHRIST THE KING!

VIVA
CRISTO
REY.ORG

DATE: MONTH   DAY   YEAR

GOALS OF THE DAY

PRAYING THE ROSARY OF 15 DECADES................... ☐

READING THE HOLY BIBLE (15 MINUTES)............... ☐

DAILY SACRIFICES... ☐

☐ _____   ☐ _____

☐ _____   ☐ _____

☐ _____   ☐ _____

☐ _____   ☐ _____

☐ _____   ☐ _____

☐ _____   ☐ _____

☐ _____   ☐ _____

☐ _____   ☐ _____

☐ _____   ☐ _____

SUGGESTIONS

If you don't know how to pray the Holy Rosary, you can get our book "Rosary for beginners" in the following link: www.vcrey.com/rosary-book

Some sacrifices that you can do include:

- Not drinking water or liquids during a meal.
- Abstain from meat on Fridays (which is also required by Holy Mother Church).
- Not eating candy or dessert during one day.
- Take a cold shower.
- Not eating meat in saturdays in honor of the Blessed Virgin Mary.
- Keep one hour of silence.
- Do not buy or sell in Sunday (which is also a commandment).
- Give food to the hungry.
- Give water to the thirsty.
- Visit the sick, and confort them.

IMPORTANT NOTES

☐ _____

☐ _____

☐ _____

☐ _____

☐ _____

☐ _____

☐ _____

☐ _____

☐ _____

YOUR SOUL'S GROWTH PLANNER

LONG LIVE CHRIST THE KING!

VIVA CRISTO REY.ORG

DATE: MONTH   DAY   YEAR

GOALS OF THE DAY

PRAYING THE ROSARY OF 15 DECADES................... ☐

READING THE HOLY BIBLE (15 MINUTES)............... ☐

DAILY SACRIFICES.. ☐

☐ _____   ☐ _____
☐ _____   ☐ _____
☐ _____   ☐ _____

☐ _____   ☐ _____
☐ _____   ☐ _____
☐ _____   ☐ _____
☐ _____   ☐ _____

☐ _____   ☐ _____
☐ _____   ☐ _____

SUGGESTIONS

If you don't know how to pray the Holy Rosary, you can get our book "Rosary for beginners" in the following link: www.vcrey.com/rosary-book

Some sacrifices that you can do include:

- Not drinking water or liquids during a meal.
- Abstain from meat on Fridays (which is also required by Holy Mother Church).
- Not eating candy or dessert during one day.
- Take a cold shower.
- Not eating meat in saturdays in honor of the Blessed Virgin Mary.
- Keep one hour of silence.
- Do not buy or sell in Sunday (which is also a commandment).
- Give food to the hungry.
- Give water to the thirsty.
- Visit the sick, and confort them.

IMPORTANT NOTES

☐ _____
☐ _____
☐ _____
☐ _____
☐ _____
☐ _____
☐ _____
☐ _____
☐ _____

YOUR SOUL'S GROWTH PLANNER

LONG LIVE CHRIST THE KING!

VIVA CRISTO REY.ORG

DATE: MONTH   DAY   YEAR

GOALS OF THE DAY

PRAYING THE ROSARY OF 15 DECADES................... ☐

READING THE HOLY BIBLE (15 MINUTES)............... ☐

DAILY SACRIFICES... ☐

☐ _____   ☐ _____

☐ _____   ☐ _____

☐ _____   ☐ _____

☐ _____   ☐ _____

☐ _____   ☐ _____

☐ _____   ☐ _____

☐ _____   ☐ _____

☐ _____   ☐ _____

☐ _____   ☐ _____

SUGGESTIONS

If you don't know how to pray the Holy Rosary, you can get our book "Rosary for beginners" in the following link: www.vcrey.com/rosary-book

Some sacrifices that you can do include:

- Not drinking water or liquids during a meal.
- Abstain from meat on Fridays (which is also required by Holy Mother Church).
- Not eating candy or dessert during one day.
- Take a cold shower.
- Not eating meat in saturdays in honor of the Blessed Virgin Mary.
- Keep one hour of silence.
- Do not buy or sell in Sunday (which is also a commandment).
- Give food to the hungry.
- Give water to the thirsty.
- Visit the sick, and confort them.

IMPORTANT NOTES

☐ _____

☐ _____

☐ _____

☐ _____

☐ _____

☐ _____

☐ _____

☐ _____

☐ _____

YOUR SOUL'S GROWTH PLANNER

LONG LIVE CHRIST THE KING!

VIVA
CRISTO
REY.ORG

DATE: MONTH   DAY   YEAR

GOALS OF THE DAY

PRAYING THE ROSARY OF 15 DECADES................... ☐

READING THE HOLY BIBLE (15 MINUTES)................ ☐

DAILY SACRIFICES... ☐

☐ _____   ☐ _____
☐ _____   ☐ _____
☐ _____   ☐ _____
☐ _____   ☐ _____
☐ _____   ☐ _____
☐ _____   ☐ _____
☐ _____   ☐ _____
☐ _____   ☐ _____
☐ _____   ☐ _____

SUGGESTIONS

If you don't know how to pray the Holy Rosary, you can get our book "Rosary for beginners" in the following link: www.vcrey.com/rosary-book

Some sacrifices that you can do include:

- Not drinking water or liquids during a meal.
- Abstain from meat on Fridays (which is also required by Holy Mother Church).
- Not eating candy or dessert during one day.
- Take a cold shower.
- Not eating meat in saturdays in honor of the Blessed Virgin Mary.
- Keep one hour of silence.
- Do not buy or sell in Sunday (which is also a commandment).
- Give food to the hungry.
- Give water to the thirsty.
- Visit the sick, and confort them.

IMPORTANT NOTES

☐ _____
☐ _____
☐ _____
☐ _____
☐ _____
☐ _____
☐ _____
☐ _____
☐ _____

YOUR SOUL'S GROWTH PLANNER

LONG LIVE CHRIST THE KING!

VIVA
CRISTO
REY.ORG

DATE: MONTH   DAY   YEAR

GOALS OF THE DAY

PRAYING THE ROSARY OF 15 DECADES.................. ☐

READING THE HOLY BIBLE (15 MINUTES)................ ☐

DAILY SACRIFICES... ☐

☐ _____   ☐ _____
☐ _____   ☐ _____
☐ _____   ☐ _____
☐ _____   ☐ _____
☐ _____   ☐ _____
☐ _____   ☐ _____
☐ _____   ☐ _____
☐ _____   ☐ _____
☐ _____   ☐ _____

SUGGESTIONS

If you don't know how to pray the Holy Rosary, you can get our book "Rosary for beginners" in the following link: www.vcrey.com/rosary-book

Some sacrifices that you can do include:

- Not drinking water or liquids during a meal.
- Abstain from meat on Fridays (which is also required by Holy Mother Church).
- Not eating candy or dessert during one day.
- Take a cold shower.
- Not eating meat in saturdays in honor of the Blessed Virgin Mary.
- Keep one hour of silence.
- Do not buy or sell in Sunday (which is also a commandment).
- Give food to the hungry.
- Give water to the thirsty.
- Visit the sick, and confort them.

IMPORTANT NOTES

☐ _____
☐ _____
☐ _____
☐ _____
☐ _____
☐ _____
☐ _____
☐ _____
☐ _____

YOUR SOUL'S GROWTH PLANNER

LONG LIVE CHRIST THE KING!

VIVA CRISTO REY.ORG

DATE: MONTH   DAY   YEAR

GOALS OF THE DAY

PRAYING THE ROSARY OF 15 DECADES.................. ☐

READING THE HOLY BIBLE (15 MINUTES)............... ☐

DAILY SACRIFICES.. ☐

☐ _____   ☐ _____
☐ _____   ☐ _____
☐ _____   ☐ _____
☐ _____   ☐ _____
☐ _____   ☐ _____
☐ _____   ☐ _____
☐ _____   ☐ _____
☐ _____   ☐ _____
☐ _____   ☐ _____

SUGGESTIONS

If you don't know how to pray the Holy Rosary, you can get our book "Rosary for beginners" in the following link: www.vcrey.com/rosary-book

Some sacrifices that you can do include:

- Not drinking water or liquids during a meal.
- Abstain from meat on Fridays (which is also required by Holy Mother Church).
- Not eating candy or dessert during one day.
- Take a cold shower.
- Not eating meat in saturdays in honor of the Blessed Virgin Mary.
- Keep one hour of silence.
- Do not buy or sell in Sunday (which is also a commandment).
- Give food to the hungry.
- Give water to the thirsty.
- Visit the sick, and confort them.

IMPORTANT NOTES

☐ _____
☐ _____
☐ _____
☐ _____
☐ _____
☐ _____
☐ _____
☐ _____
☐ _____

YOUR SOUL'S GROWTH PLANNER

LONG LIVE CHRIST THE KING!

VIVA CRISTO REY.ORG

DATE: MONTH   DAY   YEAR

GOALS OF THE DAY

PRAYING THE ROSARY OF 15 DECADES................... ☐

READING THE HOLY BIBLE (15 MINUTES)................ ☐

DAILY SACRIFICES... ☐

☐ _____   ☐ _____
☐ _____   ☐ _____
☐ _____   ☐ _____

☐ _____   ☐ _____
☐ _____   ☐ _____
☐ _____   ☐ _____

☐ _____   ☐ _____

☐ _____   ☐ _____
☐ _____   ☐ _____

SUGGESTIONS

If you don't know how to pray the Holy Rosary, you can get our book "Rosary for beginners" in the following link: www.vcrey.com/rosary-book

Some sacrifices that you can do include:

- Not drinking water or liquids during a meal.
- Abstain from meat on Fridays (which is also required by Holy Mother Church).
- Not eating candy or dessert during one day.
- Take a cold shower.
- Not eating meat in saturdays in honor of the Blessed Virgin Mary.
- Keep one hour of silence.
- Do not buy or sell in Sunday (which is also a commandment).
- Give food to the hungry.
- Give water to the thirsty.
- Visit the sick, and confort them.

IMPORTANT NOTES

☐ _____
☐ _____
☐ _____
☐ _____
☐ _____
☐ _____
☐ _____
☐ _____
☐ _____

YOUR SOUL'S GROWTH PLANNER

LONG LIVE CHRIST THE KING!

VIVA
CRISTO
REY.ORG

DATE: MONTH   DAY   YEAR

GOALS OF THE DAY

PRAYING THE ROSARY OF 15 DECADES................... ☐

READING THE HOLY BIBLE (15 MINUTES)............... ☐

DAILY SACRIFICES... ☐

☐ _____   ☐ _____
☐ _____   ☐ _____
☐ _____   ☐ _____

☐ _____   ☐ _____
☐ _____   ☐ _____
☐ _____   ☐ _____
☐ _____   ☐ _____
☐ _____   ☐ _____
☐ _____   ☐ _____

SUGGESTIONS

If you don't know how to pray the Holy Rosary, you can get our book "Rosary for beginners" in the following link: www.vcrey.com/rosary-book

Some sacrifices that you can do include:

- Not drinking water or liquids during a meal.
- Abstain from meat on Fridays (which is also required by Holy Mother Church).
- Not eating candy or dessert during one day.
- Take a cold shower.
- Not eating meat in saturdays in honor of the Blessed Virgin Mary.
- Keep one hour of silence.
- Do not buy or sell in Sunday (which is also a commandment).
- Give food to the hungry.
- Give water to the thirsty.
- Visit the sick, and confort them.

IMPORTANT NOTES

☐ _____
☐ _____
☐ _____
☐ _____
☐ _____
☐ _____
☐ _____
☐ _____
☐ _____

YOUR SOUL'S GROWTH PLANNER

LONG LIVE CHRIST THE KING!

VIVA
CRISTO
REY.ORG

DATE: MONTH   DAY   YEAR

GOALS OF THE DAY

PRAYING THE ROSARY OF 15 DECADES.................. ☐

READING THE HOLY BIBLE (15 MINUTES)............... ☐

DAILY SACRIFICES... ☐

☐ _____   ☐ _____

☐ _____   ☐ _____

☐ _____   ☐ _____

☐ _____   ☐ _____

☐ _____   ☐ _____
☐ _____   ☐ _____

☐ _____   ☐ _____

☐ _____   ☐ _____

☐ _____   ☐ _____

SUGGESTIONS

If you don't know how to pray the Holy Rosary, you can get our book "Rosary for beginners" in the following link: www.vcrey.com/rosary-book

Some sacrifices that you can do include:

- Not drinking water or liquids during a meal.
- Abstain from meat on Fridays (which is also required by Holy Mother Church).
- Not eating candy or dessert during one day.
- Take a cold shower.
- Not eating meat in saturdays in honor of the Blessed Virgin Mary.
- Keep one hour of silence.
- Do not buy or sell in Sunday (which is also a commandment).
- Give food to the hungry.
- Give water to the thirsty.
- Visit the sick, and confort them.

IMPORTANT NOTES

☐ _____

☐ _____

☐ _____

☐ _____

☐ _____

☐ _____

☐ _____

☐ _____

☐ _____

YOUR SOUL'S GROWTH PLANNER

LONG LIVE CHRIST THE KING!

VIVA
CRISTO
REY.ORG

DATE: MONTH   DAY   YEAR

GOALS OF THE DAY

PRAYING THE ROSARY OF 15 DECADES................... ☐

READING THE HOLY BIBLE (15 MINUTES)............... ☐

DAILY SACRIFICES... ☐

☐ _____ ☐ _____
☐ _____ ☐ _____
☐ _____ ☐ _____
☐ _____ ☐ _____
☐ _____ ☐ _____
☐ _____ ☐ _____
☐ _____ ☐ _____
☐ _____ ☐ _____
☐ _____ ☐ _____

SUGGESTIONS

If you don't know how to pray the Holy Rosary, you can get our book "Rosary for beginners" in the following link: www.vcrey.com/rosary-book

Some sacrifices that you can do include:

- Not drinking water or liquids during a meal.
- Abstain from meat on Fridays (which is also required by Holy Mother Church).
- Not eating candy or dessert during one day.
- Take a cold shower.
- Not eating meat in saturdays in honor of the Blessed Virgin Mary.
- Keep one hour of silence.
- Do not buy or sell in Sunday (which is also a commandment).
- Give food to the hungry.
- Give water to the thirsty.
- Visit the sick, and confort them.

IMPORTANT NOTES

☐ _____
☐ _____
☐ _____
☐ _____
☐ _____
☐ _____
☐ _____
☐ _____
☐ _____
☐ _____

YOUR SOUL'S GROWTH PLANNER

LONG LIVE CHRIST THE KING!

VIVA CRISTO REY.ORG

DATE: MONTH   DAY   YEAR

GOALS OF THE DAY

PRAYING THE ROSARY OF 15 DECADES................... ☐

READING THE HOLY BIBLE (15 MINUTES)................ ☐

DAILY SACRIFICES.. ☐

☐ _____   ☐ _____
☐ _____   ☐ _____
☐ _____   ☐ _____
☐ _____   ☐ _____
☐ _____   ☐ _____
☐ _____   ☐ _____
☐ _____   ☐ _____
☐ _____   ☐ _____
☐ _____   ☐ _____

SUGGESTIONS

If you don't know how to pray the Holy Rosary, you can get our book "Rosary for beginners" in the following link: www.vcrey.com/rosary-book

Some sacrifices that you can do include:

- Not drinking water or liquids during a meal.
- Abstain from meat on Fridays (which is also required by Holy Mother Church).
- Not eating candy or dessert during one day.
- Take a cold shower.
- Not eating meat in saturdays in honor of the Blessed Virgin Mary.
- Keep one hour of silence.
- Do not buy or sell in Sunday (which is also a commandment).
- Give food to the hungry.
- Give water to the thirsty.
- Visit the sick, and confort them.

IMPORTANT NOTES

☐ _____
☐ _____
☐ _____
☐ _____
☐ _____
☐ _____
☐ _____
☐ _____
☐ _____

YOUR SOUL'S GROWTH PLANNER

LONG LIVE CHRIST THE KING!

VIVA
CRISTO
REY.ORG

DATE: MONTH   DAY   YEAR

GOALS OF THE DAY

PRAYING THE ROSARY OF 15 DECADES.................. ☐

READING THE HOLY BIBLE (15 MINUTES)................ ☐

DAILY SACRIFICES.. ☐

☐ _____   ☐ _____
☐ _____   ☐ _____
☐ _____   ☐ _____

☐ _____   ☐ _____
☐ _____   ☐ _____
☐ _____   ☐ _____

☐ _____   ☐ _____

☐ _____   ☐ _____
☐ _____   ☐ _____

SUGGESTIONS

If you don't know how to pray the Holy Rosary, you can get our book "Rosary for beginners" in the following link: www.vcrey.com/rosary-book

Some sacrifices that you can do include:

- Not drinking water or liquids during a meal.
- Abstain from meat on Fridays (which is also required by Holy Mother Church).
- Not eating candy or dessert during one day.
- Take a cold shower.
- Not eating meat in saturdays in honor of the Blessed Virgin Mary.
- Keep one hour of silence.
- Do not buy or sell in Sunday (which is also a commandment).
- Give food to the hungry.
- Give water to the thirsty.
- Visit the sick, and confort them.

IMPORTANT NOTES

☐ _____
☐ _____
☐ _____
☐ _____
☐ _____
☐ _____
☐ _____
☐ _____
☐ _____

YOUR SOUL'S GROWTH PLANNER

LONG LIVE CHRIST THE KING!

DATE: MONTH   DAY   YEAR

GOALS OF THE DAY

PRAYING THE ROSARY OF 15 DECADES................... ☐

READING THE HOLY BIBLE (15 MINUTES)............... ☐

DAILY SACRIFICES... ☐

☐ _____   ☐ _____
☐ _____   ☐ _____
☐ _____   ☐ _____
☐ _____   ☐ _____
☐ _____   ☐ _____
☐ _____   ☐ _____
☐ _____   ☐ _____
☐ _____   ☐ _____
☐ _____   ☐ _____

SUGGESTIONS

If you don't know how to pray the Holy Rosary, you can get our book "Rosary for beginners" in the following link: www.vcrey.com/rosary-book

Some sacrifices that you can do include:

- Not drinking water or liquids during a meal.
- Abstain from meat on Fridays (which is also required by Holy Mother Church).
- Not eating candy or dessert during one day.
- Take a cold shower.
- Not eating meat in saturdays in honor of the Blessed Virgin Mary.
- Keep one hour of silence.
- Do not buy or sell in Sunday (which is also a commandment).
- Give food to the hungry.
- Give water to the thirsty.
- Visit the sick, and confort them.

IMPORTANT NOTES

☐ _____
☐ _____
☐ _____
☐ _____
☐ _____
☐ _____
☐ _____
☐ _____
☐ _____

YOUR SOUL'S GROWTH PLANNER

LONG LIVE CHRIST THE KING!

VIVA CRISTO REY.ORG

DATE: MONTH   DAY   YEAR

GOALS OF THE DAY

PRAYING THE ROSARY OF 15 DECADES................... ☐

READING THE HOLY BIBLE (15 MINUTES)............... ☐

DAILY SACRIFICES.. ☐

☐ _____   ☐ _____
☐ _____   ☐ _____
☐ _____   ☐ _____
☐ _____   ☐ _____
☐ _____   ☐ _____
☐ _____   ☐ _____
☐ _____   ☐ _____
☐ _____   ☐ _____
☐ _____   ☐ _____

SUGGESTIONS

If you don't know how to pray the Holy Rosary, you can get our book "Rosary for beginners" in the following link: www.vcrey.com/rosary-book

Some sacrifices that you can do include:

- Not drinking water or liquids during a meal.
- Abstain from meat on Fridays (which is also required by Holy Mother Church).
- Not eating candy or dessert during one day.
- Take a cold shower.
- Not eating meat in saturdays in honor of the Blessed Virgin Mary.
- Keep one hour of silence.
- Do not buy or sell in Sunday (which is also a commandment).
- Give food to the hungry.
- Give water to the thirsty.
- Visit the sick, and confort them.

IMPORTANT NOTES

☐ _____
☐ _____
☐ _____
☐ _____
☐ _____
☐ _____
☐ _____
☐ _____
☐ _____

YOUR SOUL'S GROWTH PLANNER

LONG LIVE CHRIST THE KING!

VIVA
CRISTO
REY.ORG

DATE: MONTH   DAY   YEAR

GOALS OF THE DAY

PRAYING THE ROSARY OF 15 DECADES.................... ☐

READING THE HOLY BIBLE (15 MINUTES)................ ☐

DAILY SACRIFICES.. ☐

☐ _____   ☐ _____

☐ _____   ☐ _____

☐ _____   ☐ _____

☐ _____   ☐ _____

☐ _____   ☐ _____
☐ _____   ☐ _____

☐ _____   ☐ _____

☐ _____   ☐ _____
☐ _____   ☐ _____

SUGGESTIONS

If you don't know how to pray the Holy Rosary, you can get our book "Rosary for beginners" in the following link: www.vcrey.com/rosary-book

Some sacrifices that you can do include:

- Not drinking water or liquids during a meal.
- Abstain from meat on Fridays (which is also required by Holy Mother Church).
- Not eating candy or dessert during one day.
- Take a cold shower.
- Not eating meat in saturdays in honor of the Blessed Virgin Mary.
- Keep one hour of silence.
- Do not buy or sell in Sunday (which is also a commandment).
- Give food to the hungry.
- Give water to the thirsty.
- Visit the sick, and confort them.

IMPORTANT NOTES

☐ _____

☐ _____

☐ _____

☐ _____

☐ _____

☐ _____

☐ _____

☐ _____

☐ _____

YOUR SOUL'S GROWTH PLANNER

LONG LIVE CHRIST THE KING!

VIVA CRISTO REY.ORG

DATE: MONTH   DAY   YEAR

GOALS OF THE DAY

PRAYING THE ROSARY OF 15 DECADES................... ☐

READING THE HOLY BIBLE (15 MINUTES)................ ☐

DAILY SACRIFICES... ☐

☐ _____   ☐ _____
☐ _____   ☐ _____
☐ _____   ☐ _____
☐ _____   ☐ _____
☐ _____   ☐ _____
☐ _____   ☐ _____
☐ _____   ☐ _____
☐ _____   ☐ _____
☐ _____   ☐ _____

SUGGESTIONS

If you don't know how to pray the Holy Rosary, you can get our book "Rosary for beginners" in the following link: www.vcrey.com/rosary-book

Some sacrifices that you can do include:

- Not drinking water or liquids during a meal.
- Abstain from meat on Fridays (which is also required by Holy Mother Church).
- Not eating candy or dessert during one day.
- Take a cold shower.
- Not eating meat in saturdays in honor of the Blessed Virgin Mary.
- Keep one hour of silence.
- Do not buy or sell in Sunday (which is also a commandment).
- Give food to the hungry.
- Give water to the thirsty.
- Visit the sick, and confort them.

IMPORTANT NOTES

☐ _____
☐ _____
☐ _____
☐ _____
☐ _____
☐ _____
☐ _____
☐ _____
☐ _____

YOUR SOUL'S GROWTH PLANNER

LONG LIVE CHRIST THE KING!

VIVA
CRISTO
REY.ORG

DATE: MONTH   DAY   YEAR

GOALS OF THE DAY

PRAYING THE ROSARY OF 15 DECADES................... ☐

READING THE HOLY BIBLE (15 MINUTES)................ ☐

DAILY SACRIFICES... ☐

☐ _____   ☐ _____
☐ _____   ☐ _____
☐ _____   ☐ _____
☐ _____   ☐ _____
☐ _____   ☐ _____
☐ _____   ☐ _____
☐ _____   ☐ _____
☐ _____   ☐ _____
☐ _____   ☐ _____

SUGGESTIONS

If you don't know how to pray the Holy Rosary, you can get our book "Rosary for beginners" in the following link: www.vcrey.com/rosary-book

Some sacrifices that you can do include:

- Not drinking water or liquids during a meal.
- Abstain from meat on Fridays (which is also required by Holy Mother Church).
- Not eating candy or dessert during one day.
- Take a cold shower.
- Not eating meat in saturdays in honor of the Blessed Virgin Mary.
- Keep one hour of silence.
- Do not buy or sell in Sunday (which is also a commandment).
- Give food to the hungry.
- Give water to the thirsty.
- Visit the sick, and confort them.

IMPORTANT NOTES

☐ _____
☐ _____
☐ _____
☐ _____
☐ _____
☐ _____
☐ _____
☐ _____
☐ _____

YOUR SOUL'S GROWTH PLANNER

LONG LIVE CHRIST THE KING!

VIVA
CRISTO
REY.ORG

DATE: MONTH   DAY   YEAR

GOALS OF THE DAY

PRAYING THE ROSARY OF 15 DECADES................. ☐

READING THE HOLY BIBLE (15 MINUTES)............... ☐

DAILY SACRIFICES.. ☐

☐ _____   ☐ _____
☐ _____   ☐ _____
☐ _____   ☐ _____
☐ _____   ☐ _____
☐ _____   ☐ _____
☐ _____   ☐ _____
☐ _____   ☐ _____
☐ _____   ☐ _____
☐ _____   ☐ _____

SUGGESTIONS

If you don't know how to pray the Holy Rosary, you can get our book "Rosary for beginners" in the following link: www.vcrey.com/rosary-book

Some sacrifices that you can do include:

- Not drinking water or liquids during a meal.
- Abstain from meat on Fridays (which is also required by Holy Mother Church).
- Not eating candy or dessert during one day.
- Take a cold shower.
- Not eating meat in saturdays in honor of the Blessed Virgin Mary.
- Keep one hour of silence.
- Do not buy or sell in Sunday (which is also a commandment).
- Give food to the hungry.
- Give water to the thirsty.
- Visit the sick, and confort them.

IMPORTANT NOTES

☐ _____
☐ _____
☐ _____
☐ _____
☐ _____
☐ _____
☐ _____
☐ _____
☐ _____

YOUR SOUL'S GROWTH PLANNER

LONG LIVE CHRIST THE KING!

VIVA CRISTO REY.ORG

DATE: MONTH   DAY   YEAR

GOALS OF THE DAY

PRAYING THE ROSARY OF 15 DECADES................... ☐

READING THE HOLY BIBLE (15 MINUTES)................ ☐

DAILY SACRIFICES.. ☐

☐ _____   ☐ _____
☐ _____   ☐ _____
☐ _____   ☐ _____
☐ _____   ☐ _____
☐ _____   ☐ _____
☐ _____   ☐ _____
☐ _____   ☐ _____
☐ _____   ☐ _____
☐ _____   ☐ _____

SUGGESTIONS

If you don't know how to pray the Holy Rosary, you can get our book "Rosary for beginners" in the following link: www.vcrey.com/rosary-book

Some sacrifices that you can do include:

- Not drinking water or liquids during a meal.
- Abstain from meat on Fridays (which is also required by Holy Mother Church).
- Not eating candy or dessert during one day.
- Take a cold shower.
- Not eating meat in saturdays in honor of the Blessed Virgin Mary.
- Keep one hour of silence.
- Do not buy or sell in Sunday (which is also a commandment).
- Give food to the hungry.
- Give water to the thirsty.
- Visit the sick, and confort them.

IMPORTANT NOTES

☐ _____
☐ _____
☐ _____
☐ _____
☐ _____
☐ _____
☐ _____
☐ _____
☐ _____

YOUR SOUL'S GROWTH PLANNER

LONG LIVE CHRIST THE KING!

VIVA
CRISTO
REY.ORG

DATE: MONTH   DAY   YEAR

GOALS OF THE DAY

PRAYING THE ROSARY OF 15 DECADES................... ☐

READING THE HOLY BIBLE (15 MINUTES)............... ☐

DAILY SACRIFICES.. ☐

☐ _____   ☐ _____
☐ _____   ☐ _____
☐ _____   ☐ _____

☐ _____   ☐ _____
☐ _____   ☐ _____
☐ _____   ☐ _____
☐ _____   ☐ _____

☐ _____   ☐ _____
☐ _____   ☐ _____

SUGGESTIONS

If you don't know how to pray the Holy Rosary, you can get our book "Rosary for beginners" in the following link: www.vcrey.com/rosary-book

Some sacrifices that you can do include:

- Not drinking water or liquids during a meal.
- Abstain from meat on Fridays (which is also required by Holy Mother Church).
- Not eating candy or dessert during one day.
- Take a cold shower.
- Not eating meat in saturdays in honor of the Blessed Virgin Mary.
- Keep one hour of silence.
- Do not buy or sell in Sunday (which is also a commandment).
- Give food to the hungry.
- Give water to the thirsty.
- Visit the sick, and confort them.

IMPORTANT NOTES

☐ _____
☐ _____
☐ _____
☐ _____
☐ _____
☐ _____
☐ _____
☐ _____
☐ _____

YOUR SOUL'S GROWTH PLANNER

LONG LIVE CHRIST THE KING!

VIVA CRISTO REY.ORG

DATE: MONTH   DAY   YEAR

GOALS OF THE DAY

PRAYING THE ROSARY OF 15 DECADES................... ☐

READING THE HOLY BIBLE (15 MINUTES)............... ☐

DAILY SACRIFICES.. ☐

☐ _____   ☐ _____
☐ _____   ☐ _____
☐ _____   ☐ _____
☐ _____   ☐ _____
☐ _____   ☐ _____
☐ _____   ☐ _____
☐ _____   ☐ _____
☐ _____   ☐ _____
☐ _____   ☐ _____

SUGGESTIONS

If you don't know how to pray the Holy Rosary, you can get our book "Rosary for beginners" in the following link: www.vcrey.com/rosary-book

Some sacrifices that you can do include:

- Not drinking water or liquids during a meal.
- Abstain from meat on Fridays (which is also required by Holy Mother Church).
- Not eating candy or dessert during one day.
- Take a cold shower.
- Not eating meat in saturdays in honor of the Blessed Virgin Mary.
- Keep one hour of silence.
- Do not buy or sell in Sunday (which is also a commandment).
- Give food to the hungry.
- Give water to the thirsty.
- Visit the sick, and confort them.

IMPORTANT NOTES

☐ _____
☐ _____
☐ _____
☐ _____
☐ _____
☐ _____
☐ _____
☐ _____
☐ _____

YOUR SOUL'S GROWTH PLANNER

LONG LIVE CHRIST THE KING!

VIVA
CRISTO
REY.ORG

DATE: MONTH   DAY   YEAR

GOALS OF THE DAY

PRAYING THE ROSARY OF 15 DECADES................... ☐

READING THE HOLY BIBLE (15 MINUTES)............... ☐

DAILY SACRIFICES... ☐

☐ _____   ☐ _____

☐ _____   ☐ _____

☐ _____   ☐ _____

☐ _____   ☐ _____

☐ _____   ☐ _____

☐ _____   ☐ _____

☐ _____   ☐ _____

☐ _____   ☐ _____

☐ _____   ☐ _____

SUGGESTIONS

If you don't know how to pray the Holy Rosary, you can get our book "Rosary for beginners" in the following link: www.vcrey.com/rosary-book

Some sacrifices that you can do include:

- Not drinking water or liquids during a meal.
- Abstain from meat on Fridays (which is also required by Holy Mother Church).
- Not eating candy or dessert during one day.
- Take a cold shower.
- Not eating meat in saturdays in honor of the Blessed Virgin Mary.
- Keep one hour of silence.
- Do not buy or sell in Sunday (which is also a commandment).
- Give food to the hungry.
- Give water to the thirsty.
- Visit the sick, and confort them.

IMPORTANT NOTES

☐ _____

☐ _____

☐ _____

☐ _____

☐ _____

☐ _____

☐ _____

☐ _____

☐ _____

YOUR SOUL'S GROWTH PLANNER

LONG LIVE CHRIST THE KING!

VIVA
CRISTO
REY.ORG

DATE: MONTH   DAY   YEAR

GOALS OF THE DAY

PRAYING THE ROSARY OF 15 DECADES................... ☐

READING THE HOLY BIBLE (15 MINUTES)................ ☐

DAILY SACRIFICES... ☐

☐ _____   ☐ _____
☐ _____   ☐ _____
☐ _____   ☐ _____

☐ _____   ☐ _____
☐ _____   ☐ _____
☐ _____   ☐ _____
☐ _____   ☐ _____

☐ _____   ☐ _____
☐ _____   ☐ _____

SUGGESTIONS

If you don't know how to pray the Holy Rosary, you can get our book "Rosary for beginners" in the following link: www.vcrey.com/rosary-book

Some sacrifices that you can do include:

- Not drinking water or liquids during a meal.
- Abstain from meat on Fridays (which is also required by Holy Mother Church).
- Not eating candy or dessert during one day.
- Take a cold shower.
- Not eating meat in saturdays in honor of the Blessed Virgin Mary.
- Keep one hour of silence.
- Do not buy or sell in Sunday (which is also a commandment).
- Give food to the hungry.
- Give water to the thirsty.
- Visit the sick, and confort them.

IMPORTANT NOTES

☐ _____
☐ _____
☐ _____
☐ _____
☐ _____
☐ _____
☐ _____
☐ _____
☐ _____

YOUR SOUL'S GROWTH PLANNER

LONG LIVE CHRIST THE KING!

VIVA
CRISTO
REY.ORG

DATE: MONTH   DAY   YEAR

GOALS OF THE DAY

PRAYING THE ROSARY OF 15 DECADES.................... ☐

READING THE HOLY BIBLE (15 MINUTES)............... ☐

DAILY SACRIFICES... ☐

☐ _____   ☐ _____
☐ _____   ☐ _____
☐ _____   ☐ _____
☐ _____   ☐ _____
☐ _____   ☐ _____
☐ _____   ☐ _____
☐ _____   ☐ _____
☐ _____   ☐ _____
☐ _____   ☐ _____

SUGGESTIONS

If you don't know how to pray the Holy Rosary, you can get our book "Rosary for beginners" in the following link: www.vcrey.com/rosary-book

Some sacrifices that you can do include:

- Not drinking water or liquids during a meal.
- Abstain from meat on Fridays (which is also required by Holy Mother Church).
- Not eating candy or dessert during one day.
- Take a cold shower.
- Not eating meat in saturdays in honor of the Blessed Virgin Mary.
- Keep one hour of silence.
- Do not buy or sell in Sunday (which is also a commandment).
- Give food to the hungry.
- Give water to the thirsty.
- Visit the sick, and confort them.

IMPORTANT NOTES

☐ _____
☐ _____
☐ _____
☐ _____
☐ _____
☐ _____
☐ _____
☐ _____
☐ _____

YOUR SOUL'S GROWTH PLANNER

LONG LIVE CHRIST THE KING!

VIVA
CRISTO
REY.ORG

DATE: MONTH   DAY   YEAR

GOALS OF THE DAY

PRAYING THE ROSARY OF 15 DECADES.................. ☐

READING THE HOLY BIBLE (15 MINUTES)................ ☐

DAILY SACRIFICES... ☐

☐ _____   ☐ _____
☐ _____   ☐ _____
☐ _____   ☐ _____

☐ _____   ☐ _____
☐ _____   ☐ _____
☐ _____   ☐ _____
☐ _____   ☐ _____

☐ _____   ☐ _____
☐ _____   ☐ _____

SUGGESTIONS

If you don't know how to pray the Holy Rosary, you can get our book "Rosary for beginners" in the following link: www.vcrey.com/rosary-book

Some sacrifices that you can do include:

- Not drinking water or liquids during a meal.
- Abstain from meat on Fridays (which is also required by Holy Mother Church).
- Not eating candy or dessert during one day.
- Take a cold shower.
- Not eating meat in saturdays in honor of the Blessed Virgin Mary.
- Keep one hour of silence.
- Do not buy or sell in Sunday (which is also a commandment).
- Give food to the hungry.
- Give water to the thirsty.
- Visit the sick, and confort them.

IMPORTANT NOTES

☐ _____
☐ _____
☐ _____
☐ _____
☐ _____
☐ _____
☐ _____
☐ _____
☐ _____

YOUR SOUL'S GROWTH PLANNER

LONG LIVE CHRIST THE KING!

VIVA CRISTO REY.ORG

DATE: MONTH   DAY   YEAR

GOALS OF THE DAY

PRAYING THE ROSARY OF 15 DECADES................. ☐

READING THE HOLY BIBLE (15 MINUTES)............... ☐

DAILY SACRIFICES....................................... ☐

☐ _____   ☐ _____
☐ _____   ☐ _____
☐ _____   ☐ _____
☐ _____   ☐ _____
☐ _____   ☐ _____
☐ _____   ☐ _____
☐ _____   ☐ _____
☐ _____   ☐ _____
☐ _____   ☐ _____

SUGGESTIONS

If you don't know how to pray the Holy Rosary, you can get our book "Rosary for beginners" in the following link: www.vcrey.com/rosary-book

Some sacrifices that you can do include:

- Not drinking water or liquids during a meal.
- Abstain from meat on Fridays (which is also required by Holy Mother Church).
- Not eating candy or dessert during one day.
- Take a cold shower.
- Not eating meat in saturdays in honor of the Blessed Virgin Mary.
- Keep one hour of silence.
- Do not buy or sell in Sunday (which is also a commandment).
- Give food to the hungry.
- Give water to the thirsty.
- Visit the sick, and confort them.

IMPORTANT NOTES

☐ _____
☐ _____
☐ _____
☐ _____
☐ _____
☐ _____
☐ _____
☐ _____
☐ _____

YOUR SOUL'S GROWTH PLANNER

LONG LIVE CHRIST THE KING!

VIVA CRISTO REY.ORG

DATE: MONTH   DAY   YEAR

GOALS OF THE DAY

PRAYING THE ROSARY OF 15 DECADES................. ☐

READING THE HOLY BIBLE (15 MINUTES)............... ☐

DAILY SACRIFICES.. ☐

☐ _____   ☐ _____

☐ _____   ☐ _____

☐ _____   ☐ _____

☐ _____   ☐ _____

☐ _____   ☐ _____

☐ _____   ☐ _____

☐ _____   ☐ _____

☐ _____   ☐ _____

☐ _____   ☐ _____

SUGGESTIONS

If you don't know how to pray the Holy Rosary, you can get our book "Rosary for beginners" in the following link: www.vcrey.com/rosary-book

Some sacrifices that you can do include:

- Not drinking water or liquids during a meal.
- Abstain from meat on Fridays (which is also required by Holy Mother Church).
- Not eating candy or dessert during one day.
- Take a cold shower.
- Not eating meat in saturdays in honor of the Blessed Virgin Mary.
- Keep one hour of silence.
- Do not buy or sell in Sunday (which is also a commandment).
- Give food to the hungry.
- Give water to the thirsty.
- Visit the sick, and confort them.

IMPORTANT NOTES

☐ _____

☐ _____

☐ _____

☐ _____

☐ _____

☐ _____

☐ _____

☐ _____

☐ _____

☐ _____

YOUR SOUL'S GROWTH PLANNER

LONG LIVE CHRIST THE KING!

VIVA CRISTO REY.ORG

DATE: MONTH   DAY   YEAR

GOALS OF THE DAY

PRAYING THE ROSARY OF 15 DECADES.................... ☐

READING THE HOLY BIBLE (15 MINUTES)................ ☐

DAILY SACRIFICES.. ☐

☐ _____   ☐ _____
☐ _____   ☐ _____
☐ _____   ☐ _____
☐ _____   ☐ _____
☐ _____   ☐ _____
☐ _____   ☐ _____
☐ _____   ☐ _____
☐ _____   ☐ _____
☐ _____   ☐ _____

SUGGESTIONS

If you don't know how to pray the Holy Rosary, you can get our book "Rosary for beginners" in the following link: www.vcrey.com/rosary-book

Some sacrifices that you can do include:

- Not drinking water or liquids during a meal.
- Abstain from meat on Fridays (which is also required by Holy Mother Church).
- Not eating candy or dessert during one day.
- Take a cold shower.
- Not eating meat in saturdays in honor of the Blessed Virgin Mary.
- Keep one hour of silence.
- Do not buy or sell in Sunday (which is also a commandment).
- Give food to the hungry.
- Give water to the thirsty.
- Visit the sick, and confort them.

IMPORTANT NOTES

☐ _____
☐ _____
☐ _____
☐ _____
☐ _____
☐ _____
☐ _____
☐ _____

YOUR SOUL'S GROWTH PLANNER

LONG LIVE CHRIST THE KING!

VIVA CRISTO REY.ORG

DATE: MONTH   DAY   YEAR

GOALS OF THE DAY

PRAYING THE ROSARY OF 15 DECADES................... ☐

READING THE HOLY BIBLE (15 MINUTES)................ ☐

DAILY SACRIFICES.. ☐

☐ _____   ☐ _____
☐ _____   ☐ _____
☐ _____   ☐ _____
☐ _____   ☐ _____
☐ _____   ☐ _____
☐ _____   ☐ _____
☐ _____   ☐ _____
☐ _____   ☐ _____
☐ _____   ☐ _____

SUGGESTIONS

If you don't know how to pray the Holy Rosary, you can get our book "Rosary for beginners" in the following link: www.vcrey.com/rosary-book

Some sacrifices that you can do include:

- Not drinking water or liquids during a meal.
- Abstain from meat on Fridays (which is also required by Holy Mother Church).
- Not eating candy or dessert during one day.
- Take a cold shower.
- Not eating meat in saturdays in honor of the Blessed Virgin Mary.
- Keep one hour of silence.
- Do not buy or sell in Sunday (which is also a commandment).
- Give food to the hungry.
- Give water to the thirsty.
- Visit the sick, and confort them.

IMPORTANT NOTES

☐ _____
☐ _____
☐ _____
☐ _____
☐ _____
☐ _____
☐ _____
☐ _____
☐ _____

YOUR SOUL'S GROWTH PLANNER

LONG LIVE CHRIST THE KING!

VIVA CRISTO REY.ORG

DATE: MONTH   DAY   YEAR

GOALS OF THE DAY

PRAYING THE ROSARY OF 15 DECADES.................. ☐

READING THE HOLY BIBLE (15 MINUTES)................ ☐

DAILY SACRIFICES... ☐

☐ _____   ☐ _____
☐ _____   ☐ _____
☐ _____   ☐ _____
☐ _____   ☐ _____
☐ _____   ☐ _____
☐ _____   ☐ _____
☐ _____   ☐ _____
☐ _____   ☐ _____
☐ _____   ☐ _____

SUGGESTIONS

If you don't know how to pray the Holy Rosary, you can get our book "Rosary for beginners" in the following link: www.vcrey.com/rosary-book

Some sacrifices that you can do include:

- Not drinking water or liquids during a meal.
- Abstain from meat on Fridays (which is also required by Holy Mother Church).
- Not eating candy or dessert during one day.
- Take a cold shower.
- Not eating meat in saturdays in honor of the Blessed Virgin Mary.
- Keep one hour of silence.
- Do not buy or sell in Sunday (which is also a commandment).
- Give food to the hungry.
- Give water to the thirsty.
- Visit the sick, and confort them.

IMPORTANT NOTES

☐ _____
☐ _____
☐ _____
☐ _____
☐ _____
☐ _____
☐ _____
☐ _____
☐ _____

YOUR SOUL'S GROWTH PLANNER

LONG LIVE CHRIST THE KING!

VIVA
CRISTO
REY.ORG

DATE: MONTH   DAY   YEAR

GOALS OF THE DAY

PRAYING THE ROSARY OF 15 DECADES................... ☐

READING THE HOLY BIBLE (15 MINUTES)............... ☐

DAILY SACRIFICES.. ☐

☐ _____   ☐ _____

☐ _____   ☐ _____

☐ _____   ☐ _____

☐ _____   ☐ _____

☐ _____   ☐ _____

☐ _____   ☐ _____

☐ _____   ☐ _____

☐ _____   ☐ _____

☐ _____   ☐ _____

SUGGESTIONS

If you don't know how to pray the Holy Rosary, you can get our book "Rosary for beginners" in the following link: www.vcrey.com/rosary-book

Some sacrifices that you can do include:

- Not drinking water or liquids during a meal.
- Abstain from meat on Fridays (which is also required by Holy Mother Church).
- Not eating candy or dessert during one day.
- Take a cold shower.
- Not eating meat in saturdays in honor of the Blessed Virgin Mary.
- Keep one hour of silence.
- Do not buy or sell in Sunday (which is also a commandment).
- Give food to the hungry.
- Give water to the thirsty.
- Visit the sick, and confort them.

IMPORTANT NOTES

☐ _____

☐ _____

☐ _____

☐ _____

☐ _____

☐ _____

☐ _____

☐ _____

☐ _____

YOUR SOUL'S GROWTH PLANNER

LONG LIVE CHRIST THE KING!

VIVA CRISTO REY.ORG

DATE: MONTH   DAY   YEAR

GOALS OF THE DAY

PRAYING THE ROSARY OF 15 DECADES................... ☐

READING THE HOLY BIBLE (15 MINUTES)............... ☐

DAILY SACRIFICES.. ☐

☐ _____   ☐ _____
☐ _____   ☐ _____
☐ _____   ☐ _____

☐ _____   ☐ _____
☐ _____   ☐ _____
☐ _____   ☐ _____
☐ _____   ☐ _____

☐ _____   ☐ _____
☐ _____   ☐ _____

SUGGESTIONS

If you don't know how to pray the Holy Rosary, you can get our book "Rosary for beginners" in the following link: www.vcrey.com/rosary-book

Some sacrifices that you can do include:

- Not drinking water or liquids during a meal.
- Abstain from meat on Fridays (which is also required by Holy Mother Church).
- Not eating candy or dessert during one day.
- Take a cold shower.
- Not eating meat in saturdays in honor of the Blessed Virgin Mary.
- Keep one hour of silence.
- Do not buy or sell in Sunday (which is also a commandment).
- Give food to the hungry.
- Give water to the thirsty.
- Visit the sick, and confort them.

IMPORTANT NOTES

☐ _____
☐ _____
☐ _____
☐ _____
☐ _____
☐ _____
☐ _____
☐ _____
☐ _____

YOUR SOUL'S GROWTH PLANNER

LONG LIVE CHRIST THE KING!

VIVA CRISTO REY.ORG

DATE: MONTH   DAY   YEAR

GOALS OF THE DAY

PRAYING THE ROSARY OF 15 DECADES................... ☐

READING THE HOLY BIBLE (15 MINUTES)............... ☐

DAILY SACRIFICES... ☐

☐ _____   ☐ _____
☐ _____   ☐ _____
☐ _____   ☐ _____

☐ _____   ☐ _____
☐ _____   ☐ _____
☐ _____   ☐ _____
☐ _____   ☐ _____

☐ _____   ☐ _____
☐ _____   ☐ _____

SUGGESTIONS

If you don't know how to pray the Holy Rosary, you can get our book "Rosary for beginners" in the following link: www.vcrey.com/rosary-book

Some sacrifices that you can do include:

- Not drinking water or liquids during a meal.
- Abstain from meat on Fridays (which is also required by Holy Mother Church).
- Not eating candy or dessert during one day.
- Take a cold shower.
- Not eating meat in saturdays in honor of the Blessed Virgin Mary.
- Keep one hour of silence.
- Do not buy or sell in Sunday (which is also a commandment).
- Give food to the hungry.
- Give water to the thirsty.
- Visit the sick, and confort them.

IMPORTANT NOTES

☐ _____
☐ _____
☐ _____
☐ _____
☐ _____
☐ _____
☐ _____
☐ _____
☐ _____

YOUR SOUL'S GROWTH PLANNER

LONG LIVE CHRIST THE KING!

VIVA CRISTO REY.ORG

DATE: MONTH   DAY   YEAR

GOALS OF THE DAY

PRAYING THE ROSARY OF 15 DECADES.................. ☐

READING THE HOLY BIBLE (15 MINUTES)............... ☐

DAILY SACRIFICES...................................... ☐

☐ _____   ☐ _____
☐ _____   ☐ _____
☐ _____   ☐ _____
☐ _____   ☐ _____
☐ _____   ☐ _____
☐ _____   ☐ _____
☐ _____   ☐ _____
☐ _____   ☐ _____
☐ _____   ☐ _____

SUGGESTIONS

If you don't know how to pray the Holy Rosary, you can get our book "Rosary for beginners" in the following link: www.vcrey.com/rosary-book

Some sacrifices that you can do include:

- Not drinking water or liquids during a meal.
- Abstain from meat on Fridays (which is also required by Holy Mother Church).
- Not eating candy or dessert during one day.
- Take a cold shower.
- Not eating meat in saturdays in honor of the Blessed Virgin Mary.
- Keep one hour of silence.
- Do not buy or sell in Sunday (which is also a commandment).
- Give food to the hungry.
- Give water to the thirsty.
- Visit the sick, and confort them.

IMPORTANT NOTES

☐ _____
☐ _____
☐ _____
☐ _____
☐ _____
☐ _____
☐ _____
☐ _____
☐ _____

YOUR SOUL'S GROWTH PLANNER

LONG LIVE CHRIST THE KING!

VIVA CRISTO REY.ORG

DATE: MONTH   DAY   YEAR

GOALS OF THE DAY

PRAYING THE ROSARY OF 15 DECADES................. ☐

READING THE HOLY BIBLE (15 MINUTES)............... ☐

DAILY SACRIFICES... ☐

☐ _____   ☐ _____

☐ _____   ☐ _____

☐ _____   ☐ _____

☐ _____   ☐ _____

☐ _____   ☐ _____

☐ _____   ☐ _____

☐ _____   ☐ _____

☐ _____   ☐ _____

☐ _____   ☐ _____

SUGGESTIONS

If you don't know how to pray the Holy Rosary, you can get our book "Rosary for beginners" in the following link: www.vcrey.com/rosary-book

Some sacrifices that you can do include:

- Not drinking water or liquids during a meal.
- Abstain from meat on Fridays (which is also required by Holy Mother Church).
- Not eating candy or dessert during one day.
- Take a cold shower.
- Not eating meat in saturdays in honor of the Blessed Virgin Mary.
- Keep one hour of silence.
- Do not buy or sell in Sunday (which is also a commandment).
- Give food to the hungry.
- Give water to the thirsty.
- Visit the sick, and confort them.

IMPORTANT NOTES

☐ _____

☐ _____

☐ _____

☐ _____

☐ _____

☐ _____

☐ _____

☐ _____

☐ _____

YOUR SOUL'S GROWTH PLANNER

LONG LIVE CHRIST THE KING!

VIVA CRISTO REY.ORG

DATE: MONTH   DAY   YEAR

GOALS OF THE DAY

PRAYING THE ROSARY OF 15 DECADES..................... ☐

READING THE HOLY BIBLE (15 MINUTES)............... ☐

DAILY SACRIFICES... ☐

☐ _____ ☐ _____
☐ _____ ☐ _____
☐ _____ ☐ _____

☐ _____ ☐ _____
☐ _____ ☐ _____
☐ _____ ☐ _____
☐ _____ ☐ _____

☐ _____ ☐ _____
☐ _____ ☐ _____

SUGGESTIONS

If you don't know how to pray the Holy Rosary, you can get our book "Rosary for beginners" in the following link: www.vcrey.com/rosary-book

Some sacrifices that you can do include:

- Not drinking water or liquids during a meal.
- Abstain from meat on Fridays (which is also required by Holy Mother Church).
- Not eating candy or dessert during one day.
- Take a cold shower.
- Not eating meat in saturdays in honor of the Blessed Virgin Mary.
- Keep one hour of silence.
- Do not buy or sell in Sunday (which is also a commandment).
- Give food to the hungry.
- Give water to the thirsty.
- Visit the sick, and confort them.

IMPORTANT NOTES

☐ _____
☐ _____
☐ _____
☐ _____
☐ _____
☐ _____
☐ _____
☐ _____
☐ _____
☐ _____

YOUR SOUL'S GROWTH PLANNER

LONG LIVE CHRIST THE KING!

VIVA
CRISTO
REY.ORG

DATE: MONTH   DAY   YEAR

GOALS OF THE DAY

PRAYING THE ROSARY OF 15 DECADES.................. ☐

READING THE HOLY BIBLE (15 MINUTES).............. ☐

DAILY SACRIFICES.. ☐

☐ _____   ☐ _____
☐ _____   ☐ _____
☐ _____   ☐ _____
☐ _____   ☐ _____
☐ _____   ☐ _____
☐ _____   ☐ _____
☐ _____   ☐ _____
☐ _____   ☐ _____
☐ _____   ☐ _____

SUGGESTIONS

If you don't know how to pray the Holy Rosary, you can get our book "Rosary for beginners" in the following link: www.vcrey.com/rosary-book

Some sacrifices that you can do include:

- Not drinking water or liquids during a meal.
- Abstain from meat on Fridays (which is also required by Holy Mother Church).
- Not eating candy or dessert during one day.
- Take a cold shower.
- Not eating meat in saturdays in honor of the Blessed Virgin Mary.
- Keep one hour of silence.
- Do not buy or sell in Sunday (which is also a commandment).
- Give food to the hungry.
- Give water to the thirsty.
- Visit the sick, and confort them.

IMPORTANT NOTES

☐ _____
☐ _____
☐ _____
☐ _____
☐ _____
☐ _____
☐ _____
☐ _____
☐ _____

YOUR SOUL'S GROWTH PLANNER

LONG LIVE CHRIST THE KING!

VIVA CRISTO REY.ORG

DATE: MONTH   DAY   YEAR

GOALS OF THE DAY

PRAYING THE ROSARY OF 15 DECADES................... ☐

READING THE HOLY BIBLE (15 MINUTES)............... ☐

DAILY SACRIFICES.. ☐

☐ _____   ☐ _____
☐ _____   ☐ _____
☐ _____   ☐ _____
☐ _____   ☐ _____
☐ _____   ☐ _____
☐ _____   ☐ _____
☐ _____   ☐ _____
☐ _____   ☐ _____
☐ _____   ☐ _____

SUGGESTIONS

If you don't know how to pray the Holy Rosary, you can get our book "Rosary for beginners" in the following link: www.vcrey.com/rosary-book

Some sacrifices that you can do include:

- Not drinking water or liquids during a meal.
- Abstain from meat on Fridays (which is also required by Holy Mother Church).
- Not eating candy or dessert during one day.
- Take a cold shower.
- Not eating meat in saturdays in honor of the Blessed Virgin Mary.
- Keep one hour of silence.
- Do not buy or sell in Sunday (which is also a commandment).
- Give food to the hungry.
- Give water to the thirsty.
- Visit the sick, and confort them.

IMPORTANT NOTES

☐ _____
☐ _____
☐ _____
☐ _____
☐ _____
☐ _____
☐ _____
☐ _____
☐ _____

YOUR SOUL'S GROWTH PLANNER

LONG LIVE CHRIST THE KING!

VIVA CRISTO REY.ORG

DATE: MONTH   DAY   YEAR

GOALS OF THE DAY

PRAYING THE ROSARY OF 15 DECADES................... ☐

READING THE HOLY BIBLE (15 MINUTES)................ ☐

DAILY SACRIFICES.. ☐

☐ _____   ☐ _____
☐ _____   ☐ _____
☐ _____   ☐ _____
☐ _____   ☐ _____
☐ _____   ☐ _____
☐ _____   ☐ _____
☐ _____   ☐ _____
☐ _____   ☐ _____
☐ _____   ☐ _____

SUGGESTIONS

If you don't know how to pray the Holy Rosary, you can get our book "Rosary for beginners" in the following link: www.vcrey.com/rosary-book

Some sacrifices that you can do include:

- Not drinking water or liquids during a meal.
- Abstain from meat on Fridays (which is also required by Holy Mother Church).
- Not eating candy or dessert during one day.
- Take a cold shower.
- Not eating meat in saturdays in honor of the Blessed Virgin Mary.
- Keep one hour of silence.
- Do not buy or sell in Sunday (which is also a commandment).
- Give food to the hungry.
- Give water to the thirsty.
- Visit the sick, and confort them.

IMPORTANT NOTES

☐ _____
☐ _____
☐ _____
☐ _____
☐ _____
☐ _____
☐ _____
☐ _____
☐ _____

YOUR SOUL'S GROWTH PLANNER

LONG LIVE CHRIST THE KING!

VIVA CRISTO REY.ORG

DATE: MONTH   DAY   YEAR

GOALS OF THE DAY

PRAYING THE ROSARY OF 15 DECADES................... ☐

READING THE HOLY BIBLE (15 MINUTES)............... ☐

DAILY SACRIFICES.. ☐

☐ _____   ☐ _____
☐ _____   ☐ _____
☐ _____   ☐ _____
☐ _____   ☐ _____
☐ _____   ☐ _____
☐ _____   ☐ _____
☐ _____   ☐ _____
☐ _____   ☐ _____
☐ _____   ☐ _____

SUGGESTIONS

If you don't know how to pray the Holy Rosary, you can get our book "Rosary for beginners" in the following link: www.vcrey.com/rosary-book

Some sacrifices that you can do include:

- Not drinking water or liquids during a meal.
- Abstain from meat on Fridays (which is also required by Holy Mother Church).
- Not eating candy or dessert during one day.
- Take a cold shower.
- Not eating meat in saturdays in honor of the Blessed Virgin Mary.
- Keep one hour of silence.
- Do not buy or sell in Sunday (which is also a commandment).
- Give food to the hungry.
- Give water to the thirsty.
- Visit the sick, and confort them.

IMPORTANT NOTES

☐ _____
☐ _____
☐ _____
☐ _____
☐ _____
☐ _____
☐ _____
☐ _____
☐ _____

YOUR SOUL'S GROWTH PLANNER

LONG LIVE CHRIST THE KING!

VIVA
CRISTO
REY.ORG

DATE: MONTH   DAY   YEAR

GOALS OF THE DAY

PRAYING THE ROSARY OF 15 DECADES.................... ☐

READING THE HOLY BIBLE (15 MINUTES)................ ☐

DAILY SACRIFICES.. ☐

☐ _____   ☐ _____
☐ _____   ☐ _____
☐ _____   ☐ _____
☐ _____   ☐ _____
☐ _____   ☐ _____
☐ _____   ☐ _____
☐ _____   ☐ _____
☐ _____   ☐ _____
☐ _____   ☐ _____

SUGGESTIONS

If you don't know how to pray the Holy Rosary, you can get our book "Rosary for beginners" in the following link: www.vcrey.com/rosary-book

Some sacrifices that you can do include:

- Not drinking water or liquids during a meal.
- Abstain from meat on Fridays (which is also required by Holy Mother Church).
- Not eating candy or dessert during one day.
- Take a cold shower.
- Not eating meat in saturdays in honor of the Blessed Virgin Mary.
- Keep one hour of silence.
- Do not buy or sell in Sunday (which is also a commandment).
- Give food to the hungry.
- Give water to the thirsty.
- Visit the sick, and confort them.

IMPORTANT NOTES

☐ _____
☐ _____
☐ _____
☐ _____
☐ _____
☐ _____
☐ _____
☐ _____
☐ _____

YOUR SOUL'S GROWTH PLANNER

LONG LIVE CHRIST THE KING!

VIVA
CRISTO
REY.ORG

DATE: MONTH   DAY   YEAR

GOALS OF THE DAY

PRAYING THE ROSARY OF 15 DECADES.................. ☐

READING THE HOLY BIBLE (15 MINUTES)............... ☐

DAILY SACRIFICES... ☐

☐ _____   ☐ _____
☐ _____   ☐ _____
☐ _____   ☐ _____

☐ _____   ☐ _____
☐ _____   ☐ _____
☐ _____   ☐ _____

☐ _____   ☐ _____

☐ _____   ☐ _____
☐ _____   ☐ _____

SUGGESTIONS

If you don't know how to pray the Holy Rosary, you can get our book "Rosary for beginners" in the following link: www.vcrey.com/rosary-book

Some sacrifices that you can do include:

- Not drinking water or liquids during a meal.
- Abstain from meat on Fridays (which is also required by Holy Mother Church).
- Not eating candy or dessert during one day.
- Take a cold shower.
- Not eating meat in saturdays in honor of the Blessed Virgin Mary.
- Keep one hour of silence.
- Do not buy or sell in Sunday (which is also a commandment).
- Give food to the hungry.
- Give water to the thirsty.
- Visit the sick, and confort them.

IMPORTANT NOTES

☐ _____
☐ _____
☐ _____
☐ _____
☐ _____
☐ _____
☐ _____
☐ _____
☐ _____

YOUR SOUL'S GROWTH PLANNER

LONG LIVE CHRIST THE KING!

DATE: MONTH   DAY   YEAR

GOALS OF THE DAY

PRAYING THE ROSARY OF 15 DECADES................... ☐

READING THE HOLY BIBLE (15 MINUTES)................ ☐

DAILY SACRIFICES... ☐

☐ _____   ☐ _____

☐ _____   ☐ _____

☐ _____   ☐ _____

☐ _____   ☐ _____

☐ _____   ☐ _____

☐ _____   ☐ _____

☐ _____   ☐ _____

☐ _____   ☐ _____

☐ _____   ☐ _____

SUGGESTIONS

If you don't know how to pray the Holy Rosary, you can get our book "Rosary for beginners" in the following link: www.vcrey.com/rosary-book

Some sacrifices that you can do include:

- Not drinking water or liquids during a meal.
- Abstain from meat on Fridays (which is also required by Holy Mother Church).
- Not eating candy or dessert during one day.
- Take a cold shower.
- Not eating meat in saturdays in honor of the Blessed Virgin Mary.
- Keep one hour of silence.
- Do not buy or sell in Sunday (which is also a commandment).
- Give food to the hungry.
- Give water to the thirsty.
- Visit the sick, and confort them.

IMPORTANT NOTES

☐ _____

☐ _____

☐ _____

☐ _____

☐ _____

☐ _____

☐ _____

☐ _____

☐ _____

YOUR SOUL'S GROWTH PLANNER

LONG LIVE CHRIST THE KING!

VIVA
CRISTO
REY.ORG

DATE: MONTH   DAY   YEAR

GOALS OF THE DAY

PRAYING THE ROSARY OF 15 DECADES................... ☐

READING THE HOLY BIBLE (15 MINUTES)............... ☐

DAILY SACRIFICES.. ☐

☐ _____   ☐ _____
☐ _____   ☐ _____
☐ _____   ☐ _____
☐ _____   ☐ _____
☐ _____   ☐ _____
☐ _____   ☐ _____
☐ _____   ☐ _____
☐ _____   ☐ _____
☐ _____   ☐ _____

SUGGESTIONS

If you don't know how to pray the Holy Rosary, you can get our book "Rosary for beginners" in the following link: www.vcrey.com/rosary-book

Some sacrifices that you can do include:

- Not drinking water or liquids during a meal.
- Abstain from meat on Fridays (which is also required by Holy Mother Church).
- Not eating candy or dessert during one day.
- Take a cold shower.
- Not eating meat in saturdays in honor of the Blessed Virgin Mary.
- Keep one hour of silence.
- Do not buy or sell in Sunday (which is also a commandment).
- Give food to the hungry.
- Give water to the thirsty.
- Visit the sick, and confort them.

IMPORTANT NOTES

☐ _____
☐ _____
☐ _____
☐ _____
☐ _____
☐ _____
☐ _____
☐ _____
☐ _____

YOUR SOUL'S GROWTH PLANNER

LONG LIVE CHRIST THE KING!

VIVA CRISTO REY.ORG

DATE: MONTH   DAY   YEAR

GOALS OF THE DAY

PRAYING THE ROSARY OF 15 DECADES.................. ☐

READING THE HOLY BIBLE (15 MINUTES)............... ☐

DAILY SACRIFICES....................................... ☐

☐ _____   ☐ _____
☐ _____   ☐ _____
☐ _____   ☐ _____
☐ _____   ☐ _____
☐ _____   ☐ _____
☐ _____   ☐ _____
☐ _____   ☐ _____
☐ _____   ☐ _____
☐ _____   ☐ _____

SUGGESTIONS

If you don't know how to pray the Holy Rosary, you can get our book "Rosary for beginners" in the following link: www.vcrey.com/rosary-book

Some sacrifices that you can do include:

- Not drinking water or liquids during a meal.
- Abstain from meat on Fridays (which is also required by Holy Mother Church).
- Not eating candy or dessert during one day.
- Take a cold shower.
- Not eating meat in saturdays in honor of the Blessed Virgin Mary.
- Keep one hour of silence.
- Do not buy or sell in Sunday (which is also a commandment).
- Give food to the hungry.
- Give water to the thirsty.
- Visit the sick, and confort them.

IMPORTANT NOTES

☐ _____
☐ _____
☐ _____
☐ _____
☐ _____
☐ _____
☐ _____
☐ _____
☐ _____

YOUR SOUL'S GROWTH PLANNER

LONG LIVE CHRIST THE KING!

VIVA CRISTO REY.ORG

DATE: MONTH   DAY   YEAR

GOALS OF THE DAY

PRAYING THE ROSARY OF 15 DECADES.................. ☐

READING THE HOLY BIBLE (15 MINUTES)............... ☐

DAILY SACRIFICES... ☐

☐ _____   ☐ _____

☐ _____   ☐ _____

☐ _____   ☐ _____

☐ _____   ☐ _____

☐ _____   ☐ _____

☐ _____   ☐ _____

☐ _____   ☐ _____

☐ _____   ☐ _____

☐ _____

SUGGESTIONS

If you don't know how to pray the Holy Rosary, you can get our book "Rosary for beginners" in the following link: www.vcrey.com/rosary-book

Some sacrifices that you can do include:

- Not drinking water or liquids during a meal.
- Abstain from meat on Fridays (which is also required by Holy Mother Church).
- Not eating candy or dessert during one day.
- Take a cold shower.
- Not eating meat in saturdays in honor of the Blessed Virgin Mary.
- Keep one hour of silence.
- Do not buy or sell in Sunday (which is also a commandment).
- Give food to the hungry.
- Give water to the thirsty.
- Visit the sick, and confort them.

IMPORTANT NOTES

☐ _____

☐ _____

☐ _____

☐ _____

☐ _____

☐ _____

☐ _____

☐ _____

☐ _____

YOUR SOUL'S GROWTH PLANNER

LONG LIVE CHRIST THE KING!

VIVA CRISTO REY.ORG

DATE: MONTH   DAY   YEAR

GOALS OF THE DAY

PRAYING THE ROSARY OF 15 DECADES.................... ☐

READING THE HOLY BIBLE (15 MINUTES)................ ☐

DAILY SACRIFICES... ☐

☐ _____   ☐ _____
☐ _____   ☐ _____
☐ _____   ☐ _____
☐ _____   ☐ _____
☐ _____   ☐ _____
☐ _____   ☐ _____
☐ _____   ☐ _____
☐ _____   ☐ _____
☐ _____   ☐ _____

SUGGESTIONS

If you don't know how to pray the Holy Rosary, you can get our book "Rosary for beginners" in the following link: www.vcrey.com/rosary-book

Some sacrifices that you can do include:

- Not drinking water or liquids during a meal.
- Abstain from meat on Fridays (which is also required by Holy Mother Church).
- Not eating candy or dessert during one day.
- Take a cold shower.
- Not eating meat in saturdays in honor of the Blessed Virgin Mary.
- Keep one hour of silence.
- Do not buy or sell in Sunday (which is also a commandment).
- Give food to the hungry.
- Give water to the thirsty.
- Visit the sick, and confort them.

IMPORTANT NOTES

☐ _____
☐ _____
☐ _____
☐ _____
☐ _____
☐ _____
☐ _____
☐ _____
☐ _____

YOUR SOUL'S GROWTH PLANNER

LONG LIVE CHRIST THE KING!

VIVA
CRISTO
REY.ORG

DATE: MONTH   DAY   YEAR

GOALS OF THE DAY

PRAYING THE ROSARY OF 15 DECADES.................. ☐

READING THE HOLY BIBLE (15 MINUTES)............... ☐

DAILY SACRIFICES.. ☐

☐ _____   ☐ _____
☐ _____   ☐ _____
☐ _____   ☐ _____
☐ _____   ☐ _____
☐ _____   ☐ _____
☐ _____   ☐ _____
☐ _____   ☐ _____
☐ _____   ☐ _____
☐ _____   ☐ _____

SUGGESTIONS

If you don't know how to pray the Holy Rosary, you can get our book "Rosary for beginners" in the following link: www.vcrey.com/rosary-book

Some sacrifices that you can do include:

- Not drinking water or liquids during a meal.
- Abstain from meat on Fridays (which is also required by Holy Mother Church).
- Not eating candy or dessert during one day.
- Take a cold shower.
- Not eating meat in saturdays in honor of the Blessed Virgin Mary.
- Keep one hour of silence.
- Do not buy or sell in Sunday (which is also a commandment).
- Give food to the hungry.
- Give water to the thirsty.
- Visit the sick, and confort them.

IMPORTANT NOTES

☐ _____
☐ _____
☐ _____
☐ _____
☐ _____
☐ _____
☐ _____
☐ _____
☐ _____

YOUR SOUL'S GROWTH PLANNER

LONG LIVE CHRIST THE KING!

VIVA
CRISTO
REY.ORG

DATE: MONTH   DAY   YEAR

GOALS OF THE DAY

PRAYING THE ROSARY OF 15 DECADES................... ☐

READING THE HOLY BIBLE (15 MINUTES)................ ☐

DAILY SACRIFICES... ☐

☐ _____   ☐ _____

☐ _____   ☐ _____

☐ _____   ☐ _____

☐ _____   ☐ _____

☐ _____   ☐ _____

☐ _____   ☐ _____

☐ _____   ☐ _____

☐ _____   ☐ _____

☐ _____   ☐ _____

SUGGESTIONS

If you don't know how to pray the Holy Rosary, you can get our book "Rosary for beginners" in the following link: www.vcrey.com/rosary-book

Some sacrifices that you can do include:

- Not drinking water or liquids during a meal.
- Abstain from meat on Fridays (which is also required by Holy Mother Church).
- Not eating candy or dessert during one day.
- Take a cold shower.
- Not eating meat in saturdays in honor of the Blessed Virgin Mary.
- Keep one hour of silence.
- Do not buy or sell in Sunday (which is also a commandment).
- Give food to the hungry.
- Give water to the thirsty.
- Visit the sick, and confort them.

IMPORTANT NOTES

☐ _____

☐ _____

☐ _____

☐ _____

☐ _____

☐ _____

☐ _____

☐ _____

☐ _____

YOUR SOUL'S GROWTH PLANNER

LONG LIVE CHRIST THE KING!

VIVA
CRISTO
REY.ORG

DATE: MONTH   DAY   YEAR

GOALS OF THE DAY

PRAYING THE ROSARY OF 15 DECADES................... ☐

READING THE HOLY BIBLE (15 MINUTES)................ ☐

DAILY SACRIFICES... ☐

☐ _____   ☐ _____
☐ _____   ☐ _____
☐ _____   ☐ _____

☐ _____   ☐ _____
☐ _____   ☐ _____
☐ _____   ☐ _____
☐ _____   ☐ _____

☐ _____   ☐ _____
☐ _____   ☐ _____

SUGGESTIONS

If you don't know how to pray the Holy Rosary, you can get our book "Rosary for beginners" in the following link: www.vcrey.com/rosary-book

Some sacrifices that you can do include:

- Not drinking water or liquids during a meal.
- Abstain from meat on Fridays (which is also required by Holy Mother Church).
- Not eating candy or dessert during one day.
- Take a cold shower.
- Not eating meat in saturdays in honor of the Blessed Virgin Mary.
- Keep one hour of silence.
- Do not buy or sell in Sunday (which is also a commandment).
- Give food to the hungry.
- Give water to the thirsty.
- Visit the sick, and confort them.

IMPORTANT NOTES

☐ _____
☐ _____
☐ _____
☐ _____
☐ _____
☐ _____
☐ _____
☐ _____
☐ _____

YOUR SOUL'S GROWTH PLANNER

LONG LIVE CHRIST THE KING!

VIVA CRISTO REY.ORG

DATE: MONTH   DAY   YEAR

GOALS OF THE DAY

PRAYING THE ROSARY OF 15 DECADES..................☐

READING THE HOLY BIBLE (15 MINUTES)...............☐

DAILY SACRIFICES...☐

☐ _____   ☐ _____
☐ _____   ☐ _____
☐ _____   ☐ _____
☐ _____   ☐ _____
☐ _____   ☐ _____
☐ _____   ☐ _____
☐ _____   ☐ _____
☐ _____   ☐ _____
☐ _____   ☐ _____

SUGGESTIONS

If you don't know how to pray the Holy Rosary, you can get our book "Rosary for beginners" in the following link: www.vcrey.com/rosary-book

Some sacrifices that you can do include:

- Not drinking water or liquids during a meal.
- Abstain from meat on Fridays (which is also required by Holy Mother Church).
- Not eating candy or dessert during one day.
- Take a cold shower.
- Not eating meat in saturdays in honor of the Blessed Virgin Mary.
- Keep one hour of silence.
- Do not buy or sell in Sunday (which is also a commandment).
- Give food to the hungry.
- Give water to the thirsty.
- Visit the sick, and confort them.

IMPORTANT NOTES

☐ _____
☐ _____
☐ _____
☐ _____
☐ _____
☐ _____
☐ _____
☐ _____
☐ _____

YOUR SOUL'S GROWTH PLANNER

LONG LIVE CHRIST THE KING!

VIVA CRISTO REY.ORG

DATE: MONTH   DAY   YEAR

GOALS OF THE DAY

PRAYING THE ROSARY OF 15 DECADES................... ☐

READING THE HOLY BIBLE (15 MINUTES)................ ☐

DAILY SACRIFICES.. ☐

☐ _____   ☐ _____
☐ _____   ☐ _____
☐ _____   ☐ _____
☐ _____   ☐ _____
☐ _____   ☐ _____
☐ _____   ☐ _____
☐ _____   ☐ _____
☐ _____   ☐ _____
☐ _____   ☐ _____

SUGGESTIONS

If you don't know how to pray the Holy Rosary, you can get our book "Rosary for beginners" in the following link: www.vcrey.com/rosary-book

Some sacrifices that you can do include:

- Not drinking water or liquids during a meal.
- Abstain from meat on Fridays (which is also required by Holy Mother Church).
- Not eating candy or dessert during one day.
- Take a cold shower.
- Not eating meat in saturdays in honor of the Blessed Virgin Mary.
- Keep one hour of silence.
- Do not buy or sell in Sunday (which is also a commandment).
- Give food to the hungry.
- Give water to the thirsty.
- Visit the sick, and confort them.

IMPORTANT NOTES

☐ _____
☐ _____
☐ _____
☐ _____
☐ _____
☐ _____
☐ _____
☐ _____
☐ _____

YOUR SOUL'S GROWTH PLANNER

LONG LIVE CHRIST THE KING!

VIVA CRISTO REY.ORG

DATE: MONTH   DAY   YEAR

GOALS OF THE DAY

PRAYING THE ROSARY OF 15 DECADES.................... ☐

READING THE HOLY BIBLE (15 MINUTES)................ ☐

DAILY SACRIFICES.. ☐

☐ _____   ☐ _____
☐ _____   ☐ _____
☐ _____   ☐ _____
☐ _____   ☐ _____
☐ _____   ☐ _____
☐ _____   ☐ _____
☐ _____   ☐ _____
☐ _____   ☐ _____
☐ _____   ☐ _____

SUGGESTIONS

If you don't know how to pray the Holy Rosary, you can get our book "Rosary for beginners" in the following link: www.vcrey.com/rosary-book

Some sacrifices that you can do include:

- Not drinking water or liquids during a meal.
- Abstain from meat on Fridays (which is also required by Holy Mother Church).
- Not eating candy or dessert during one day.
- Take a cold shower.
- Not eating meat in saturdays in honor of the Blessed Virgin Mary.
- Keep one hour of silence.
- Do not buy or sell in Sunday (which is also a commandment).
- Give food to the hungry.
- Give water to the thirsty.
- Visit the sick, and confort them.

IMPORTANT NOTES

☐ _____
☐ _____
☐ _____
☐ _____
☐ _____
☐ _____
☐ _____
☐ _____
☐ _____

YOUR SOUL'S GROWTH PLANNER

LONG LIVE CHRIST THE KING!

VIVA
CRISTO
REY.ORG

DATE: MONTH   DAY   YEAR

GOALS OF THE DAY

PRAYING THE ROSARY OF 15 DECADES.................. ☐

READING THE HOLY BIBLE (15 MINUTES)............... ☐

DAILY SACRIFICES... ☐

☐ _____   ☐ _____
☐ _____   ☐ _____
☐ _____   ☐ _____
☐ _____   ☐ _____
☐ _____   ☐ _____
☐ _____   ☐ _____
☐ _____   ☐ _____
☐ _____   ☐ _____
☐ _____   ☐ _____

SUGGESTIONS

If you don't know how to pray the Holy Rosary, you can get our book "Rosary for beginners" in the following link: www.vcrey.com/rosary-book

Some sacrifices that you can do include:

- Not drinking water or liquids during a meal.
- Abstain from meat on Fridays (which is also required by Holy Mother Church).
- Not eating candy or dessert during one day.
- Take a cold shower.
- Not eating meat in saturdays in honor of the Blessed Virgin Mary.
- Keep one hour of silence.
- Do not buy or sell in Sunday (which is also a commandment).
- Give food to the hungry.
- Give water to the thirsty.
- Visit the sick, and confort them.

IMPORTANT NOTES

☐ _____
☐ _____
☐ _____
☐ _____
☐ _____
☐ _____
☐ _____
☐ _____
☐ _____
☐ _____

YOUR SOUL'S GROWTH PLANNER

LONG LIVE CHRIST THE KING!

VIVA
CRISTO
REY.ORG

DATE: MONTH   DAY   YEAR

GOALS OF THE DAY

PRAYING THE ROSARY OF 15 DECADES................... ☐

READING THE HOLY BIBLE (15 MINUTES)................ ☐

DAILY SACRIFICES... ☐

☐ _____   ☐ _____

☐ _____   ☐ _____

☐ _____   ☐ _____

☐ _____   ☐ _____

☐ _____   ☐ _____

☐ _____   ☐ _____

☐ _____   ☐ _____

☐ _____   ☐ _____

☐ _____   ☐ _____

SUGGESTIONS

If you don't know how to pray the Holy Rosary, you can get our book "Rosary for beginners" in the following link: www.vcrey.com/rosary-book

Some sacrifices that you can do include:

- Not drinking water or liquids during a meal.
- Abstain from meat on Fridays (which is also required by Holy Mother Church).
- Not eating candy or dessert during one day.
- Take a cold shower.
- Not eating meat in saturdays in honor of the Blessed Virgin Mary.
- Keep one hour of silence.
- Do not buy or sell in Sunday (which is also a commandment).
- Give food to the hungry.
- Give water to the thirsty.
- Visit the sick, and confort them.

IMPORTANT NOTES

☐ _____

☐ _____

☐ _____

☐ _____

☐ _____

☐ _____

☐ _____

☐ _____

☐ _____

YOUR SOUL'S GROWTH PLANNER

LONG LIVE CHRIST THE KING!

VIVA
CRISTO
REY.ORG

DATE: MONTH   DAY   YEAR

GOALS OF THE DAY

PRAYING THE ROSARY OF 15 DECADES................... ☐

READING THE HOLY BIBLE (15 MINUTES)............... ☐

DAILY SACRIFICES... ☐

☐ _____   ☐ _____
☐ _____   ☐ _____
☐ _____   ☐ _____

☐ _____   ☐ _____
☐ _____   ☐ _____
☐ _____   ☐ _____
☐ _____   ☐ _____

☐ _____   ☐ _____
☐ _____   ☐ _____

SUGGESTIONS

If you don't know how to pray the Holy Rosary, you can get our book "Rosary for beginners" in the following link: www.vcrey.com/rosary-book

Some sacrifices that you can do include:

- Not drinking water or liquids during a meal.
- Abstain from meat on Fridays (which is also required by Holy Mother Church).
- Not eating candy or dessert during one day.
- Take a cold shower.
- Not eating meat in saturdays in honor of the Blessed Virgin Mary.
- Keep one hour of silence.
- Do not buy or sell in Sunday (which is also a commandment).
- Give food to the hungry.
- Give water to the thirsty.
- Visit the sick, and confort them.

IMPORTANT NOTES

☐ _____
☐ _____
☐ _____
☐ _____
☐ _____
☐ _____
☐ _____
☐ _____
☐ _____

YOUR SOUL'S GROWTH PLANNER

LONG LIVE CHRIST THE KING!

VIVA CRISTO REY.ORG

DATE: MONTH   DAY   YEAR

GOALS OF THE DAY

PRAYING THE ROSARY OF 15 DECADES................... ☐

READING THE HOLY BIBLE (15 MINUTES)............... ☐

DAILY SACRIFICES.. ☐

☐ _____   ☐ _____

☐ _____   ☐ _____

☐ _____   ☐ _____

☐ _____   ☐ _____

☐ _____   ☐ _____

☐ _____   ☐ _____

☐ _____   ☐ _____

☐ _____   ☐ _____

☐ _____   ☐ _____

SUGGESTIONS

If you don't know how to pray the Holy Rosary, you can get our book "Rosary for beginners" in the following link: www.vcrey.com/rosary-book

Some sacrifices that you can do include:

- Not drinking water or liquids during a meal.
- Abstain from meat on Fridays (which is also required by Holy Mother Church).
- Not eating candy or dessert during one day.
- Take a cold shower.
- Not eating meat in saturdays in honor of the Blessed Virgin Mary.
- Keep one hour of silence.
- Do not buy or sell in Sunday (which is also a commandment).
- Give food to the hungry.
- Give water to the thirsty.
- Visit the sick, and confort them.

IMPORTANT NOTES

☐ _____

☐ _____

☐ _____

☐ _____

☐ _____

☐ _____

☐ _____

☐ _____

☐ _____

YOUR SOUL'S GROWTH PLANNER

LONG LIVE CHRIST THE KING!

VIVA
CRISTO
REY.ORG

DATE: MONTH   DAY   YEAR

GOALS OF THE DAY

PRAYING THE ROSARY OF 15 DECADES................... ☐

READING THE HOLY BIBLE (15 MINUTES)............... ☐

DAILY SACRIFICES.. ☐

☐ _____   ☐ _____
☐ _____   ☐ _____
☐ _____   ☐ _____
☐ _____   ☐ _____
☐ _____   ☐ _____
☐ _____   ☐ _____
☐ _____   ☐ _____
☐ _____   ☐ _____
☐ _____   ☐ _____

SUGGESTIONS

If you don't know how to pray the Holy Rosary, you can get our book "Rosary for beginners" in the following link: www.vcrey.com/rosary-book

Some sacrifices that you can do include:

- Not drinking water or liquids during a meal.
- Abstain from meat on Fridays (which is also required by Holy Mother Church).
- Not eating candy or dessert during one day.
- Take a cold shower.
- Not eating meat in saturdays in honor of the Blessed Virgin Mary.
- Keep one hour of silence.
- Do not buy or sell in Sunday (which is also a commandment).
- Give food to the hungry.
- Give water to the thirsty.
- Visit the sick, and confort them.

IMPORTANT NOTES

☐ _____
☐ _____
☐ _____
☐ _____
☐ _____
☐ _____
☐ _____
☐ _____
☐ _____

YOUR SOUL'S GROWTH PLANNER

LONG LIVE CHRIST THE KING!

VIVA CRISTO REY.ORG

DATE: MONTH   DAY   YEAR

GOALS OF THE DAY

PRAYING THE ROSARY OF 15 DECADES.................. ☐

READING THE HOLY BIBLE (15 MINUTES)............... ☐

DAILY SACRIFICES... ☐

☐ _____   ☐ _____

☐ _____   ☐ _____

☐ _____   ☐ _____

☐ _____   ☐ _____

☐ _____   ☐ _____

☐ _____   ☐ _____

☐ _____   ☐ _____

☐ _____   ☐ _____

☐ _____   ☐ _____

SUGGESTIONS

If you don't know how to pray the Holy Rosary, you can get our book "Rosary for beginners" in the following link: www.vcrey.com/rosary-book

Some sacrifices that you can do include:

- Not drinking water or liquids during a meal.
- Abstain from meat on Fridays (which is also required by Holy Mother Church).
- Not eating candy or dessert during one day.
- Take a cold shower.
- Not eating meat in saturdays in honor of the Blessed Virgin Mary.
- Keep one hour of silence.
- Do not buy or sell in Sunday (which is also a commandment).
- Give food to the hungry.
- Give water to the thirsty.
- Visit the sick, and confort them.

IMPORTANT NOTES

☐ _____

☐ _____

☐ _____

☐ _____

☐ _____

☐ _____

☐ _____

☐ _____

☐ _____

YOUR SOUL'S GROWTH PLANNER

LONG LIVE CHRIST THE KING!

VIVA CRISTO REY.ORG

DATE: MONTH   DAY   YEAR

GOALS OF THE DAY

PRAYING THE ROSARY OF 15 DECADES................... ☐

READING THE HOLY BIBLE (15 MINUTES)................ ☐

DAILY SACRIFICES.. ☐

☐ _____   ☐ _____
☐ _____   ☐ _____
☐ _____   ☐ _____
☐ _____   ☐ _____
☐ _____   ☐ _____
☐ _____   ☐ _____
☐ _____   ☐ _____
☐ _____   ☐ _____
☐ _____   ☐ _____

SUGGESTIONS

If you don't know how to pray the Holy Rosary, you can get our book "Rosary for beginners" in the following link: www.vcrey.com/rosary-book

Some sacrifices that you can do include:

- Not drinking water or liquids during a meal.
- Abstain from meat on Fridays (which is also required by Holy Mother Church).
- Not eating candy or dessert during one day.
- Take a cold shower.
- Not eating meat in saturdays in honor of the Blessed Virgin Mary.
- Keep one hour of silence.
- Do not buy or sell in Sunday (which is also a commandment).
- Give food to the hungry.
- Give water to the thirsty.
- Visit the sick, and confort them.

IMPORTANT NOTES

☐ _____
☐ _____
☐ _____
☐ _____
☐ _____
☐ _____
☐ _____
☐ _____
☐ _____

YOUR SOUL'S GROWTH PLANNER

LONG LIVE CHRIST THE KING!

VIVA
CRISTO
REY.ORG

DATE: MONTH   DAY   YEAR

GOALS OF THE DAY

PRAYING THE ROSARY OF 15 DECADES.................. ☐

READING THE HOLY BIBLE (15 MINUTES)............... ☐

DAILY SACRIFICES... ☐

☐ _____   ☐ _____
☐ _____   ☐ _____
☐ _____   ☐ _____
☐ _____   ☐ _____
☐ _____   ☐ _____
☐ _____   ☐ _____
☐ _____   ☐ _____
☐ _____   ☐ _____
☐ _____   ☐ _____

SUGGESTIONS

If you don't know how to pray the Holy Rosary, you can get our book "Rosary for beginners" in the following link: www.vcrey.com/rosary-book

Some sacrifices that you can do include:

- Not drinking water or liquids during a meal.
- Abstain from meat on Fridays (which is also required by Holy Mother Church).
- Not eating candy or dessert during one day.
- Take a cold shower.
- Not eating meat in saturdays in honor of the Blessed Virgin Mary.
- Keep one hour of silence.
- Do not buy or sell in Sunday (which is also a commandment).
- Give food to the hungry.
- Give water to the thirsty.
- Visit the sick, and confort them.

IMPORTANT NOTES

☐ _____
☐ _____
☐ _____
☐ _____
☐ _____
☐ _____
☐ _____
☐ _____
☐ _____

YOUR SOUL'S GROWTH PLANNER

LONG LIVE CHRIST THE KING!

VIVA CRISTO REY.ORG

DATE: MONTH   DAY   YEAR

GOALS OF THE DAY

PRAYING THE ROSARY OF 15 DECADES.................. ☐

READING THE HOLY BIBLE (15 MINUTES)............... ☐

DAILY SACRIFICES.. ☐

☐ _____   ☐ _____
☐ _____   ☐ _____
☐ _____   ☐ _____
☐ _____   ☐ _____
☐ _____   ☐ _____
☐ _____   ☐ _____
☐ _____   ☐ _____
☐ _____   ☐ _____
☐ _____   ☐ _____

SUGGESTIONS

If you don't know how to pray the Holy Rosary, you can get our book "Rosary for beginners" in the following link: www.vcrey.com/rosary-book

Some sacrifices that you can do include:

- Not drinking water or liquids during a meal.
- Abstain from meat on Fridays (which is also required by Holy Mother Church).
- Not eating candy or dessert during one day.
- Take a cold shower.
- Not eating meat in saturdays in honor of the Blessed Virgin Mary.
- Keep one hour of silence.
- Do not buy or sell in Sunday (which is also a commandment).
- Give food to the hungry.
- Give water to the thirsty.
- Visit the sick, and confort them.

IMPORTANT NOTES

☐ _____
☐ _____
☐ _____
☐ _____
☐ _____
☐ _____
☐ _____
☐ _____
☐ _____

YOUR SOUL'S GROWTH PLANNER

LONG LIVE CHRIST THE KING!

VIVA
CRISTO
REY.ORG

DATE: MONTH   DAY   YEAR

GOALS OF THE DAY

PRAYING THE ROSARY OF 15 DECADES................... ☐

READING THE HOLY BIBLE (15 MINUTES)............... ☐

DAILY SACRIFICES.. ☐

☐ _____   ☐ _____

☐ _____   ☐ _____

☐ _____   ☐ _____

☐ _____   ☐ _____

☐ _____   ☐ _____

☐ _____   ☐ _____

☐ _____   ☐ _____

☐ _____   ☐ _____

☐ _____   ☐ _____

SUGGESTIONS

If you don't know how to pray the Holy Rosary, you can get our book "Rosary for beginners" in the following link: www.vcrey.com/rosary-book

Some sacrifices that you can do include:

- Not drinking water or liquids during a meal.
- Abstain from meat on Fridays (which is also required by Holy Mother Church).
- Not eating candy or dessert during one day.
- Take a cold shower.
- Not eating meat in saturdays in honor of the Blessed Virgin Mary.
- Keep one hour of silence.
- Do not buy or sell in Sunday (which is also a commandment).
- Give food to the hungry.
- Give water to the thirsty.
- Visit the sick, and confort them.

IMPORTANT NOTES

☐ _____

☐ _____

☐ _____

☐ _____

☐ _____

☐ _____

☐ _____

☐ _____

☐ _____

YOUR SOUL'S GROWTH PLANNER

LONG LIVE CHRIST THE KING!

VIVA CRISTO REY.ORG

DATE: MONTH   DAY   YEAR

GOALS OF THE DAY

PRAYING THE ROSARY OF 15 DECADES................... ☐

READING THE HOLY BIBLE (15 MINUTES)................ ☐

DAILY SACRIFICES.. ☐

☐ _____   ☐ _____
☐ _____   ☐ _____
☐ _____   ☐ _____
☐ _____   ☐ _____
☐ _____   ☐ _____
☐ _____
☐ _____   ☐ _____
☐ _____   ☐ _____
☐ _____

IMPORTANT NOTES

☐ _____
☐ _____
☐ _____
☐ _____
☐ _____
☐ _____
☐ _____
☐ _____
☐ _____

YOUR SOUL'S GROWTH PLANNER

LONG LIVE CHRIST THE KING!

VIVA
CRISTO
REY.ORG

DATE: MONTH   DAY   YEAR

GOALS OF THE DAY

PRAYING THE ROSARY OF 15 DECADES................... ☐

READING THE HOLY BIBLE (15 MINUTES)............... ☐

DAILY SACRIFICES... ☐

☐ _____   ☐ _____

☐ _____   ☐ _____

☐ _____   ☐ _____

☐ _____   ☐ _____

☐ _____   ☐ _____
☐ _____   ☐ _____

☐ _____   ☐ _____

☐ _____   ☐ _____

☐ _____   ☐ _____

SUGGESTIONS

If you don't know how to pray the Holy Rosary, you can get our book "Rosary for beginners" in the following link: www.vcrey.com/rosary-book

Some sacrifices that you can do include:

- Not drinking water or liquids during a meal.
- Abstain from meat on Fridays (which is also required by Holy Mother Church).
- Not eating candy or dessert during one day.
- Take a cold shower.
- Not eating meat in saturdays in honor of the Blessed Virgin Mary.
- Keep one hour of silence.
- Do not buy or sell in Sunday (which is also a commandment).
- Give food to the hungry.
- Give water to the thirsty.
- Visit the sick, and confort them.

IMPORTANT NOTES

☐ _____

☐ _____

☐ _____

☐ _____

☐ _____

☐ _____

☐ _____

☐ _____

☐ _____

YOUR SOUL'S GROWTH PLANNER

LONG LIVE CHRIST THE KING!

VIVA CRISTO REY.ORG

DATE: MONTH   DAY   YEAR

GOALS OF THE DAY

PRAYING THE ROSARY OF 15 DECADES................... ☐

READING THE HOLY BIBLE (15 MINUTES)................ ☐

DAILY SACRIFICES... ☐

☐ _____   ☐ _____
☐ _____   ☐ _____
☐ _____   ☐ _____
☐ _____   ☐ _____
☐ _____   ☐ _____
☐ _____   ☐ _____
☐ _____   ☐ _____
☐ _____   ☐ _____
☐ _____   ☐ _____

SUGGESTIONS

If you don't know how to pray the Holy Rosary, you can get our book "Rosary for beginners" in the following link: www.vcrey.com/rosary-book

Some sacrifices that you can do include:

- Not drinking water or liquids during a meal.
- Abstain from meat on Fridays (which is also required by Holy Mother Church).
- Not eating candy or dessert during one day.
- Take a cold shower.
- Not eating meat in saturdays in honor of the Blessed Virgin Mary.
- Keep one hour of silence.
- Do not buy or sell in Sunday (which is also a commandment).
- Give food to the hungry.
- Give water to the thirsty.
- Visit the sick, and confort them.

IMPORTANT NOTES

☐ _____
☐ _____
☐ _____
☐ _____
☐ _____
☐ _____
☐ _____
☐ _____
☐ _____

YOUR SOUL'S GROWTH PLANNER

LONG LIVE CHRIST THE KING!

VIVA
CRISTO
REY.ORG

DATE: MONTH   DAY   YEAR

GOALS OF THE DAY

PRAYING THE ROSARY OF 15 DECADES................... ☐

READING THE HOLY BIBLE (15 MINUTES)................ ☐

DAILY SACRIFICES... ☐

☐ _____   ☐ _____
☐ _____   ☐ _____
☐ _____   ☐ _____
☐ _____   ☐ _____
☐ _____   ☐ _____
☐ _____   ☐ _____
☐ _____   ☐ _____
☐ _____   ☐ _____
☐ _____   ☐ _____

SUGGESTIONS

If you don't know how to pray the Holy Rosary, you can get our book "Rosary for beginners" in the following link: www.vcrey.com/rosary-book

Some sacrifices that you can do include:

- Not drinking water or liquids during a meal.
- Abstain from meat on Fridays (which is also required by Holy Mother Church).
- Not eating candy or dessert during one day.
- Take a cold shower.
- Not eating meat in saturdays in honor of the Blessed Virgin Mary.
- Keep one hour of silence.
- Do not buy or sell in Sunday (which is also a commandment).
- Give food to the hungry.
- Give water to the thirsty.
- Visit the sick, and confort them.

IMPORTANT NOTES

☐ _____
☐ _____
☐ _____
☐ _____
☐ _____
☐ _____
☐ _____
☐ _____
☐ _____

YOUR SOUL'S GROWTH PLANNER

LONG LIVE CHRIST THE KING!

VIVA CRISTO REY.ORG

DATE: MONTH   DAY   YEAR

GOALS OF THE DAY

PRAYING THE ROSARY OF 15 DECADES.................. ☐

READING THE HOLY BIBLE (15 MINUTES)............... ☐

DAILY SACRIFICES... ☐

☐ _____   ☐ _____
☐ _____   ☐ _____
☐ _____   ☐ _____
☐ _____   ☐ _____
☐ _____   ☐ _____
☐ _____   ☐ _____
☐ _____   ☐ _____
☐ _____   ☐ _____
☐ _____   ☐ _____

SUGGESTIONS

If you don't know how to pray the Holy Rosary, you can get our book "Rosary for beginners" in the following link: www.vcrey.com/rosary-book

Some sacrifices that you can do include:

- Not drinking water or liquids during a meal.
- Abstain from meat on Fridays (which is also required by Holy Mother Church).
- Not eating candy or dessert during one day.
- Take a cold shower.
- Not eating meat in saturdays in honor of the Blessed Virgin Mary.
- Keep one hour of silence.
- Do not buy or sell in Sunday (which is also a commandment).
- Give food to the hungry.
- Give water to the thirsty.
- Visit the sick, and confort them.

IMPORTANT NOTES

☐ _____
☐ _____
☐ _____
☐ _____
☐ _____
☐ _____
☐ _____
☐ _____
☐ _____

YOUR SOUL'S GROWTH PLANNER

LONG LIVE CHRIST THE KING!

VIVA
CRISTO
REY.ORG

DATE: MONTH   DAY   YEAR

GOALS OF THE DAY

PRAYING THE ROSARY OF 15 DECADES.................. ☐

READING THE HOLY BIBLE (15 MINUTES).............. ☐

DAILY SACRIFICES.. ☐

☐ _____   ☐ _____
☐ _____   ☐ _____
☐ _____   ☐ _____
☐ _____   ☐ _____
☐ _____   ☐ _____
☐ _____   ☐ _____
☐ _____   ☐ _____
☐ _____   ☐ _____
☐ _____   ☐ _____

SUGGESTIONS

If you don't know how to pray the Holy Rosary, you can get our book "Rosary for beginners" in the following link: www.vcrey.com/rosary-book

Some sacrifices that you can do include:

- Not drinking water or liquids during a meal.
- Abstain from meat on Fridays (which is also required by Holy Mother Church).
- Not eating candy or dessert during one day.
- Take a cold shower.
- Not eating meat in saturdays in honor of the Blessed Virgin Mary.
- Keep one hour of silence.
- Do not buy or sell in Sunday (which is also a commandment).
- Give food to the hungry.
- Give water to the thirsty.
- Visit the sick, and confort them.

IMPORTANT NOTES

☐ _____
☐ _____
☐ _____
☐ _____
☐ _____
☐ _____
☐ _____
☐ _____
☐ _____

YOUR SOUL'S GROWTH PLANNER

LONG LIVE CHRIST THE KING!

VIVA CRISTO REY.ORG

DATE: MONTH   DAY   YEAR

GOALS OF THE DAY

PRAYING THE ROSARY OF 15 DECADES................... ☐

READING THE HOLY BIBLE (15 MINUTES)............... ☐

DAILY SACRIFICES.. ☐

☐ _____   ☐ _____

☐ _____   ☐ _____

☐ _____   ☐ _____

☐ _____   ☐ _____

☐ _____   ☐ _____

☐ _____   ☐ _____

☐ _____   ☐ _____

☐ _____   ☐ _____

☐ _____   ☐ _____

SUGGESTIONS

If you don't know how to pray the Holy Rosary, you can get our book "Rosary for beginners" in the following link: www.vcrey.com/rosary-book

Some sacrifices that you can do include:

- Not drinking water or liquids during a meal.
- Abstain from meat on Fridays (which is also required by Holy Mother Church).
- Not eating candy or dessert during one day.
- Take a cold shower.
- Not eating meat in saturdays in honor of the Blessed Virgin Mary.
- Keep one hour of silence.
- Do not buy or sell in Sunday (which is also a commandment).
- Give food to the hungry.
- Give water to the thirsty.
- Visit the sick, and confort them.

IMPORTANT NOTES

☐ _____

☐ _____

☐ _____

☐ _____

☐ _____

☐ _____

☐ _____

☐ _____

☐ _____

YOUR SOUL'S GROWTH PLANNER

LONG LIVE CHRIST THE KING!

VIVA
CRISTO
REY.ORG

DATE: MONTH   DAY   YEAR

GOALS OF THE DAY

PRAYING THE ROSARY OF 15 DECADES................... ☐

READING THE HOLY BIBLE (15 MINUTES)................ ☐

DAILY SACRIFICES.. ☐

☐ _____   ☐ _____

☐ _____   ☐ _____

☐ _____   ☐ _____

☐ _____   ☐ _____

☐ _____   ☐ _____

☐ _____   ☐ _____

☐ _____   ☐ _____

☐ _____   ☐ _____

☐ _____   ☐ _____

SUGGESTIONS

If you don't know how to pray the Holy Rosary, you can get our book "Rosary for beginners" in the following link: www.vcrey.com/rosary-book

Some sacrifices that you can do include:

- Not drinking water or liquids during a meal.
- Abstain from meat on Fridays (which is also required by Holy Mother Church).
- Not eating candy or dessert during one day.
- Take a cold shower.
- Not eating meat in saturdays in honor of the Blessed Virgin Mary.
- Keep one hour of silence.
- Do not buy or sell in Sunday (which is also a commandment).
- Give food to the hungry.
- Give water to the thirsty.
- Visit the sick, and confort them.

IMPORTANT NOTES

☐ _____

☐ _____

☐ _____

☐ _____

☐ _____

☐ _____

☐ _____

☐ _____

☐ _____

YOUR SOUL'S GROWTH PLANNER

LONG LIVE CHRIST THE KING!

VIVA
CRISTO
REY.ORG

DATE: MONTH   DAY   YEAR

GOALS OF THE DAY

PRAYING THE ROSARY OF 15 DECADES................... ☐

READING THE HOLY BIBLE (15 MINUTES)................ ☐

DAILY SACRIFICES... ☐

☐ _____   ☐ _____
☐ _____   ☐ _____
☐ _____   ☐ _____
☐ _____   ☐ _____
☐ _____   ☐ _____
☐ _____   ☐ _____
☐ _____   ☐ _____
☐ _____   ☐ _____
☐ _____   ☐ _____

SUGGESTIONS

If you don't know how to pray the Holy Rosary, you can get our book "Rosary for beginners" in the following link: www.vcrey.com/rosary-book

Some sacrifices that you can do include:

- Not drinking water or liquids during a meal.
- Abstain from meat on Fridays (which is also required by Holy Mother Church).
- Not eating candy or dessert during one day.
- Take a cold shower.
- Not eating meat in saturdays in honor of the Blessed Virgin Mary.
- Keep one hour of silence.
- Do not buy or sell in Sunday (which is also a commandment).
- Give food to the hungry.
- Give water to the thirsty.
- Visit the sick, and confort them.

IMPORTANT NOTES

☐ _____
☐ _____
☐ _____
☐ _____
☐ _____
☐ _____
☐ _____
☐ _____
☐ _____

YOUR SOUL'S GROWTH PLANNER

LONG LIVE CHRIST THE KING!

VIVA
CRISTO
REY.ORG

DATE: MONTH   DAY   YEAR

GOALS OF THE DAY

PRAYING THE ROSARY OF 15 DECADES.................. ☐

READING THE HOLY BIBLE (15 MINUTES)............... ☐

DAILY SACRIFICES... ☐

☐ _____   ☐ _____

☐ _____   ☐ _____

☐ _____   ☐ _____

☐ _____   ☐ _____

☐ _____   ☐ _____

☐ _____   ☐ _____

☐ _____   ☐ _____

☐ _____   ☐ _____

☐ _____   ☐ _____

SUGGESTIONS

If you don't know how to pray the Holy Rosary, you can get our book "Rosary for beginners" in the following link: www.vcrey.com/rosary-book

Some sacrifices that you can do include:

- Not drinking water or liquids during a meal.
- Abstain from meat on Fridays (which is also required by Holy Mother Church).
- Not eating candy or dessert during one day.
- Take a cold shower.
- Not eating meat in saturdays in honor of the Blessed Virgin Mary.
- Keep one hour of silence.
- Do not buy or sell in Sunday (which is also a commandment).
- Give food to the hungry.
- Give water to the thirsty.
- Visit the sick, and confort them.

IMPORTANT NOTES

☐ _____

☐ _____

☐ _____

☐ _____

☐ _____

☐ _____

☐ _____

☐ _____

☐ _____

YOUR SOUL'S GROWTH PLANNER

LONG LIVE CHRIST THE KING!

VIVA CRISTO REY.ORG

DATE: MONTH   DAY   YEAR

GOALS OF THE DAY

PRAYING THE ROSARY OF 15 DECADES................... ☐

READING THE HOLY BIBLE (15 MINUTES)................ ☐

DAILY SACRIFICES.. ☐

☐ _____   ☐ _____
☐ _____   ☐ _____
☐ _____   ☐ _____
☐ _____   ☐ _____
☐ _____   ☐ _____
☐ _____   ☐ _____
☐ _____   ☐ _____
☐ _____   ☐ _____
☐ _____   ☐ _____

SUGGESTIONS

If you don't know how to pray the Holy Rosary, you can get our book "Rosary for beginners" in the following link: www.vcrey.com/rosary-book

Some sacrifices that you can do include:

- Not drinking water or liquids during a meal.
- Abstain from meat on Fridays (which is also required by Holy Mother Church).
- Not eating candy or dessert during one day.
- Take a cold shower.
- Not eating meat in saturdays in honor of the Blessed Virgin Mary.
- Keep one hour of silence.
- Do not buy or sell in Sunday (which is also a commandment).
- Give food to the hungry.
- Give water to the thirsty.
- Visit the sick, and confort them.

IMPORTANT NOTES

☐ _____
☐ _____
☐ _____
☐ _____
☐ _____
☐ _____
☐ _____
☐ _____
☐ _____

YOUR SOUL'S GROWTH PLANNER

LONG LIVE CHRIST THE KING!

DATE: MONTH   DAY   YEAR

GOALS OF THE DAY

PRAYING THE ROSARY OF 15 DECADES................... ☐

READING THE HOLY BIBLE (15 MINUTES)................ ☐

DAILY SACRIFICES... ☐

☐ _____   ☐ _____
☐ _____   ☐ _____
☐ _____   ☐ _____
☐ _____   ☐ _____
☐ _____   ☐ _____
☐ _____   ☐ _____
☐ _____   ☐ _____
☐ _____   ☐ _____
☐ _____   ☐ _____

SUGGESTIONS

If you don't know how to pray the Holy Rosary, you can get our book "Rosary for beginners" in the following link: www.vcrey.com/rosary-book

Some sacrifices that you can do include:

- Not drinking water or liquids during a meal.
- Abstain from meat on Fridays (which is also required by Holy Mother Church).
- Not eating candy or dessert during one day.
- Take a cold shower.
- Not eating meat in saturdays in honor of the Blessed Virgin Mary.
- Keep one hour of silence.
- Do not buy or sell in Sunday (which is also a commandment).
- Give food to the hungry.
- Give water to the thirsty.
- Visit the sick, and confort them.

IMPORTANT NOTES

☐ _____
☐ _____
☐ _____
☐ _____
☐ _____
☐ _____
☐ _____
☐ _____
☐ _____

YOUR SOUL'S GROWTH PLANNER

LONG LIVE CHRIST THE KING!

VIVA CRISTO REY.ORG

DATE: MONTH   DAY   YEAR

GOALS OF THE DAY

PRAYING THE ROSARY OF 15 DECADES................... ☐

READING THE HOLY BIBLE (15 MINUTES)............... ☐

DAILY SACRIFICES.. ☐

☐ _____   ☐ _____
☐ _____   ☐ _____
☐ _____   ☐ _____

☐ _____   ☐ _____
☐ _____   ☐ _____
☐ _____   ☐ _____
☐ _____   ☐ _____

☐ _____   ☐ _____
☐ _____   ☐ _____

SUGGESTIONS

If you don't know how to pray the Holy Rosary, you can get our book "Rosary for beginners" in the following link: www.vcrey.com/rosary-book

Some sacrifices that you can do include:

- Not drinking water or liquids during a meal.
- Abstain from meat on Fridays (which is also required by Holy Mother Church).
- Not eating candy or dessert during one day.
- Take a cold shower.
- Not eating meat in saturdays in honor of the Blessed Virgin Mary.
- Keep one hour of silence.
- Do not buy or sell in Sunday (which is also a commandment).
- Give food to the hungry.
- Give water to the thirsty.
- Visit the sick, and confort them.

IMPORTANT NOTES

☐ _____
☐ _____
☐ _____
☐ _____
☐ _____
☐ _____
☐ _____
☐ _____
☐ _____

YOUR SOUL'S GROWTH PLANNER

LONG LIVE CHRIST THE KING!

VIVA CRISTO REY.ORG

DATE: MONTH   DAY   YEAR

GOALS OF THE DAY

PRAYING THE ROSARY OF 15 DECADES.................. ☐

READING THE HOLY BIBLE (15 MINUTES)............... ☐

DAILY SACRIFICES... ☐

☐ _____   ☐ _____

☐ _____   ☐ _____

☐ _____   ☐ _____

☐ _____   ☐ _____

☐ _____   ☐ _____

☐ _____   ☐ _____

☐ _____   ☐ _____

☐ _____   ☐ _____

☐ _____   ☐ _____

SUGGESTIONS

If you don't know how to pray the Holy Rosary, you can get our book "Rosary for beginners" in the following link: www.vcrey.com/rosary-book

Some sacrifices that you can do include:

- Not drinking water or liquids during a meal.
- Abstain from meat on Fridays (which is also required by Holy Mother Church).
- Not eating candy or dessert during one day.
- Take a cold shower.
- Not eating meat in saturdays in honor of the Blessed Virgin Mary.
- Keep one hour of silence.
- Do not buy or sell in Sunday (which is also a commandment).
- Give food to the hungry.
- Give water to the thirsty.
- Visit the sick, and confort them.

IMPORTANT NOTES

☐ _____

☐ _____

☐ _____

☐ _____

☐ _____

☐ _____

☐ _____

☐ _____

☐ _____

YOUR SOUL'S GROWTH PLANNER

LONG LIVE CHRIST THE KING!

VIVA CRISTO REY.ORG

DATE: MONTH   DAY   YEAR

GOALS OF THE DAY

PRAYING THE ROSARY OF 15 DECADES................... ☐

READING THE HOLY BIBLE (15 MINUTES)................ ☐

DAILY SACRIFICES.. ☐

☐ _____   ☐ _____
☐ _____   ☐ _____
☐ _____   ☐ _____
☐ _____   ☐ _____
☐ _____   ☐ _____
☐ _____   ☐ _____
☐ _____   ☐ _____
☐ _____   ☐ _____
☐ _____   ☐ _____

SUGGESTIONS

If you don't know how to pray the Holy Rosary, you can get our book "Rosary for beginners" in the following link: www.vcrey.com/rosary-book

Some sacrifices that you can do include:

- Not drinking water or liquids during a meal.
- Abstain from meat on Fridays (which is also required by Holy Mother Church).
- Not eating candy or dessert during one day.
- Take a cold shower.
- Not eating meat in saturdays in honor of the Blessed Virgin Mary.
- Keep one hour of silence.
- Do not buy or sell in Sunday (which is also a commandment).
- Give food to the hungry.
- Give water to the thirsty.
- Visit the sick, and confort them.

IMPORTANT NOTES

☐ _____
☐ _____
☐ _____
☐ _____
☐ _____
☐ _____
☐ _____
☐ _____
☐ _____

YOUR SOUL'S GROWTH PLANNER

LONG LIVE CHRIST THE KING!

VIVA
CRISTO
REY.ORG

DATE: MONTH   DAY   YEAR

GOALS OF THE DAY

PRAYING THE ROSARY OF 15 DECADES................... ☐

READING THE HOLY BIBLE (15 MINUTES)................ ☐

DAILY SACRIFICES... ☐

☐ _____   ☐ _____
☐ _____   ☐ _____
☐ _____   ☐ _____
☐ _____   ☐ _____
☐ _____   ☐ _____
☐ _____   ☐ _____
☐ _____   ☐ _____
☐ _____   ☐ _____
☐ _____   ☐ _____

SUGGESTIONS

If you don't know how to pray the Holy Rosary, you can get our book "Rosary for beginners" in the following link: www.vcrey.com/rosary-book

Some sacrifices that you can do include:

- Not drinking water or liquids during a meal.
- Abstain from meat on Fridays (which is also required by Holy Mother Church).
- Not eating candy or dessert during one day.
- Take a cold shower.
- Not eating meat in saturdays in honor of the Blessed Virgin Mary.
- Keep one hour of silence.
- Do not buy or sell in Sunday (which is also a commandment).
- Give food to the hungry.
- Give water to the thirsty.
- Visit the sick, and confort them.

IMPORTANT NOTES

☐ _____
☐ _____
☐ _____
☐ _____
☐ _____
☐ _____
☐ _____
☐ _____
☐ _____

YOUR SOUL'S GROWTH PLANNER

LONG LIVE CHRIST THE KING!

VIVA CRISTO REY.ORG

DATE: MONTH   DAY   YEAR

GOALS OF THE DAY

PRAYING THE ROSARY OF 15 DECADES................... ☐

READING THE HOLY BIBLE (15 MINUTES)............... ☐

DAILY SACRIFICES.. ☐

☐ _____   ☐ _____
☐ _____   ☐ _____
☐ _____   ☐ _____
☐ _____   ☐ _____
☐ _____   ☐ _____
☐ _____   ☐ _____
☐ _____   ☐ _____
☐ _____   ☐ _____
☐ _____   ☐ _____

SUGGESTIONS

If you don't know how to pray the Holy Rosary, you can get our book "Rosary for beginners" in the following link: www.vcrey.com/rosary-book

Some sacrifices that you can do include:

- Not drinking water or liquids during a meal.
- Abstain from meat on Fridays (which is also required by Holy Mother Church).
- Not eating candy or dessert during one day.
- Take a cold shower.
- Not eating meat in saturdays in honor of the Blessed Virgin Mary.
- Keep one hour of silence.
- Do not buy or sell in Sunday (which is also a commandment).
- Give food to the hungry.
- Give water to the thirsty.
- Visit the sick, and confort them.

IMPORTANT NOTES

☐ _____
☐ _____
☐ _____
☐ _____
☐ _____
☐ _____
☐ _____
☐ _____
☐ _____

YOUR SOUL'S GROWTH PLANNER

LONG LIVE CHRIST THE KING!

VIVA
CRISTO
REY.ORG

DATE: MONTH   DAY   YEAR

GOALS OF THE DAY

PRAYING THE ROSARY OF 15 DECADES................... ☐

READING THE HOLY BIBLE (15 MINUTES)................ ☐

DAILY SACRIFICES... ☐

☐ _____   ☐ _____

☐ _____   ☐ _____

☐ _____   ☐ _____

☐ _____   ☐ _____

☐ _____   ☐ _____

☐ _____   ☐ _____

☐ _____   ☐ _____

☐ _____   ☐ _____

SUGGESTIONS

If you don't know how to pray the Holy Rosary, you can get our book "Rosary for beginners" in the following link: www.vcrey.com/rosary-book

Some sacrifices that you can do include:

- Not drinking water or liquids during a meal.
- Abstain from meat on Fridays (which is also required by Holy Mother Church).
- Not eating candy or dessert during one day.
- Take a cold shower.
- Not eating meat in saturdays in honor of the Blessed Virgin Mary.
- Keep one hour of silence.
- Do not buy or sell in Sunday (which is also a commandment).
- Give food to the hungry.
- Give water to the thirsty.
- Visit the sick, and confort them.

IMPORTANT NOTES

☐ _____

☐ _____

☐ _____

☐ _____

☐ _____

☐ _____

☐ _____

☐ _____

☐ _____

YOUR SOUL'S GROWTH PLANNER

LONG LIVE CHRIST THE KING!

VIVA CRISTO REY.ORG

DATE: MONTH   DAY   YEAR

GOALS OF THE DAY

PRAYING THE ROSARY OF 15 DECADES.................. ☐

READING THE HOLY BIBLE (15 MINUTES)............... ☐

DAILY SACRIFICES... ☐

☐ _____   ☐ _____
☐ _____   ☐ _____
☐ _____   ☐ _____
☐ _____   ☐ _____
☐ _____   ☐ _____
☐ _____   ☐ _____
☐ _____   ☐ _____
☐ _____   ☐ _____
☐ _____   ☐ _____

SUGGESTIONS

If you don't know how to pray the Holy Rosary, you can get our book "Rosary for beginners" in the following link: www.vcrey.com/rosary-book

Some sacrifices that you can do include:

- Not drinking water or liquids during a meal.
- Abstain from meat on Fridays (which is also required by Holy Mother Church).
- Not eating candy or dessert during one day.
- Take a cold shower.
- Not eating meat in saturdays in honor of the Blessed Virgin Mary.
- Keep one hour of silence.
- Do not buy or sell in Sunday (which is also a commandment).
- Give food to the hungry.
- Give water to the thirsty.
- Visit the sick, and confort them.

IMPORTANT NOTES

☐ _____
☐ _____
☐ _____
☐ _____
☐ _____
☐ _____
☐ _____
☐ _____
☐ _____

YOUR SOUL'S GROWTH PLANNER

LONG LIVE CHRIST THE KING!

VIVA
CRISTO
REY.ORG

DATE: MONTH   DAY   YEAR

GOALS OF THE DAY

PRAYING THE ROSARY OF 15 DECADES................... ☐

READING THE HOLY BIBLE (15 MINUTES)............... ☐

DAILY SACRIFICES... ☐

☐ _____   ☐ _____

☐ _____   ☐ _____

☐ _____   ☐ _____

☐ _____   ☐ _____

☐ _____   ☐ _____

☐ _____   ☐ _____

☐ _____   ☐ _____

☐ _____   ☐ _____

☐ _____   ☐ _____

SUGGESTIONS

If you don't know how to pray the Holy Rosary, you can get our book "Rosary for beginners" in the following link: www.vcrey.com/rosary-book

Some sacrifices that you can do include:

- Not drinking water or liquids during a meal.
- Abstain from meat on Fridays (which is also required by Holy Mother Church).
- Not eating candy or dessert during one day.
- Take a cold shower.
- Not eating meat in saturdays in honor of the Blessed Virgin Mary.
- Keep one hour of silence.
- Do not buy or sell in Sunday (which is also a commandment).
- Give food to the hungry.
- Give water to the thirsty.
- Visit the sick, and confort them.

IMPORTANT NOTES

☐ _____

☐ _____

☐ _____

☐ _____

☐ _____

☐ _____

☐ _____

☐ _____

☐ _____

YOUR SOUL'S GROWTH PLANNER

LONG LIVE CHRIST THE KING!

DATE: MONTH   DAY   YEAR

GOALS OF THE DAY

PRAYING THE ROSARY OF 15 DECADES.................. ☐

READING THE HOLY BIBLE (15 MINUTES).............. ☐

DAILY SACRIFICES.. ☐

☐ _____   ☐ _____
☐ _____   ☐ _____
☐ _____   ☐ _____
☐ _____   ☐ _____
☐ _____   ☐ _____
☐ _____   ☐ _____
☐ _____   ☐ _____
☐ _____   ☐ _____
☐ _____   ☐ _____

SUGGESTIONS

If you don't know how to pray the Holy Rosary, you can get our book "Rosary for beginners" in the following link: www.vcrey.com/rosary-book

Some sacrifices that you can do include:

- Not drinking water or liquids during a meal.
- Abstain from meat on Fridays (which is also required by Holy Mother Church).
- Not eating candy or dessert during one day.
- Take a cold shower.
- Not eating meat in saturdays in honor of the Blessed Virgin Mary.
- Keep one hour of silence.
- Do not buy or sell in Sunday (which is also a commandment).
- Give food to the hungry.
- Give water to the thirsty.
- Visit the sick, and confort them.

IMPORTANT NOTES

☐ _____
☐ _____
☐ _____
☐ _____
☐ _____
☐ _____
☐ _____
☐ _____
☐ _____

YOUR SOUL'S GROWTH PLANNER

LONG LIVE CHRIST THE KING!

VIVA
CRISTO
REY.ORG

DATE: MONTH   DAY   YEAR

GOALS OF THE DAY

PRAYING THE ROSARY OF 15 DECADES................... ☐

READING THE HOLY BIBLE (15 MINUTES)............... ☐

DAILY SACRIFICES... ☐

☐ _____   ☐ _____
☐ _____   ☐ _____
☐ _____   ☐ _____
☐ _____   ☐ _____
☐ _____   ☐ _____
☐ _____   ☐ _____
☐ _____   ☐ _____
☐ _____   ☐ _____
☐ _____   ☐ _____

SUGGESTIONS

If you don't know how to pray the Holy Rosary, you can get our book "Rosary for beginners" in the following link: www.vcrey.com/rosary-book

Some sacrifices that you can do include:

- Not drinking water or liquids during a meal.
- Abstain from meat on Fridays (which is also required by Holy Mother Church).
- Not eating candy or dessert during one day.
- Take a cold shower.
- Not eating meat in saturdays in honor of the Blessed Virgin Mary.
- Keep one hour of silence.
- Do not buy or sell in Sunday (which is also a commandment).
- Give food to the hungry.
- Give water to the thirsty.
- Visit the sick, and confort them.

IMPORTANT NOTES

☐ _____
☐ _____
☐ _____
☐ _____
☐ _____
☐ _____
☐ _____
☐ _____
☐ _____

YOUR SOUL'S GROWTH PLANNER

LONG LIVE CHRIST THE KING!

VIVA
CRISTO
REY.ORG

DATE: MONTH   DAY   YEAR

GOALS OF THE DAY

PRAYING THE ROSARY OF 15 DECADES.................. ☐

READING THE HOLY BIBLE (15 MINUTES)................ ☐

DAILY SACRIFICES... ☐

☐ _____   ☐ _____
☐ _____   ☐ _____
☐ _____   ☐ _____
☐ _____   ☐ _____
☐ _____   ☐ _____
☐ _____   ☐ _____
☐ _____   ☐ _____
☐ _____   ☐ _____
☐ _____   ☐ _____

SUGGESTIONS

If you don't know how to pray the Holy Rosary, you can get our book "Rosary for beginners" in the following link: www.vcrey.com/rosary-book

Some sacrifices that you can do include:

- Not drinking water or liquids during a meal.
- Abstain from meat on Fridays (which is also required by Holy Mother Church).
- Not eating candy or dessert during one day.
- Take a cold shower.
- Not eating meat in saturdays in honor of the Blessed Virgin Mary.
- Keep one hour of silence.
- Do not buy or sell in Sunday (which is also a commandment).
- Give food to the hungry.
- Give water to the thirsty.
- Visit the sick, and confort them.

IMPORTANT NOTES

☐ _____
☐ _____
☐ _____
☐ _____
☐ _____
☐ _____
☐ _____
☐ _____
☐ _____

YOUR SOUL'S GROWTH PLANNER

LONG LIVE CHRIST THE KING!

VIVA
CRISTO
REY.ORG

DATE: MONTH   DAY   YEAR

GOALS OF THE DAY

PRAYING THE ROSARY OF 15 DECADES.................. ☐

READING THE HOLY BIBLE (15 MINUTES)............... ☐

DAILY SACRIFICES... ☐

☐ _____   ☐ _____
☐ _____   ☐ _____
☐ _____   ☐ _____
☐ _____   ☐ _____
☐ _____   ☐ _____
☐ _____   ☐ _____
☐ _____   ☐ _____
☐ _____   ☐ _____
☐ _____   ☐ _____

SUGGESTIONS

If you don't know how to pray the Holy Rosary, you can get our book "Rosary for beginners" in the following link: www.vcrey.com/rosary-book

Some sacrifices that you can do include:

- Not drinking water or liquids during a meal.
- Abstain from meat on Fridays (which is also required by Holy Mother Church).
- Not eating candy or dessert during one day.
- Take a cold shower.
- Not eating meat in saturdays in honor of the Blessed Virgin Mary.
- Keep one hour of silence.
- Do not buy or sell in Sunday (which is also a commandment).
- Give food to the hungry.
- Give water to the thirsty.
- Visit the sick, and confort them.

IMPORTANT NOTES

☐ _____
☐ _____
☐ _____
☐ _____
☐ _____
☐ _____
☐ _____
☐ _____
☐ _____

YOUR SOUL'S GROWTH PLANNER

LONG LIVE CHRIST THE KING!

DATE: MONTH   DAY   YEAR

GOALS OF THE DAY

PRAYING THE ROSARY OF 15 DECADES................... ☐

READING THE HOLY BIBLE (15 MINUTES)................ ☐

DAILY SACRIFICES... ☐

☐ _____   ☐ _____
☐ _____   ☐ _____
☐ _____   ☐ _____
☐ _____   ☐ _____
☐ _____   ☐ _____
☐ _____   ☐ _____
☐ _____   ☐ _____
☐ _____   ☐ _____
☐ _____   ☐ _____

SUGGESTIONS

If you don't know how to pray the Holy Rosary, you can get our book "Rosary for beginners" in the following link: www.vcrey.com/rosary-book

Some sacrifices that you can do include:

- Not drinking water or liquids during a meal.
- Abstain from meat on Fridays (which is also required by Holy Mother Church).
- Not eating candy or dessert during one day.
- Take a cold shower.
- Not eating meat in saturdays in honor of the Blessed Virgin Mary.
- Keep one hour of silence.
- Do not buy or sell in Sunday (which is also a commandment).
- Give food to the hungry.
- Give water to the thirsty.
- Visit the sick, and confort them.

IMPORTANT NOTES

☐ _____
☐ _____
☐ _____
☐ _____
☐ _____
☐ _____
☐ _____
☐ _____
☐ _____

YOUR SOUL'S GROWTH PLANNER

LONG LIVE CHRIST THE KING!

VIVA
CRISTO
REY.ORG

DATE: MONTH   DAY   YEAR

GOALS OF THE DAY

PRAYING THE ROSARY OF 15 DECADES................... ☐

READING THE HOLY BIBLE (15 MINUTES)............... ☐

DAILY SACRIFICES.. ☐

☐ _____   ☐ _____

☐ _____   ☐ _____

☐ _____   ☐ _____

☐ _____   ☐ _____

☐ _____   ☐ _____

☐ _____   ☐ _____

☐ _____   ☐ _____

☐ _____   ☐ _____

☐ _____   ☐ _____

SUGGESTIONS

If you don't know how to pray the Holy Rosary, you can get our book "Rosary for beginners" in the following link: www.vcrey.com/rosary-book

Some sacrifices that you can do include:

- Not drinking water or liquids during a meal.
- Abstain from meat on Fridays (which is also required by Holy Mother Church).
- Not eating candy or dessert during one day.
- Take a cold shower.
- Not eating meat in saturdays in honor of the Blessed Virgin Mary.
- Keep one hour of silence.
- Do not buy or sell in Sunday (which is also a commandment).
- Give food to the hungry.
- Give water to the thirsty.
- Visit the sick, and confort them.

IMPORTANT NOTES

☐ _____

☐ _____

☐ _____

☐ _____

☐ _____

☐ _____

☐ _____

☐ _____

☐ _____

YOUR SOUL'S GROWTH PLANNER

LONG LIVE CHRIST THE KING!

VIVA
CRISTO
REY.ORG

DATE: MONTH   DAY   YEAR

GOALS OF THE DAY

PRAYING THE ROSARY OF 15 DECADES................... ☐

READING THE HOLY BIBLE (15 MINUTES)............... ☐

DAILY SACRIFICES... ☐

☐ _____   ☐ _____
☐ _____   ☐ _____
☐ _____   ☐ _____
☐ _____   ☐ _____
☐ _____   ☐ _____
☐ _____   ☐ _____
☐ _____   ☐ _____
☐ _____   ☐ _____
☐ _____   ☐ _____

SUGGESTIONS

If you don't know how to pray the Holy Rosary, you can get our book "Rosary for beginners" in the following link: www.vcrey.com/rosary-book

Some sacrifices that you can do include:

- Not drinking water or liquids during a meal.
- Abstain from meat on Fridays (which is also required by Holy Mother Church).
- Not eating candy or dessert during one day.
- Take a cold shower.
- Not eating meat in saturdays in honor of the Blessed Virgin Mary.
- Keep one hour of silence.
- Do not buy or sell in Sunday (which is also a commandment).
- Give food to the hungry.
- Give water to the thirsty.
- Visit the sick, and confort them.

IMPORTANT NOTES

☐ _____
☐ _____
☐ _____
☐ _____
☐ _____
☐ _____
☐ _____
☐ _____
☐ _____

YOUR SOUL'S GROWTH PLANNER

LONG LIVE CHRIST THE KING!

VIVA
CRISTO
REY.ORG

DATE: MONTH   DAY   YEAR

GOALS OF THE DAY

PRAYING THE ROSARY OF 15 DECADES.................. ☐

READING THE HOLY BIBLE (15 MINUTES)............... ☐

DAILY SACRIFICES... ☐

☐ _____   ☐ _____
☐ _____   ☐ _____
☐ _____   ☐ _____
☐ _____   ☐ _____
☐ _____   ☐ _____
☐ _____   ☐ _____
☐ _____   ☐ _____
☐ _____   ☐ _____
☐ _____   ☐ _____

SUGGESTIONS

If you don't know how to pray the Holy Rosary, you can get our book "Rosary for beginners" in the following link: www.vcrey.com/rosary-book

Some sacrifices that you can do include:

- Not drinking water or liquids during a meal.
- Abstain from meat on Fridays (which is also required by Holy Mother Church).
- Not eating candy or dessert during one day.
- Take a cold shower.
- Not eating meat in saturdays in honor of the Blessed Virgin Mary.
- Keep one hour of silence.
- Do not buy or sell in Sunday (which is also a commandment).
- Give food to the hungry.
- Give water to the thirsty.
- Visit the sick, and confort them.

IMPORTANT NOTES

☐ _____
☐ _____
☐ _____
☐ _____
☐ _____
☐ _____
☐ _____
☐ _____
☐ _____

YOUR SOUL'S GROWTH PLANNER

LONG LIVE CHRIST THE KING!

VIVA CRISTO REY.ORG

DATE: MONTH   DAY   YEAR

GOALS OF THE DAY

PRAYING THE ROSARY OF 15 DECADES.................. ☐

READING THE HOLY BIBLE (15 MINUTES)............... ☐

DAILY SACRIFICES... ☐

☐ _____   ☐ _____

☐ _____   ☐ _____

☐ _____   ☐ _____

☐ _____   ☐ _____

☐ _____   ☐ _____

☐ _____   ☐ _____

☐ _____   ☐ _____

☐ _____   ☐ _____

☐ _____   ☐ _____

SUGGESTIONS

If you don't know how to pray the Holy Rosary, you can get our book "Rosary for beginners" in the following link: www.vcrey.com/rosary-book

Some sacrifices that you can do include:

- Not drinking water or liquids during a meal.
- Abstain from meat on Fridays (which is also required by Holy Mother Church).
- Not eating candy or dessert during one day.
- Take a cold shower.
- Not eating meat in saturdays in honor of the Blessed Virgin Mary.
- Keep one hour of silence.
- Do not buy or sell in Sunday (which is also a commandment).
- Give food to the hungry.
- Give water to the thirsty.
- Visit the sick, and confort them.

IMPORTANT NOTES

☐ _____

☐ _____

☐ _____

☐ _____

☐ _____

☐ _____

☐ _____

☐ _____

☐ _____

YOUR SOUL'S GROWTH PLANNER

LONG LIVE CHRIST THE KING!

VIVA CRISTO REY.ORG

DATE: MONTH   DAY   YEAR

GOALS OF THE DAY

PRAYING THE ROSARY OF 15 DECADES.................. ☐

READING THE HOLY BIBLE (15 MINUTES)................ ☐

DAILY SACRIFICES... ☐

☐ _____   ☐ _____
☐ _____   ☐ _____
☐ _____   ☐ _____

☐ _____   ☐ _____
☐ _____   ☐ _____
☐ _____   ☐ _____
☐ _____   ☐ _____

☐ _____   ☐ _____
☐ _____   ☐ _____

SUGGESTIONS

If you don't know how to pray the Holy Rosary, you can get our book "Rosary for beginners" in the following link: www.vcrey.com/rosary-book

Some sacrifices that you can do include:

- Not drinking water or liquids during a meal.
- Abstain from meat on Fridays (which is also required by Holy Mother Church).
- Not eating candy or dessert during one day.
- Take a cold shower.
- Not eating meat in saturdays in honor of the Blessed Virgin Mary.
- Keep one hour of silence.
- Do not buy or sell in Sunday (which is also a commandment).
- Give food to the hungry.
- Give water to the thirsty.
- Visit the sick, and confort them.

IMPORTANT NOTES

☐ _____
☐ _____
☐ _____
☐ _____
☐ _____
☐ _____
☐ _____
☐ _____
☐ _____

YOUR SOUL'S GROWTH PLANNER

LONG LIVE CHRIST THE KING!

VIVA CRISTO REY.ORG

DATE: MONTH   DAY   YEAR

GOALS OF THE DAY

PRAYING THE ROSARY OF 15 DECADES................... ☐

READING THE HOLY BIBLE (15 MINUTES)............... ☐

DAILY SACRIFICES.. ☐

☐ _____   ☐ _____
☐ _____   ☐ _____
☐ _____   ☐ _____

☐ _____   ☐ _____
☐ _____   ☐ _____
☐ _____   ☐ _____
☐ _____   ☐ _____

☐ _____   ☐ _____
☐ _____   ☐ _____

SUGGESTIONS

If you don't know how to pray the Holy Rosary, you can get our book "Rosary for beginners" in the following link: www.vcrey.com/rosary-book

Some sacrifices that you can do include:

- Not drinking water or liquids during a meal.
- Abstain from meat on Fridays (which is also required by Holy Mother Church).
- Not eating candy or dessert during one day.
- Take a cold shower.
- Not eating meat in saturdays in honor of the Blessed Virgin Mary.
- Keep one hour of silence.
- Do not buy or sell in Sunday (which is also a commandment).
- Give food to the hungry.
- Give water to the thirsty.
- Visit the sick, and confort them.

IMPORTANT NOTES

☐ _____
☐ _____
☐ _____
☐ _____
☐ _____
☐ _____
☐ _____
☐ _____
☐ _____

YOUR SOUL'S GROWTH PLANNER

LONG LIVE CHRIST THE KING!

VIVA
CRISTO
REY.ORG

DATE: MONTH   DAY   YEAR

GOALS OF THE DAY

PRAYING THE ROSARY OF 15 DECADES................... ☐

READING THE HOLY BIBLE (15 MINUTES)............... ☐

DAILY SACRIFICES... ☐

☐ _____   ☐ _____
☐ _____   ☐ _____
☐ _____   ☐ _____
☐ _____   ☐ _____
☐ _____   ☐ _____
☐ _____   ☐ _____
☐ _____   ☐ _____
☐ _____   ☐ _____
☐ _____   ☐ _____

SUGGESTIONS

If you don't know how to pray the Holy Rosary, you can get our book "Rosary for beginners" in the following link: www.vcrey.com/rosary-book

Some sacrifices that you can do include:

- Not drinking water or liquids during a meal.
- Abstain from meat on Fridays (which is also required by Holy Mother Church).
- Not eating candy or dessert during one day.
- Take a cold shower.
- Not eating meat in saturdays in honor of the Blessed Virgin Mary.
- Keep one hour of silence.
- Do not buy or sell in Sunday (which is also a commandment).
- Give food to the hungry.
- Give water to the thirsty.
- Visit the sick, and confort them.

IMPORTANT NOTES

☐ _____
☐ _____
☐ _____
☐ _____
☐ _____
☐ _____
☐ _____
☐ _____
☐ _____

YOUR SOUL'S GROWTH PLANNER

LONG LIVE CHRIST THE KING!

VIVA CRISTO REY.ORG

DATE: MONTH   DAY   YEAR

GOALS OF THE DAY

PRAYING THE ROSARY OF 15 DECADES.................. ☐

READING THE HOLY BIBLE (15 MINUTES).............. ☐

DAILY SACRIFICES.. ☐

☐ _____   ☐ _____
☐ _____   ☐ _____
☐ _____   ☐ _____

☐ _____   ☐ _____
☐ _____   ☐ _____
☐ _____   ☐ _____

☐ _____   ☐ _____

☐ _____   ☐ _____
☐ _____   ☐ _____

SUGGESTIONS

If you don't know how to pray the Holy Rosary, you can get our book "Rosary for beginners" in the following link: www.vcrey.com/rosary-book

Some sacrifices that you can do include:

- Not drinking water or liquids during a meal.
- Abstain from meat on Fridays (which is also required by Holy Mother Church).
- Not eating candy or dessert during one day.
- Take a cold shower.
- Not eating meat in saturdays in honor of the Blessed Virgin Mary.
- Keep one hour of silence.
- Do not buy or sell in Sunday (which is also a commandment).
- Give food to the hungry.
- Give water to the thirsty.
- Visit the sick, and confort them.

IMPORTANT NOTES

☐ _____
☐ _____
☐ _____
☐ _____
☐ _____
☐ _____
☐ _____
☐ _____
☐ _____

YOUR SOUL'S GROWTH PLANNER

LONG LIVE CHRIST THE KING!

VIVA CRISTO REY.ORG

DATE: MONTH   DAY   YEAR

GOALS OF THE DAY

PRAYING THE ROSARY OF 15 DECADES................... ☐

READING THE HOLY BIBLE (15 MINUTES)................ ☐

DAILY SACRIFICES... ☐

☐ _____   ☐ _____
☐ _____   ☐ _____
☐ _____   ☐ _____
☐ _____   ☐ _____
☐ _____   ☐ _____
☐ _____   ☐ _____
☐ _____   ☐ _____
☐ _____   ☐ _____
☐ _____   ☐ _____

SUGGESTIONS

If you don't know how to pray the Holy Rosary, you can get our book "Rosary for beginners" in the following link: www.vcrey.com/rosary-book

Some sacrifices that you can do include:

- Not drinking water or liquids during a meal.
- Abstain from meat on Fridays (which is also required by Holy Mother Church).
- Not eating candy or dessert during one day.
- Take a cold shower.
- Not eating meat in saturdays in honor of the Blessed Virgin Mary.
- Keep one hour of silence.
- Do not buy or sell in Sunday (which is also a commandment).
- Give food to the hungry.
- Give water to the thirsty.
- Visit the sick, and confort them.

IMPORTANT NOTES

☐ _____
☐ _____
☐ _____
☐ _____
☐ _____
☐ _____
☐ _____
☐ _____
☐ _____

YOUR SOUL'S GROWTH PLANNER

LONG LIVE CHRIST THE KING!

VIVA CRISTO REY.ORG

DATE: MONTH   DAY   YEAR

GOALS OF THE DAY

PRAYING THE ROSARY OF 15 DECADES................... ☐

READING THE HOLY BIBLE (15 MINUTES)............... ☐

DAILY SACRIFICES.. ☐

☐ _____   ☐ _____
☐ _____   ☐ _____
☐ _____   ☐ _____
☐ _____   ☐ _____
☐ _____   ☐ _____
☐ _____   ☐ _____
☐ _____   ☐ _____
☐ _____   ☐ _____
☐ _____   ☐ _____

SUGGESTIONS

If you don't know how to pray the Holy Rosary, you can get our book "Rosary for beginners" in the following link: www.vcrey.com/rosary-book

Some sacrifices that you can do include:

- Not drinking water or liquids during a meal.
- Abstain from meat on Fridays (which is also required by Holy Mother Church).
- Not eating candy or dessert during one day.
- Take a cold shower.
- Not eating meat in saturdays in honor of the Blessed Virgin Mary.
- Keep one hour of silence.
- Do not buy or sell in Sunday (which is also a commandment).
- Give food to the hungry.
- Give water to the thirsty.
- Visit the sick, and confort them.

IMPORTANT NOTES

☐ _____
☐ _____
☐ _____
☐ _____
☐ _____
☐ _____
☐ _____
☐ _____
☐ _____

YOUR SOUL'S GROWTH PLANNER

LONG LIVE CHRIST THE KING!

VIVA CRISTO REY.ORG

DATE: MONTH   DAY   YEAR

GOALS OF THE DAY

PRAYING THE ROSARY OF 15 DECADES................... ☐

READING THE HOLY BIBLE (15 MINUTES)................ ☐

DAILY SACRIFICES... ☐

☐ _____   ☐ _____

☐ _____   ☐ _____

☐ _____   ☐ _____

☐ _____   ☐ _____

☐ _____   ☐ _____

☐ _____   ☐ _____

☐ _____   ☐ _____

☐ _____   ☐ _____

☐ _____   ☐ _____

SUGGESTIONS

If you don't know how to pray the Holy Rosary, you can get our book "Rosary for beginners" in the following link: www.vcrey.com/rosary-book

Some sacrifices that you can do include:

- Not drinking water or liquids during a meal.
- Abstain from meat on Fridays (which is also required by Holy Mother Church).
- Not eating candy or dessert during one day.
- Take a cold shower.
- Not eating meat in saturdays in honor of the Blessed Virgin Mary.
- Keep one hour of silence.
- Do not buy or sell in Sunday (which is also a commandment).
- Give food to the hungry.
- Give water to the thirsty.
- Visit the sick, and confort them.

IMPORTANT NOTES

☐ _____

☐ _____

☐ _____

☐ _____

☐ _____

☐ _____

☐ _____

☐ _____

☐ _____

☐ _____

YOUR SOUL'S GROWTH PLANNER

LONG LIVE CHRIST THE KING!

VIVA
CRISTO
REY.ORG

DATE: MONTH   DAY   YEAR

GOALS OF THE DAY

PRAYING THE ROSARY OF 15 DECADES................... ☐

READING THE HOLY BIBLE (15 MINUTES)............... ☐

DAILY SACRIFICES... ☐

☐ _____   ☐ _____
☐ _____   ☐ _____
☐ _____   ☐ _____
☐ _____   ☐ _____
☐ _____   ☐ _____
☐ _____   ☐ _____
☐ _____   ☐ _____
☐ _____   ☐ _____

SUGGESTIONS

If you don't know how to pray the Holy Rosary, you can get our book "Rosary for beginners" in the following link: www.vcrey.com/rosary-book

Some sacrifices that you can do include:

- Not drinking water or liquids during a meal.
- Abstain from meat on Fridays (which is also required by Holy Mother Church).
- Not eating candy or dessert during one day.
- Take a cold shower.
- Not eating meat in saturdays in honor of the Blessed Virgin Mary.
- Keep one hour of silence.
- Do not buy or sell in Sunday (which is also a commandment).
- Give food to the hungry.
- Give water to the thirsty.
- Visit the sick, and confort them.

IMPORTANT NOTES

☐ _____
☐ _____
☐ _____
☐ _____
☐ _____
☐ _____
☐ _____
☐ _____
☐ _____

YOUR SOUL'S GROWTH PLANNER

LONG LIVE CHRIST THE KING!

VIVA CRISTO REY.ORG

DATE: MONTH   DAY   YEAR

GOALS OF THE DAY

PRAYING THE ROSARY OF 15 DECADES.................... ☐

READING THE HOLY BIBLE (15 MINUTES)................ ☐

DAILY SACRIFICES... ☐

☐ _____   ☐ _____
☐ _____   ☐ _____
☐ _____   ☐ _____
☐ _____   ☐ _____
☐ _____   ☐ _____
☐ _____   ☐ _____
☐ _____   ☐ _____
☐ _____   ☐ _____
☐ _____   ☐ _____

SUGGESTIONS

If you don't know how to pray the Holy Rosary, you can get our book "Rosary for beginners" in the following link: www.vcrey.com/rosary-book

Some sacrifices that you can do include:

- Not drinking water or liquids during a meal.
- Abstain from meat on Fridays (which is also required by Holy Mother Church).
- Not eating candy or dessert during one day.
- Take a cold shower.
- Not eating meat in saturdays in honor of the Blessed Virgin Mary.
- Keep one hour of silence.
- Do not buy or sell in Sunday (which is also a commandment).
- Give food to the hungry.
- Give water to the thirsty.
- Visit the sick, and confort them.

IMPORTANT NOTES

☐ _____
☐ _____
☐ _____
☐ _____
☐ _____
☐ _____
☐ _____
☐ _____
☐ _____

YOUR SOUL'S GROWTH PLANNER

LONG LIVE CHRIST THE KING!

VIVA CRISTO REY.ORG

DATE: MONTH   DAY   YEAR

GOALS OF THE DAY

PRAYING THE ROSARY OF 15 DECADES................... ☐

READING THE HOLY BIBLE (15 MINUTES)................ ☐

DAILY SACRIFICES.. ☐

☐ _____   ☐ _____
☐ _____   ☐ _____
☐ _____   ☐ _____
☐ _____   ☐ _____
☐ _____   ☐ _____
☐ _____   ☐ _____
☐ _____   ☐ _____
☐ _____   ☐ _____
☐ _____   ☐ _____

SUGGESTIONS

If you don't know how to pray the Holy Rosary, you can get our book "Rosary for beginners" in the following link: www.vcrey.com/rosary-book

Some sacrifices that you can do include:

- Not drinking water or liquids during a meal.
- Abstain from meat on Fridays (which is also required by Holy Mother Church).
- Not eating candy or dessert during one day.
- Take a cold shower.
- Not eating meat in saturdays in honor of the Blessed Virgin Mary.
- Keep one hour of silence.
- Do not buy or sell in Sunday (which is also a commandment).
- Give food to the hungry.
- Give water to the thirsty.
- Visit the sick, and confort them.

IMPORTANT NOTES

☐ _____
☐ _____
☐ _____
☐ _____
☐ _____
☐ _____
☐ _____
☐ _____
☐ _____

YOUR SOUL'S GROWTH PLANNER

LONG LIVE CHRIST THE KING!

VIVA
CRISTO
REY.ORG

DATE: MONTH   DAY   YEAR

GOALS OF THE DAY

PRAYING THE ROSARY OF 15 DECADES................... ☐

READING THE HOLY BIBLE (15 MINUTES)............... ☐

DAILY SACRIFICES.. ☐

☐ _____   ☐ _____
☐ _____   ☐ _____
☐ _____   ☐ _____
☐ _____   ☐ _____
☐ _____   ☐ _____
☐ _____   ☐ _____
☐ _____   ☐ _____
☐ _____   ☐ _____
☐ _____   ☐ _____

SUGGESTIONS

If you don't know how to pray the Holy Rosary, you can get our book "Rosary for beginners" in the following link: www.vcrey.com/rosary-book

Some sacrifices that you can do include:

- Not drinking water or liquids during a meal.
- Abstain from meat on Fridays (which is also required by Holy Mother Church).
- Not eating candy or dessert during one day.
- Take a cold shower.
- Not eating meat in saturdays in honor of the Blessed Virgin Mary.
- Keep one hour of silence.
- Do not buy or sell in Sunday (which is also a commandment).
- Give food to the hungry.
- Give water to the thirsty.
- Visit the sick, and confort them.

IMPORTANT NOTES

☐ _____
☐ _____
☐ _____
☐ _____
☐ _____
☐ _____
☐ _____
☐ _____
☐ _____

YOUR SOUL'S GROWTH PLANNER

LONG LIVE CHRIST THE KING!

VIVA
CRISTO
REY.ORG

DATE: MONTH   DAY   YEAR

GOALS OF THE DAY

PRAYING THE ROSARY OF 15 DECADES................... ☐

READING THE HOLY BIBLE (15 MINUTES)................ ☐

DAILY SACRIFICES.. ☐

☐ _____   ☐ _____
☐ _____   ☐ _____
☐ _____   ☐ _____
☐ _____   ☐ _____
☐ _____   ☐ _____
☐ _____   ☐ _____
☐ _____   ☐ _____
☐ _____   ☐ _____
☐ _____   ☐ _____

SUGGESTIONS

If you don't know how to pray the Holy Rosary, you can get our book "Rosary for beginners" in the following link: www.vcrey.com/rosary-book

Some sacrifices that you can do include:

- Not drinking water or liquids during a meal.
- Abstain from meat on Fridays (which is also required by Holy Mother Church).
- Not eating candy or dessert during one day.
- Take a cold shower.
- Not eating meat in saturdays in honor of the Blessed Virgin Mary.
- Keep one hour of silence.
- Do not buy or sell in Sunday (which is also a commandment).
- Give food to the hungry.
- Give water to the thirsty.
- Visit the sick, and confort them.

IMPORTANT NOTES

☐ _____
☐ _____
☐ _____
☐ _____
☐ _____
☐ _____
☐ _____
☐ _____
☐ _____

YOUR SOUL'S GROWTH PLANNER

LONG LIVE CHRIST THE KING!

VIVA
CRISTO
REY.ORG

DATE: MONTH   DAY   YEAR

GOALS OF THE DAY

PRAYING THE ROSARY OF 15 DECADES.................. ☐

READING THE HOLY BIBLE (15 MINUTES)................ ☐

DAILY SACRIFICES....................................... ☐

☐ _____   ☐ _____

☐ _____   ☐ _____

☐ _____   ☐ _____

☐ _____   ☐ _____

☐ _____   ☐ _____

☐ _____   ☐ _____

☐ _____   ☐ _____

☐ _____   ☐ _____

☐ _____   ☐ _____

SUGGESTIONS

If you don't know how to pray the Holy Rosary, you can get our book "Rosary for beginners" in the following link: www.vcrey.com/rosary-book

Some sacrifices that you can do include:

- Not drinking water or liquids during a meal.
- Abstain from meat on Fridays (which is also required by Holy Mother Church).
- Not eating candy or dessert during one day.
- Take a cold shower.
- Not eating meat in saturdays in honor of the Blessed Virgin Mary.
- Keep one hour of silence.
- Do not buy or sell in Sunday (which is also a commandment).
- Give food to the hungry.
- Give water to the thirsty.
- Visit the sick, and confort them.

IMPORTANT NOTES

☐ _____

☐ _____

☐ _____

☐ _____

☐ _____

☐ _____

☐ _____

☐ _____

☐ _____

YOUR SOUL'S GROWTH PLANNER

LONG LIVE CHRIST THE KING!

VIVA CRISTO REY.ORG

DATE: MONTH   DAY   YEAR

GOALS OF THE DAY

PRAYING THE ROSARY OF 15 DECADES................... ☐

READING THE HOLY BIBLE (15 MINUTES)................ ☐

DAILY SACRIFICES.. ☐

☐ _____   ☐ _____
☐ _____   ☐ _____
☐ _____   ☐ _____
☐ _____   ☐ _____
☐ _____   ☐ _____
☐ _____   ☐ _____
☐ _____   ☐ _____
☐ _____   ☐ _____
☐ _____   ☐ _____

SUGGESTIONS

If you don't know how to pray the Holy Rosary, you can get our book "Rosary for beginners" in the following link: www.vcrey.com/rosary-book

Some sacrifices that you can do include:

- Not drinking water or liquids during a meal.
- Abstain from meat on Fridays (which is also required by Holy Mother Church).
- Not eating candy or dessert during one day.
- Take a cold shower.
- Not eating meat in saturdays in honor of the Blessed Virgin Mary.
- Keep one hour of silence.
- Do not buy or sell in Sunday (which is also a commandment).
- Give food to the hungry.
- Give water to the thirsty.
- Visit the sick, and confort them.

IMPORTANT NOTES

☐ _____
☐ _____
☐ _____
☐ _____
☐ _____
☐ _____
☐ _____
☐ _____
☐ _____

YOUR SOUL'S GROWTH PLANNER

LONG LIVE CHRIST THE KING!

VIVA CRISTO REY.ORG

DATE: MONTH   DAY   YEAR

GOALS OF THE DAY

PRAYING THE ROSARY OF 15 DECADES................... ☐

READING THE HOLY BIBLE (15 MINUTES)................ ☐

DAILY SACRIFICES.. ☐

☐ _____   ☐ _____
☐ _____   ☐ _____
☐ _____   ☐ _____
☐ _____   ☐ _____
☐ _____   ☐ _____
☐ _____   ☐ _____
☐ _____   ☐ _____
☐ _____   ☐ _____
☐ _____   ☐ _____

SUGGESTIONS

If you don't know how to pray the Holy Rosary, you can get our book "Rosary for beginners" in the following link: www.vcrey.com/rosary-book

Some sacrifices that you can do include:

- Not drinking water or liquids during a meal.
- Abstain from meat on Fridays (which is also required by Holy Mother Church).
- Not eating candy or dessert during one day.
- Take a cold shower.
- Not eating meat in saturdays in honor of the Blessed Virgin Mary.
- Keep one hour of silence.
- Do not buy or sell in Sunday (which is also a commandment).
- Give food to the hungry.
- Give water to the thirsty.
- Visit the sick, and confort them.

IMPORTANT NOTES

☐ _____
☐ _____
☐ _____
☐ _____
☐ _____
☐ _____
☐ _____
☐ _____
☐ _____

YOUR SOUL'S GROWTH PLANNER

LONG LIVE CHRIST THE KING!

VIVA
CRISTO
REY.ORG

DATE: MONTH   DAY   YEAR

GOALS OF THE DAY

PRAYING THE ROSARY OF 15 DECADES.................. ☐

READING THE HOLY BIBLE (15 MINUTES)............... ☐

DAILY SACRIFICES.. ☐

☐ _____   ☐ _____
☐ _____   ☐ _____
☐ _____   ☐ _____
☐ _____   ☐ _____
☐ _____   ☐ _____
☐ _____   ☐ _____
☐ _____   ☐ _____
☐ _____   ☐ _____
☐ _____   ☐ _____

SUGGESTIONS

If you don't know how to pray the Holy Rosary, you can get our book "Rosary for beginners" in the following link: www.vcrey.com/rosary-book

Some sacrifices that you can do include:

- Not drinking water or liquids during a meal.
- Abstain from meat on Fridays (which is also required by Holy Mother Church).
- Not eating candy or dessert during one day.
- Take a cold shower.
- Not eating meat in saturdays in honor of the Blessed Virgin Mary.
- Keep one hour of silence.
- Do not buy or sell in Sunday (which is also a commandment).
- Give food to the hungry.
- Give water to the thirsty.
- Visit the sick, and confort them.

IMPORTANT NOTES

☐ _____
☐ _____
☐ _____
☐ _____
☐ _____
☐ _____
☐ _____
☐ _____
☐ _____

YOUR SOUL'S GROWTH PLANNER

LONG LIVE CHRIST THE KING!

VIVA
CRISTO
REY.ORG

DATE: MONTH   DAY   YEAR

GOALS OF THE DAY

PRAYING THE ROSARY OF 15 DECADES................... ☐

READING THE HOLY BIBLE (15 MINUTES)............... ☐

DAILY SACRIFICES.. ☐

☐ _____   ☐ _____
☐ _____   ☐ _____
☐ _____   ☐ _____
☐ _____   ☐ _____
☐ _____   ☐ _____
☐ _____   ☐ _____
☐ _____   ☐ _____
☐ _____   ☐ _____
☐ _____   ☐ _____

SUGGESTIONS

If you don't know how to pray the Holy Rosary, you can get our book "Rosary for beginners" in the following link: www.vcrey.com/rosary-book

Some sacrifices that you can do include:

- Not drinking water or liquids during a meal.
- Abstain from meat on Fridays (which is also required by Holy Mother Church).
- Not eating candy or dessert during one day.
- Take a cold shower.
- Not eating meat in saturdays in honor of the Blessed Virgin Mary.
- Keep one hour of silence.
- Do not buy or sell in Sunday (which is also a commandment).
- Give food to the hungry.
- Give water to the thirsty.
- Visit the sick, and confort them.

IMPORTANT NOTES

☐ _____
☐ _____
☐ _____
☐ _____
☐ _____
☐ _____
☐ _____
☐ _____
☐ _____

YOUR SOUL'S GROWTH PLANNER

LONG LIVE CHRIST THE KING!

VIVA
CRISTO
REY.ORG

DATE: MONTH   DAY   YEAR

GOALS OF THE DAY

PRAYING THE ROSARY OF 15 DECADES.................... ☐

READING THE HOLY BIBLE (15 MINUTES)............... ☐

DAILY SACRIFICES... ☐

☐ _____   ☐ _____
☐ _____   ☐ _____
☐ _____   ☐ _____
☐ _____   ☐ _____
☐ _____   ☐ _____
☐ _____   ☐ _____
☐ _____   ☐ _____
☐ _____   ☐ _____
☐ _____   ☐ _____

SUGGESTIONS

If you don't know how to pray the Holy Rosary, you can get our book "Rosary for beginners" in the following link: www.vcrey.com/rosary-book

Some sacrifices that you can do include:

- Not drinking water or liquids during a meal.
- Abstain from meat on Fridays (which is also required by Holy Mother Church).
- Not eating candy or dessert during one day.
- Take a cold shower.
- Not eating meat in saturdays in honor of the Blessed Virgin Mary.
- Keep one hour of silence.
- Do not buy or sell in Sunday (which is also a commandment).
- Give food to the hungry.
- Give water to the thirsty.
- Visit the sick, and confort them.

IMPORTANT NOTES

☐ _____
☐ _____
☐ _____
☐ _____
☐ _____
☐ _____
☐ _____
☐ _____
☐ _____

YOUR SOUL'S GROWTH PLANNER

LONG LIVE CHRIST THE KING!

VIVA CRISTO REY.ORG

DATE: MONTH   DAY   YEAR

GOALS OF THE DAY

PRAYING THE ROSARY OF 15 DECADES................... ☐

READING THE HOLY BIBLE (15 MINUTES)............... ☐

DAILY SACRIFICES.. ☐

☐ _____   ☐ _____

☐ _____   ☐ _____

☐ _____   ☐ _____

☐ _____   ☐ _____

☐ _____   ☐ _____

☐ _____   ☐ _____

☐ _____   ☐ _____

☐ _____   ☐ _____

☐ _____   ☐ _____

SUGGESTIONS

If you don't know how to pray the Holy Rosary, you can get our book "Rosary for beginners" in the following link: www.vcrey.com/rosary-book

Some sacrifices that you can do include:

- Not drinking water or liquids during a meal.
- Abstain from meat on Fridays (which is also required by Holy Mother Church).
- Not eating candy or dessert during one day.
- Take a cold shower.
- Not eating meat in saturdays in honor of the Blessed Virgin Mary.
- Keep one hour of silence.
- Do not buy or sell in Sunday (which is also a commandment).
- Give food to the hungry.
- Give water to the thirsty.
- Visit the sick, and confort them.

IMPORTANT NOTES

☐ _____

☐ _____

☐ _____

☐ _____

☐ _____

☐ _____

☐ _____

☐ _____

☐ _____

YOUR SOUL'S GROWTH PLANNER

LONG LIVE CHRIST THE KING!

VIVA
CRISTO
REY.ORG

DATE: MONTH   DAY   YEAR

GOALS OF THE DAY

PRAYING THE ROSARY OF 15 DECADES................... ☐

READING THE HOLY BIBLE (15 MINUTES)............... ☐

DAILY SACRIFICES.. ☐

☐ _____   ☐ _____

☐ _____   ☐ _____

☐ _____   ☐ _____

☐ _____   ☐ _____

☐ _____   ☐ _____

☐ _____   ☐ _____

☐ _____   ☐ _____

☐ _____   ☐ _____

☐ _____   ☐ _____

IMPORTANT NOTES

☐ _____

☐ _____

☐ _____

☐ _____

☐ _____

☐ _____

☐ _____

☐ _____

☐ _____

YOUR SOUL'S GROWTH PLANNER

LONG LIVE CHRIST THE KING!

VIVA
CRISTO
REY.ORG

DATE: MONTH   DAY   YEAR

GOALS OF THE DAY

PRAYING THE ROSARY OF 15 DECADES................... ☐

READING THE HOLY BIBLE (15 MINUTES)................ ☐

DAILY SACRIFICES... ☐

☐ _____ ☐ _____

☐ _____ ☐ _____

☐ _____ ☐ _____

☐ _____ ☐ _____

☐ _____ ☐ _____
☐ _____ ☐ _____

☐ _____ ☐ _____

☐ _____ ☐ _____

☐ _____ ☐ _____

SUGGESTIONS

If you don't know how to pray the Holy Rosary, you can get our book "Rosary for beginners" in the following link: www.vcrey.com/rosary-book

Some sacrifices that you can do include:

- Not drinking water or liquids during a meal.
- Abstain from meat on Fridays (which is also required by Holy Mother Church).
- Not eating candy or dessert during one day.
- Take a cold shower.
- Not eating meat in saturdays in honor of the Blessed Virgin Mary.
- Keep one hour of silence.
- Do not buy or sell in Sunday (which is also a commandment).
- Give food to the hungry.
- Give water to the thirsty.
- Visit the sick, and confort them.

IMPORTANT NOTES

☐ _____

☐ _____

☐ _____

☐ _____

☐ _____

☐ _____

☐ _____

☐ _____

☐ _____

YOUR SOUL'S GROWTH PLANNER

LONG LIVE CHRIST THE KING!

VIVA CRISTO REY.ORG

DATE: MONTH   DAY   YEAR

GOALS OF THE DAY

PRAYING THE ROSARY OF 15 DECADES................... ☐

READING THE HOLY BIBLE (15 MINUTES)................ ☐

DAILY SACRIFICES.. ☐

☐ _____   ☐ _____
☐ _____   ☐ _____
☐ _____   ☐ _____
☐ _____   ☐ _____
☐ _____   ☐ _____
☐ _____   ☐ _____
☐ _____   ☐ _____
☐ _____   ☐ _____
☐ _____   ☐ _____

SUGGESTIONS

If you don't know how to pray the Holy Rosary, you can get our book "Rosary for beginners" in the following link: www.vcrey.com/rosary-book

Some sacrifices that you can do include:

- Not drinking water or liquids during a meal.
- Abstain from meat on Fridays (which is also required by Holy Mother Church).
- Not eating candy or dessert during one day.
- Take a cold shower.
- Not eating meat in saturdays in honor of the Blessed Virgin Mary.
- Keep one hour of silence.
- Do not buy or sell in Sunday (which is also a commandment).
- Give food to the hungry.
- Give water to the thirsty.
- Visit the sick, and confort them.

IMPORTANT NOTES

☐ _____
☐ _____
☐ _____
☐ _____
☐ _____
☐ _____
☐ _____
☐ _____
☐ _____

YOUR SOUL'S GROWTH PLANNER

LONG LIVE CHRIST THE KING!

VIVA CRISTO REY.ORG

DATE: MONTH   DAY   YEAR

GOALS OF THE DAY

PRAYING THE ROSARY OF 15 DECADES................... ☐

READING THE HOLY BIBLE (15 MINUTES)................ ☐

DAILY SACRIFICES.. ☐

☐ _____   ☐ _____
☐ _____   ☐ _____
☐ _____   ☐ _____
☐ _____   ☐ _____
☐ _____   ☐ _____
☐ _____   ☐ _____
☐ _____   ☐ _____
☐ _____   ☐ _____
☐ _____   ☐ _____

SUGGESTIONS

If you don't know how to pray the Holy Rosary, you can get our book "Rosary for beginners" in the following link: www.vcrey.com/rosary-book

Some sacrifices that you can do include:

- Not drinking water or liquids during a meal.
- Abstain from meat on Fridays (which is also required by Holy Mother Church).
- Not eating candy or dessert during one day.
- Take a cold shower.
- Not eating meat in saturdays in honor of the Blessed Virgin Mary.
- Keep one hour of silence.
- Do not buy or sell in Sunday (which is also a commandment).
- Give food to the hungry.
- Give water to the thirsty.
- Visit the sick, and confort them.

IMPORTANT NOTES

☐ _____
☐ _____
☐ _____
☐ _____
☐ _____
☐ _____
☐ _____
☐ _____
☐ _____

YOUR SOUL'S GROWTH PLANNER

LONG LIVE CHRIST THE KING!

VIVA CRISTO REY.ORG

DATE: MONTH   DAY   YEAR

GOALS OF THE DAY

PRAYING THE ROSARY OF 15 DECADES................... ☐

READING THE HOLY BIBLE (15 MINUTES)................ ☐

DAILY SACRIFICES... ☐

☐ _____   ☐ _____

☐ _____   ☐ _____

☐ _____   ☐ _____

☐ _____   ☐ _____

☐ _____   ☐ _____

☐ _____   ☐ _____

☐ _____   ☐ _____

☐ _____   ☐ _____

☐ _____   ☐ _____

SUGGESTIONS

If you don't know how to pray the Holy Rosary, you can get our book "Rosary for beginners" in the following link: www.vcrey.com/rosary-book

Some sacrifices that you can do include:

- Not drinking water or liquids during a meal.
- Abstain from meat on Fridays (which is also required by Holy Mother Church).
- Not eating candy or dessert during one day.
- Take a cold shower.
- Not eating meat in saturdays in honor of the Blessed Virgin Mary.
- Keep one hour of silence.
- Do not buy or sell in Sunday (which is also a commandment).
- Give food to the hungry.
- Give water to the thirsty.
- Visit the sick, and confort them.

IMPORTANT NOTES

☐ _____

☐ _____

☐ _____

☐ _____

☐ _____

☐ _____

☐ _____

☐ _____

☐ _____

YOUR SOUL'S GROWTH PLANNER

LONG LIVE CHRIST THE KING!

VIVA
CRISTO
REY.ORG

DATE: MONTH   DAY   YEAR

GOALS OF THE DAY

PRAYING THE ROSARY OF 15 DECADES................... ☐

READING THE HOLY BIBLE (15 MINUTES)................. ☐

DAILY SACRIFICES... ☐

☐ _____   ☐ _____

☐ _____   ☐ _____

☐ _____   ☐ _____

☐ _____   ☐ _____

☐ _____   ☐ _____

☐ _____   ☐ _____

☐ _____   ☐ _____

☐ _____   ☐ _____

☐ _____   ☐ _____

SUGGESTIONS

If you don't know how to pray the Holy Rosary, you can get our book "Rosary for beginners" in the following link: www.vcrey.com/rosary-book

Some sacrifices that you can do include:

- Not drinking water or liquids during a meal.
- Abstain from meat on Fridays (which is also required by Holy Mother Church).
- Not eating candy or dessert during one day.
- Take a cold shower.
- Not eating meat in saturdays in honor of the Blessed Virgin Mary.
- Keep one hour of silence.
- Do not buy or sell in Sunday (which is also a commandment).
- Give food to the hungry.
- Give water to the thirsty.
- Visit the sick, and confort them.

IMPORTANT NOTES

☐ _____

☐ _____

☐ _____

☐ _____

☐ _____

☐ _____

☐ _____

☐ _____

☐ _____

YOUR SOUL'S GROWTH PLANNER

LONG LIVE CHRIST THE KING!

VIVA CRISTO REY.ORG

DATE: MONTH   DAY   YEAR

GOALS OF THE DAY

PRAYING THE ROSARY OF 15 DECADES................... ☐

READING THE HOLY BIBLE (15 MINUTES)............... ☐

DAILY SACRIFICES... ☐

☐ _____   ☐ _____
☐ _____   ☐ _____
☐ _____   ☐ _____
☐ _____   ☐ _____
☐ _____   ☐ _____
☐ _____   ☐ _____
☐ _____   ☐ _____
☐ _____   ☐ _____
☐ _____   ☐ _____

SUGGESTIONS

If you don't know how to pray the Holy Rosary, you can get our book "Rosary for beginners" in the following link: www.vcrey.com/rosary-book

Some sacrifices that you can do include:

- Not drinking water or liquids during a meal.
- Abstain from meat on Fridays (which is also required by Holy Mother Church).
- Not eating candy or dessert during one day.
- Take a cold shower.
- Not eating meat in saturdays in honor of the Blessed Virgin Mary.
- Keep one hour of silence.
- Do not buy or sell in Sunday (which is also a commandment).
- Give food to the hungry.
- Give water to the thirsty.
- Visit the sick, and confort them.

IMPORTANT NOTES

☐ _____
☐ _____
☐ _____
☐ _____
☐ _____
☐ _____
☐ _____
☐ _____
☐ _____

YOUR SOUL'S GROWTH PLANNER

LONG LIVE CHRIST THE KING!

VIVA CRISTO REY.ORG

DATE: MONTH   DAY   YEAR

GOALS OF THE DAY

PRAYING THE ROSARY OF 15 DECADES................... ☐

READING THE HOLY BIBLE (15 MINUTES)................ ☐

DAILY SACRIFICES.. ☐

☐ _____   ☐ _____

☐ _____   ☐ _____

☐ _____   ☐ _____

☐ _____   ☐ _____

☐ _____   ☐ _____
☐ _____   ☐ _____

☐ _____   ☐ _____

☐ _____   ☐ _____

☐ _____   ☐ _____

SUGGESTIONS

If you don't know how to pray the Holy Rosary, you can get our book "Rosary for beginners" in the following link: www.vcrey.com/rosary-book

Some sacrifices that you can do include:

- Not drinking water or liquids during a meal.
- Abstain from meat on Fridays (which is also required by Holy Mother Church).
- Not eating candy or dessert during one day.
- Take a cold shower.
- Not eating meat in saturdays in honor of the Blessed Virgin Mary.
- Keep one hour of silence.
- Do not buy or sell in Sunday (which is also a commandment).
- Give food to the hungry.
- Give water to the thirsty.
- Visit the sick, and confort them.

IMPORTANT NOTES

☐ _____

☐ _____

☐ _____

☐ _____

☐ _____

☐ _____

☐ _____

☐ _____

☐ _____

YOUR SOUL'S GROWTH PLANNER

LONG LIVE CHRIST THE KING!

VIVA CRISTO REY.ORG

DATE: MONTH   DAY   YEAR

GOALS OF THE DAY

PRAYING THE ROSARY OF 15 DECADES.................. ☐

READING THE HOLY BIBLE (15 MINUTES)............... ☐

DAILY SACRIFICES... ☐

☐ _____   ☐ _____
☐ _____   ☐ _____
☐ _____   ☐ _____
☐ _____   ☐ _____
☐ _____   ☐ _____
☐ _____   ☐ _____
☐ _____   ☐ _____
☐ _____   ☐ _____
☐ _____   ☐ _____

SUGGESTIONS

If you don't know how to pray the Holy Rosary, you can get our book "Rosary for beginners" in the following link: www.vcrey.com/rosary-book

Some sacrifices that you can do include:

- Not drinking water or liquids during a meal.
- Abstain from meat on Fridays (which is also required by Holy Mother Church).
- Not eating candy or dessert during one day.
- Take a cold shower.
- Not eating meat in saturdays in honor of the Blessed Virgin Mary.
- Keep one hour of silence.
- Do not buy or sell in Sunday (which is also a commandment).
- Give food to the hungry.
- Give water to the thirsty.
- Visit the sick, and confort them.

IMPORTANT NOTES

☐ _____
☐ _____
☐ _____
☐ _____
☐ _____
☐ _____
☐ _____
☐ _____
☐ _____

YOUR SOUL'S GROWTH PLANNER

LONG LIVE CHRIST THE KING!

VIVA CRISTO REY.ORG

DATE: MONTH   DAY   YEAR

GOALS OF THE DAY

PRAYING THE ROSARY OF 15 DECADES.................. ☐

READING THE HOLY BIBLE (15 MINUTES)............... ☐

DAILY SACRIFICES... ☐

☐ _____   ☐ _____
☐ _____   ☐ _____
☐ _____   ☐ _____
☐ _____   ☐ _____
☐ _____   ☐ _____
☐ _____   ☐ _____
☐ _____   ☐ _____
☐ _____   ☐ _____
☐ _____   ☐ _____

SUGGESTIONS

If you don't know how to pray the Holy Rosary, you can get our book "Rosary for beginners" in the following link: www.vcrey.com/rosary-book

Some sacrifices that you can do include:

- Not drinking water or liquids during a meal.
- Abstain from meat on Fridays (which is also required by Holy Mother Church).
- Not eating candy or dessert during one day.
- Take a cold shower.
- Not eating meat in saturdays in honor of the Blessed Virgin Mary.
- Keep one hour of silence.
- Do not buy or sell in Sunday (which is also a commandment).
- Give food to the hungry.
- Give water to the thirsty.
- Visit the sick, and confort them.

IMPORTANT NOTES

☐ _____
☐ _____
☐ _____
☐ _____
☐ _____
☐ _____
☐ _____
☐ _____
☐ _____

YOUR SOUL'S GROWTH PLANNER

LONG LIVE CHRIST THE KING!

VIVA CRISTO REY.ORG

DATE: MONTH   DAY   YEAR

GOALS OF THE DAY

PRAYING THE ROSARY OF 15 DECADES................... ☐

READING THE HOLY BIBLE (15 MINUTES)............... ☐

DAILY SACRIFICES... ☐

☐ _____   ☐ _____
☐ _____   ☐ _____
☐ _____   ☐ _____
☐ _____   ☐ _____
☐ _____   ☐ _____
☐ _____   ☐ _____
☐ _____   ☐ _____
☐ _____   ☐ _____
☐ _____   ☐ _____

SUGGESTIONS

If you don't know how to pray the Holy Rosary, you can get our book "Rosary for beginners" in the following link: www.vcrey.com/rosary-book

Some sacrifices that you can do include:

- Not drinking water or liquids during a meal.
- Abstain from meat on Fridays (which is also required by Holy Mother Church).
- Not eating candy or dessert during one day.
- Take a cold shower.
- Not eating meat in saturdays in honor of the Blessed Virgin Mary.
- Keep one hour of silence.
- Do not buy or sell in Sunday (which is also a commandment).
- Give food to the hungry.
- Give water to the thirsty.
- Visit the sick, and confort them.

IMPORTANT NOTES

☐ _____
☐ _____
☐ _____
☐ _____
☐ _____
☐ _____
☐ _____
☐ _____
☐ _____

YOUR SOUL'S GROWTH PLANNER

LONG LIVE CHRIST THE KING!

VIVA CRISTO REY.ORG

DATE: MONTH   DAY   YEAR

GOALS OF THE DAY

PRAYING THE ROSARY OF 15 DECADES.................. ☐

READING THE HOLY BIBLE (15 MINUTES)............... ☐

DAILY SACRIFICES... ☐

☐ _____   ☐ _____

☐ _____   ☐ _____

☐ _____   ☐ _____

☐ _____   ☐ _____

☐ _____   ☐ _____

☐ _____   ☐ _____

☐ _____   ☐ _____

☐ _____   ☐ _____

☐ _____   ☐ _____

SUGGESTIONS

If you don't know how to pray the Holy Rosary, you can get our book "Rosary for beginners" in the following link: www.vcrey.com/rosary-book

Some sacrifices that you can do include:

- Not drinking water or liquids during a meal.
- Abstain from meat on Fridays (which is also required by Holy Mother Church).
- Not eating candy or dessert during one day.
- Take a cold shower.
- Not eating meat in saturdays in honor of the Blessed Virgin Mary.
- Keep one hour of silence.
- Do not buy or sell in Sunday (which is also a commandment).
- Give food to the hungry.
- Give water to the thirsty.
- Visit the sick, and confort them.

IMPORTANT NOTES

☐ _____

☐ _____

☐ _____

☐ _____

☐ _____

☐ _____

☐ _____

☐ _____

☐ _____

YOUR SOUL'S GROWTH PLANNER

LONG LIVE CHRIST THE KING!

DATE: MONTH   DAY   YEAR

GOALS OF THE DAY

PRAYING THE ROSARY OF 15 DECADES................... ☐

READING THE HOLY BIBLE (15 MINUTES)............... ☐

DAILY SACRIFICES.. ☐

☐ _____   ☐ _____
☐ _____   ☐ _____
☐ _____   ☐ _____
☐ _____   ☐ _____
☐ _____   ☐ _____
☐ _____
☐ _____   ☐ _____
☐ _____   ☐ _____
☐ _____

SUGGESTIONS

If you don't know how to pray the Holy Rosary, you can get our book "Rosary for beginners" in the following link: www.vcrey.com/rosary-book

Some sacrifices that you can do include:

- Not drinking water or liquids during a meal.
- Abstain from meat on Fridays (which is also required by Holy Mother Church).
- Not eating candy or dessert during one day.
- Take a cold shower.
- Not eating meat in saturdays in honor of the Blessed Virgin Mary.
- Keep one hour of silence.
- Do not buy or sell in Sunday (which is also a commandment).
- Give food to the hungry.
- Give water to the thirsty.
- Visit the sick, and confort them.

IMPORTANT NOTES

☐ _____
☐ _____
☐ _____
☐ _____
☐ _____
☐ _____
☐ _____
☐ _____
☐ _____

YOUR SOUL'S GROWTH PLANNER

LONG LIVE CHRIST THE KING!

VIVA CRISTO REY.ORG

DATE: MONTH   DAY   YEAR

GOALS OF THE DAY

PRAYING THE ROSARY OF 15 DECADES................... ☐

READING THE HOLY BIBLE (15 MINUTES)................ ☐

DAILY SACRIFICES.. ☐

☐ _____   ☐ _____

☐ _____   ☐ _____

☐ _____   ☐ _____

☐ _____   ☐ _____

☐ _____   ☐ _____

☐ _____   ☐ _____

☐ _____   ☐ _____

☐ _____   ☐ _____

☐ _____   ☐ _____

SUGGESTIONS

If you don't know how to pray the Holy Rosary, you can get our book "Rosary for beginners" in the following link: www.vcrey.com/rosary-book

Some sacrifices that you can do include:

- Not drinking water or liquids during a meal.
- Abstain from meat on Fridays (which is also required by Holy Mother Church).
- Not eating candy or dessert during one day.
- Take a cold shower.
- Not eating meat in saturdays in honor of the Blessed Virgin Mary.
- Keep one hour of silence.
- Do not buy or sell in Sunday (which is also a commandment).
- Give food to the hungry.
- Give water to the thirsty.
- Visit the sick, and confort them.

IMPORTANT NOTES

☐ _____

☐ _____

☐ _____

☐ _____

☐ _____

☐ _____

☐ _____

☐ _____

☐ _____

YOUR SOUL'S GROWTH PLANNER

LONG LIVE CHRIST THE KING!

VIVA CRISTO REY.ORG

DATE: MONTH   DAY   YEAR

GOALS OF THE DAY

PRAYING THE ROSARY OF 15 DECADES.................. ☐

READING THE HOLY BIBLE (15 MINUTES)............... ☐

DAILY SACRIFICES.. ☐

☐ _____   ☐ _____
☐ _____   ☐ _____
☐ _____   ☐ _____
☐ _____   ☐ _____
☐ _____   ☐ _____
☐ _____   ☐ _____
☐ _____   ☐ _____
☐ _____   ☐ _____
☐ _____   ☐ _____

SUGGESTIONS

If you don't know how to pray the Holy Rosary, you can get our book "Rosary for beginners" in the following link: www.vcrey.com/rosary-book

Some sacrifices that you can do include:

- Not drinking water or liquids during a meal.
- Abstain from meat on Fridays (which is also required by Holy Mother Church).
- Not eating candy or dessert during one day.
- Take a cold shower.
- Not eating meat in saturdays in honor of the Blessed Virgin Mary.
- Keep one hour of silence.
- Do not buy or sell in Sunday (which is also a commandment).
- Give food to the hungry.
- Give water to the thirsty.
- Visit the sick, and confort them.

IMPORTANT NOTES

☐ _____
☐ _____
☐ _____
☐ _____
☐ _____
☐ _____
☐ _____
☐ _____
☐ _____

YOUR SOUL'S GROWTH PLANNER

LONG LIVE CHRIST THE KING!

VIVA
CRISTO
REY.ORG

DATE: MONTH   DAY   YEAR

GOALS OF THE DAY

PRAYING THE ROSARY OF 15 DECADES.................... ☐

READING THE HOLY BIBLE (15 MINUTES)................ ☐

DAILY SACRIFICES.. ☐

☐ _____   ☐ _____
☐ _____   ☐ _____
☐ _____   ☐ _____
☐ _____   ☐ _____
☐ _____   ☐ _____
☐ _____   ☐ _____
☐ _____   ☐ _____
☐ _____   ☐ _____
☐ _____   ☐ _____

SUGGESTIONS

If you don't know how to pray the Holy Rosary, you can get our book "Rosary for beginners" in the following link: www.vcrey.com/rosary-book

Some sacrifices that you can do include:

- Not drinking water or liquids during a meal.
- Abstain from meat on Fridays (which is also required by Holy Mother Church).
- Not eating candy or dessert during one day.
- Take a cold shower.
- Not eating meat in saturdays in honor of the Blessed Virgin Mary.
- Keep one hour of silence.
- Do not buy or sell in Sunday (which is also a commandment).
- Give food to the hungry.
- Give water to the thirsty.
- Visit the sick, and confort them.

IMPORTANT NOTES

☐ _____
☐ _____
☐ _____
☐ _____
☐ _____
☐ _____
☐ _____
☐ _____
☐ _____

YOUR SOUL'S GROWTH PLANNER

LONG LIVE CHRIST THE KING!

VIVA
CRISTO
REY.ORG

DATE: MONTH   DAY   YEAR

GOALS OF THE DAY

PRAYING THE ROSARY OF 15 DECADES.................. ☐

READING THE HOLY BIBLE (15 MINUTES)............... ☐

DAILY SACRIFICES.. ☐

☐ _____   ☐ _____
☐ _____   ☐ _____
☐ _____   ☐ _____

☐ _____   ☐ _____
☐ _____   ☐ _____
☐ _____   ☐ _____

☐ _____   ☐ _____

☐ _____   ☐ _____
☐ _____   ☐ _____

SUGGESTIONS

If you don't know how to pray the Holy Rosary, you can get our book "Rosary for beginners" in the following link: www.vcrey.com/rosary-book

Some sacrifices that you can do include:

- Not drinking water or liquids during a meal.
- Abstain from meat on Fridays (which is also required by Holy Mother Church).
- Not eating candy or dessert during one day.
- Take a cold shower.
- Not eating meat in saturdays in honor of the Blessed Virgin Mary.
- Keep one hour of silence.
- Do not buy or sell in Sunday (which is also a commandment).
- Give food to the hungry.
- Give water to the thirsty.
- Visit the sick, and confort them.

IMPORTANT NOTES

☐ _____
☐ _____
☐ _____
☐ _____
☐ _____
☐ _____
☐ _____
☐ _____
☐ _____

YOUR SOUL'S GROWTH PLANNER

LONG LIVE CHRIST THE KING!

VIVA
CRISTO
REY.ORG

DATE: MONTH   DAY   YEAR

GOALS OF THE DAY

PRAYING THE ROSARY OF 15 DECADES................... ☐

READING THE HOLY BIBLE (15 MINUTES)................ ☐

DAILY SACRIFICES.. ☐

☐ _____   ☐ _____

☐ _____   ☐ _____

☐ _____   ☐ _____

☐ _____   ☐ _____

☐ _____   ☐ _____

☐ _____   ☐ _____

☐ _____   ☐ _____

☐ _____   ☐ _____

☐ _____   ☐ _____

SUGGESTIONS

If you don't know how to pray the Holy Rosary, you can get our book "Rosary for beginners" in the following link: www.vcrey.com/rosary-book

Some sacrifices that you can do include:

- Not drinking water or liquids during a meal.
- Abstain from meat on Fridays (which is also required by Holy Mother Church).
- Not eating candy or dessert during one day.
- Take a cold shower.
- Not eating meat in saturdays in honor of the Blessed Virgin Mary.
- Keep one hour of silence.
- Do not buy or sell in Sunday (which is also a commandment).
- Give food to the hungry.
- Give water to the thirsty.
- Visit the sick, and confort them.

IMPORTANT NOTES

☐ _____

☐ _____

☐ _____

☐ _____

☐ _____

☐ _____

☐ _____

☐ _____

☐ _____

YOUR SOUL'S GROWTH PLANNER

LONG LIVE CHRIST THE KING!

DATE: MONTH   DAY   YEAR

GOALS OF THE DAY

PRAYING THE ROSARY OF 15 DECADES................... ☐

READING THE HOLY BIBLE (15 MINUTES)................ ☐

DAILY SACRIFICES... ☐

☐ _____   ☐ _____
☐ _____   ☐ _____
☐ _____   ☐ _____
☐ _____   ☐ _____
☐ _____   ☐ _____
☐ _____   ☐ _____
☐ _____   ☐ _____
☐ _____   ☐ _____
☐ _____   ☐ _____

SUGGESTIONS

If you don't know how to pray the Holy Rosary, you can get our book "Rosary for beginners" in the following link: www.vcrey.com/rosary-book

Some sacrifices that you can do include:

- Not drinking water or liquids during a meal.
- Abstain from meat on Fridays (which is also required by Holy Mother Church).
- Not eating candy or dessert during one day.
- Take a cold shower.
- Not eating meat in saturdays in honor of the Blessed Virgin Mary.
- Keep one hour of silence.
- Do not buy or sell in Sunday (which is also a commandment).
- Give food to the hungry.
- Give water to the thirsty.
- Visit the sick, and confort them.

IMPORTANT NOTES

☐ _____
☐ _____
☐ _____
☐ _____
☐ _____
☐ _____
☐ _____
☐ _____
☐ _____

YOUR SOUL'S GROWTH PLANNER

LONG LIVE CHRIST THE KING!

DATE: MONTH   DAY   YEAR

GOALS OF THE DAY

PRAYING THE ROSARY OF 15 DECADES................... ☐

READING THE HOLY BIBLE (15 MINUTES)................ ☐

DAILY SACRIFICES.. ☐

☐ _____   ☐ _____
☐ _____   ☐ _____
☐ _____   ☐ _____
☐ _____   ☐ _____
☐ _____   ☐ _____
☐ _____   ☐ _____
☐ _____   ☐ _____
☐ _____   ☐ _____
☐ _____   ☐ _____

SUGGESTIONS

If you don't know how to pray the Holy Rosary, you can get our book "Rosary for beginners" in the following link: www.vcrey.com/rosary-book

Some sacrifices that you can do include:

- Not drinking water or liquids during a meal.
- Abstain from meat on Fridays (which is also required by Holy Mother Church).
- Not eating candy or dessert during one day.
- Take a cold shower.
- Not eating meat in saturdays in honor of the Blessed Virgin Mary.
- Keep one hour of silence.
- Do not buy or sell in Sunday (which is also a commandment).
- Give food to the hungry.
- Give water to the thirsty.
- Visit the sick, and confort them.

IMPORTANT NOTES

☐ _____
☐ _____
☐ _____
☐ _____
☐ _____
☐ _____
☐ _____
☐ _____
☐ _____

YOUR SOUL'S GROWTH PLANNER

LONG LIVE CHRIST THE KING!

VIVA
CRISTO
REY.ORG

DATE: MONTH   DAY   YEAR

GOALS OF THE DAY

PRAYING THE ROSARY OF 15 DECADES................... ☐

READING THE HOLY BIBLE (15 MINUTES)................ ☐

DAILY SACRIFICES.. ☐

☐ _____   ☐ _____
☐ _____   ☐ _____
☐ _____   ☐ _____
☐ _____   ☐ _____
☐ _____   ☐ _____
☐ _____   ☐ _____
☐ _____   ☐ _____
☐ _____   ☐ _____
☐ _____   ☐ _____

SUGGESTIONS

If you don't know how to pray the Holy Rosary, you can get our book "Rosary for beginners" in the following link: www.vcrey.com/rosary-book

Some sacrifices that you can do include:

- Not drinking water or liquids during a meal.
- Abstain from meat on Fridays (which is also required by Holy Mother Church).
- Not eating candy or dessert during one day.
- Take a cold shower.
- Not eating meat in saturdays in honor of the Blessed Virgin Mary.
- Keep one hour of silence.
- Do not buy or sell in Sunday (which is also a commandment).
- Give food to the hungry.
- Give water to the thirsty.
- Visit the sick, and confort them.

IMPORTANT NOTES

☐ _____
☐ _____
☐ _____
☐ _____
☐ _____
☐ _____
☐ _____
☐ _____
☐ _____

YOUR SOUL'S GROWTH PLANNER

LONG LIVE CHRIST THE KING!

VIVA
CRISTO
REY.ORG

DATE: MONTH   DAY   YEAR

GOALS OF THE DAY

PRAYING THE ROSARY OF 15 DECADES................... ☐

READING THE HOLY BIBLE (15 MINUTES)............... ☐

DAILY SACRIFICES... ☐

☐ _____   ☐ _____

☐ _____   ☐ _____

☐ _____   ☐ _____

☐ _____   ☐ _____

☐ _____   ☐ _____

☐ _____   ☐ _____

☐ _____   ☐ _____

☐ _____   ☐ _____

☐ _____   ☐ _____

SUGGESTIONS

If you don't know how to pray the Holy Rosary, you can get our book "Rosary for beginners" in the following link: www.vcrey.com/rosary-book

Some sacrifices that you can do include:

- Not drinking water or liquids during a meal.
- Abstain from meat on Fridays (which is also required by Holy Mother Church).
- Not eating candy or dessert during one day.
- Take a cold shower.
- Not eating meat in saturdays in honor of the Blessed Virgin Mary.
- Keep one hour of silence.
- Do not buy or sell in Sunday (which is also a commandment).
- Give food to the hungry.
- Give water to the thirsty.
- Visit the sick, and confort them.

IMPORTANT NOTES

☐ _____

☐ _____

☐ _____

☐ _____

☐ _____

☐ _____

☐ _____

☐ _____

☐ _____

YOUR SOUL'S GROWTH PLANNER

LONG LIVE CHRIST THE KING!

VIVA CRISTO REY.ORG

DATE: MONTH   DAY   YEAR

GOALS OF THE DAY

PRAYING THE ROSARY OF 15 DECADES................... ☐

READING THE HOLY BIBLE (15 MINUTES)................ ☐

DAILY SACRIFICES... ☐

☐ _____   ☐ _____
☐ _____   ☐ _____
☐ _____   ☐ _____
☐ _____   ☐ _____
☐ _____   ☐ _____
☐ _____   ☐ _____
☐ _____   ☐ _____
☐ _____   ☐ _____
☐ _____   ☐ _____

SUGGESTIONS

If you don't know how to pray the Holy Rosary, you can get our book "Rosary for beginners" in the following link: www.vcrey.com/rosary-book

Some sacrifices that you can do include:

- Not drinking water or liquids during a meal.
- Abstain from meat on Fridays (which is also required by Holy Mother Church).
- Not eating candy or dessert during one day.
- Take a cold shower.
- Not eating meat in saturdays in honor of the Blessed Virgin Mary.
- Keep one hour of silence.
- Do not buy or sell in Sunday (which is also a commandment).
- Give food to the hungry.
- Give water to the thirsty.
- Visit the sick, and confort them.

IMPORTANT NOTES

☐ _____
☐ _____
☐ _____
☐ _____
☐ _____
☐ _____
☐ _____
☐ _____
☐ _____

YOUR SOUL'S GROWTH PLANNER

LONG LIVE CHRIST THE KING!

VIVA
CRISTO
REY.ORG

DATE: MONTH   DAY   YEAR

GOALS OF THE DAY

PRAYING THE ROSARY OF 15 DECADES.................... ☐

READING THE HOLY BIBLE (15 MINUTES).............. ☐

DAILY SACRIFICES... ☐

☐ _____   ☐ _____
☐ _____   ☐ _____
☐ _____   ☐ _____
☐ _____   ☐ _____
☐ _____   ☐ _____
☐ _____   ☐ _____
☐ _____   ☐ _____
☐ _____   ☐ _____
☐ _____   ☐ _____

SUGGESTIONS

If you don't know how to pray the Holy Rosary, you can get our book "Rosary for beginners" in the following link: www.vcrey.com/rosary-book

Some sacrifices that you can do include:

- Not drinking water or liquids during a meal.
- Abstain from meat on Fridays (which is also required by Holy Mother Church).
- Not eating candy or dessert during one day.
- Take a cold shower.
- Not eating meat in saturdays in honor of the Blessed Virgin Mary.
- Keep one hour of silence.
- Do not buy or sell in Sunday (which is also a commandment).
- Give food to the hungry.
- Give water to the thirsty.
- Visit the sick, and confort them.

IMPORTANT NOTES

☐ _____
☐ _____
☐ _____
☐ _____
☐ _____
☐ _____
☐ _____
☐ _____
☐ _____

YOUR SOUL'S GROWTH PLANNER

LONG LIVE CHRIST THE KING!

VIVA
CRISTO
REY.ORG

DATE: MONTH   DAY   YEAR

GOALS OF THE DAY

PRAYING THE ROSARY OF 15 DECADES.................. ☐

READING THE HOLY BIBLE (15 MINUTES).............. ☐

DAILY SACRIFICES....................................... ☐

☐ _____   ☐ _____
☐ _____   ☐ _____
☐ _____   ☐ _____
☐ _____   ☐ _____
☐ _____   ☐ _____
☐ _____   ☐ _____
☐ _____   ☐ _____
☐ _____   ☐ _____
☐ _____   ☐ _____

SUGGESTIONS

If you don't know how to pray the Holy Rosary, you can get our book "Rosary for beginners" in the following link: www.vcrey.com/rosary-book

Some sacrifices that you can do include:

- Not drinking water or liquids during a meal.
- Abstain from meat on Fridays (which is also required by Holy Mother Church).
- Not eating candy or dessert during one day.
- Take a cold shower.
- Not eating meat in saturdays in honor of the Blessed Virgin Mary.
- Keep one hour of silence.
- Do not buy or sell in Sunday (which is also a commandment).
- Give food to the hungry.
- Give water to the thirsty.
- Visit the sick, and confort them.

IMPORTANT NOTES

☐ _____
☐ _____
☐ _____
☐ _____
☐ _____
☐ _____
☐ _____
☐ _____
☐ _____

YOUR SOUL'S GROWTH PLANNER

LONG LIVE CHRIST THE KING!

VIVA
CRISTO
REY.ORG

DATE: MONTH   DAY   YEAR

GOALS OF THE DAY

PRAYING THE ROSARY OF 15 DECADES.................. ☐

READING THE HOLY BIBLE (15 MINUTES)............... ☐

DAILY SACRIFICES... ☐

☐ _____   ☐ _____

☐ _____   ☐ _____

☐ _____   ☐ _____

☐ _____   ☐ _____

☐ _____   ☐ _____

☐ _____   ☐ _____

☐ _____   ☐ _____

☐ _____   ☐ _____

☐ _____   ☐ _____

SUGGESTIONS

If you don't know how to pray the Holy Rosary, you can get our book "Rosary for beginners" in the following link: www.vcrey.com/rosary-book

Some sacrifices that you can do include:

- Not drinking water or liquids during a meal.
- Abstain from meat on Fridays (which is also required by Holy Mother Church).
- Not eating candy or dessert during one day.
- Take a cold shower.
- Not eating meat in saturdays in honor of the Blessed Virgin Mary.
- Keep one hour of silence.
- Do not buy or sell in Sunday (which is also a commandment).
- Give food to the hungry.
- Give water to the thirsty.
- Visit the sick, and confort them.

IMPORTANT NOTES

☐ _____

☐ _____

☐ _____

☐ _____

☐ _____

☐ _____

☐ _____

☐ _____

☐ _____

YOUR SOUL'S GROWTH PLANNER

LONG LIVE CHRIST THE KING!

VIVA CRISTO REY.ORG

DATE: MONTH   DAY   YEAR

GOALS OF THE DAY

PRAYING THE ROSARY OF 15 DECADES.................. ☐

READING THE HOLY BIBLE (15 MINUTES)............... ☐

DAILY SACRIFICES... ☐

☐ _____   ☐ _____

☐ _____   ☐ _____

☐ _____   ☐ _____

☐ _____   ☐ _____

☐ _____   ☐ _____

☐ _____   ☐ _____

☐ _____   ☐ _____

☐ _____   ☐ _____

☐ _____   ☐ _____

SUGGESTIONS

If you don't know how to pray the Holy Rosary, you can get our book "Rosary for beginners" in the following link: www.vcrey.com/rosary-book

Some sacrifices that you can do include:

- Not drinking water or liquids during a meal.
- Abstain from meat on Fridays (which is also required by Holy Mother Church).
- Not eating candy or dessert during one day.
- Take a cold shower.
- Not eating meat in saturdays in honor of the Blessed Virgin Mary.
- Keep one hour of silence.
- Do not buy or sell in Sunday (which is also a commandment).
- Give food to the hungry.
- Give water to the thirsty.
- Visit the sick, and confort them.

IMPORTANT NOTES

☐ _____

☐ _____

☐ _____

☐ _____

☐ _____

☐ _____

☐ _____

☐ _____

☐ _____

YOUR SOUL'S GROWTH PLANNER

LONG LIVE CHRIST THE KING!

VIVA
CRISTO
REY.ORG

DATE: MONTH   DAY   YEAR

GOALS OF THE DAY

PRAYING THE ROSARY OF 15 DECADES................. ☐

READING THE HOLY BIBLE (15 MINUTES)............... ☐

DAILY SACRIFICES... ☐

☐ _____   ☐ _____
☐ _____   ☐ _____
☐ _____   ☐ _____
☐ _____   ☐ _____
☐ _____   ☐ _____
☐ _____   ☐ _____
☐ _____   ☐ _____
☐ _____   ☐ _____
☐ _____   ☐ _____

SUGGESTIONS

If you don't know how to pray the Holy Rosary, you can get our book "Rosary for beginners" in the following link: www.vcrey.com/rosary-book

Some sacrifices that you can do include:

- Not drinking water or liquids during a meal.
- Abstain from meat on Fridays (which is also required by Holy Mother Church).
- Not eating candy or dessert during one day.
- Take a cold shower.
- Not eating meat in saturdays in honor of the Blessed Virgin Mary.
- Keep one hour of silence.
- Do not buy or sell in Sunday (which is also a commandment).
- Give food to the hungry.
- Give water to the thirsty.
- Visit the sick, and confort them.

IMPORTANT NOTES

☐ _____
☐ _____
☐ _____
☐ _____
☐ _____
☐ _____
☐ _____
☐ _____
☐ _____

YOUR SOUL'S GROWTH PLANNER

LONG LIVE CHRIST THE KING!

VIVA CRISTO REY.ORG

DATE: MONTH   DAY   YEAR

GOALS OF THE DAY

PRAYING THE ROSARY OF 15 DECADES................... ☐

READING THE HOLY BIBLE (15 MINUTES).............. ☐

DAILY SACRIFICES... ☐

☐ _____   ☐ _____

☐ _____   ☐ _____

☐ _____   ☐ _____

☐ _____   ☐ _____

☐ _____   ☐ _____
☐ _____   ☐ _____

☐ _____   ☐ _____

☐ _____   ☐ _____
☐ _____   ☐ _____

SUGGESTIONS

If you don't know how to pray the Holy Rosary, you can get our book "Rosary for beginners" in the following link: www.vcrey.com/rosary-book

Some sacrifices that you can do include:

- Not drinking water or liquids during a meal.
- Abstain from meat on Fridays (which is also required by Holy Mother Church).
- Not eating candy or dessert during one day.
- Take a cold shower.
- Not eating meat in saturdays in honor of the Blessed Virgin Mary.
- Keep one hour of silence.
- Do not buy or sell in Sunday (which is also a commandment).
- Give food to the hungry.
- Give water to the thirsty.
- Visit the sick, and confort them.

IMPORTANT NOTES

☐ _____

☐ _____

☐ _____

☐ _____

☐ _____

☐ _____

☐ _____

☐ _____

☐ _____

Our Store of Catholic Products

With the grace of God and our sincere desire to bring to the world products with a Catholic theme, we have started a store for different products, such as clothing, canvas, mugs, phone cases, etc.

These products are aimed at people who want to remember the Catholic faith more frequently, with the idea of keeping the promises of Jesus Christ more close to the memory, and thus, to the heart.

> *"Come to me, all you that labour, and are burdened, and I will refresh you. Take up my yoke upon you, and learn of me, because I am meek, and humble of heart: and you shall find rest to your souls. For my yoke is sweet and my burden light."*
> *The Bible, New Testament, Gospel according to the Apostle Saint Matthew, chapter 11, verses 28 through 30*

If you are like us, and have in you a deep longing and desire to see in more places the face of Our Lord Jesus Christ, or to discover devotion for a saint for centuries ago that has been unjustly forgotten by the world. If you are tired of seeing people focused their attention at charachters that strive to attack the message of God in the flesh (the Messiah, Jesus Christ) then you are going to love our stores, that you can visit in the following links:

Our English Store: https://vcrey.com/vcrm-en-teespring
In Spanish: https://vcrey.com/teespring-vivacristorey

Here is just a sample of the products that you can find at our store.

Canvas that you can put in your dinner table or studio

Or a hoodie with our logo and motto "Viva Cristo Rey" (Long live Christ the King)

Buy Our Book!
"Rosary for Beginners"

You have already finished this book about the four last things. We hope that it will be of great help in ordering the affairs of your soul, and that you may say at the end of the world:

> *"Lord Jesus Christ, because I applied myself to praying the Rosary daily and doing sacrifices for your love, now I see you with joy and not with sadness"*

But it is important to emphasize that reading without prayer is of little benefit, so we invite you to please acquire our book *"Rosary For Beginners, Step By Step Tutorial"* with which you can start praying the Holy Rosary daily, which is essential for the conversion of your soul. You can obtain this book from the following link: vcrey.com/rosary-book

How did you like this book? Include your Review!

If this book has been to your liking. We would like to know about it, leave us a review of this book, just look for the title *"Food for your Soul: 365-day Catholic Planner to pray the Holy Rosary, read the Holy Bible and make daily sacrifices."* on the platform that you bought it.

When leaving your review you can include the following:

- What is something you learned from this book?
- What things stood out to you in this book?
- What are you going to implement after reading this book?
- Who would you recommend this book to?

If you wish, you can include a photo of the book in your hands, so that people can see the version of the book you have, as well as the size of the book. This will help us out a lot so that other readers may decide to buy this book, which will help us to reach more people.

Our Project
Viva Cristo Rey
Multimedia

Greetings!

On this occasion, we have decided to include our mission and some of the plans that, if it is the will of God, we want to complete in the near future.

Our Mission

We are a traditional Catholic multimedia organization that wants to fight publishers and institutions that are consumed in their desire to produce content full of impurities, blasphemy, heresy and apostasy. We want to oppose them and provide souls with an option contrary to all the evil that exists in the media today. We want to be able to produce enough professional content to give refuge to all the souls that are thirsty for educational and moral content.

Our Plans

Here is a short list of the projects in which we are involved in at the moment:

- We are making a concerted effort to bring new editions of unknown books of saints to the market.
- We are doing research on forgotten devotions that have been approved by previous Popes in previous centuries and we wish to bring these forgotten devotions to the general public.

- We want to translate books of saints who are only available in English to other languages. Primarily Spanish.
- We want to translate books of saints that are only available in Latin to English and Spanish, primarily.
- We want to design products such as board games, clothing, and similar items, but with a catholic theme.

This organization is starting. We were established in the year 2017. Please support us by sharing this book with your friends and family.

CATALOGUE OF BOOKS
VIVA CRISTO REY MULTIMEDIA

SHARE THIS CATALOG WITH YOUR FAMILY AND FRIENDS

VIA WHATSAPP

VIA MESSENGER

VIA TELEGRAM

You can download a pdf version of this catalog on the following link: vcrey.com/catalogue

VIVA
CRISTO
REY.ORG

BOOKS & AUDIOBOOKS

IN ENGLISH

CATALOG OF BOOKS AND AUDIOBOOKS

Title: How to Pray the Rosary for Beginners Step by Step Tutorial
Author: Pablo Claret
Get it as an Ebook:
https://vcrey.com/rosary-ebook
Get it as a Paperback:
vcrey.com/rosary-book

Title: The Four Last Things: Death. Judgment. Hell. Heaven. "Remember thy last end, and thou shalt never sin." a Traditional Catholic Classic for Spiritual Reform.
Author: Father Martin Von Cochem
Editor: Pablo Claret
Get it as an Ebook:
https://vcrey.com/4-last-things-ebook
Get it as a Paperback:
vcrey.com/4-last-things-book
Get it as an Audiobook:
vcrey.com/4-last-things-audiobook

CATALOG OF BOOKS AND AUDIOBOOKS

Title: Autobiography of St. Ignatius of Loyola, Catholic Priest, Theologian, Founder of the Company of Jesus (Jesuits) and Servant of Christ for the Greater Glory of God, Ad Maiorem Dei Gloriam. With Images.

Author: St. Ignatius of Loyola // **Editor**: Pablo Claret

Get it as an Ebook:
https://vcrey.com/st-ignatius-ebook
Get it as a Paperback:
https://vcrey.com/st-ignatius-book

Title: Saint Alphonsus Maria Ligori on the Patience and Imitation of Christ. With Biblical Wisdom of the Gospels, Psalms, Proverbs, Ecclesiastical + quotes from St. Francis of Assisi, and many more.

Author: St. Alphonsus Liguori
Editor: Pablo Claret
Get it as an Ebook:
https://vcrey.com/patience-ebook
Get it as a Paperback:
vcrey.com/patience-book

CATALOG OF BOOKS AND AUDIOBOOKS

Title: St. Alphonsus Maria Liguori on How to accept and love the will of God and his Divine Providence Includes quotations from St. John, Isaias, the Song of Songs, St. Bernard, etc.
Author: St. Alphonsus Liguori // **Editor**: Pablo Claret
Get it as an Ebook:
https://vcrey.com/providence-ebook
Get it as a Paperback:
vcrey.com/providence-book
Get it as an Audiobook:
vcrey.com/providence-audio

Title: God Made the Violet Too, Life of Leonie, Sister of St. Therese of the Child Jesus and the Holy Face. With Beautiful Lessons of Faith, Hope & Charity, for the Glory of The Most Holy Trinity & Our Lady.
Author: Rev. Albert H. Dolan
Editor: Pablo Claret
Get it as an Ebook:
https://vcrey.com/leoni-ebook
Get it as a Paperback:
https://vcrey.com/leoni-book
Get it as an Audiobook:
vcrey.com/leoni-audibook

CATALOG OF BOOKS AND AUDIOBOOKS

Title: The End of the World and the Signs which will precede The Final Culmination.
Catholic Meditations For Souls Who Thirst For Truth and Justice
Author: Father Charles Arminjon
Editor: Pablo Claret
Get it as an Ebook:
https://vcrey.com/end-of-the-world-ebook
Get it as a Paperback:
vcrey.com/end-of-the-world

Title: The Persecution of the Antichrist and the Conversion of the Jews in the last days.
Analyzing Catholic Prophecies With the Help
of The Fathers of The Church.
Author: Father Charles Arminjon
Editor: Pablo Claret
Get it as an Ebook:
https://vcrey.com/conversion-jews-ebooks
Get it as a Paperback:
vcrey.com/conversion-jews

CATALOG OF BOOKS
AND AUDIOBOOKS

Title: Christus Vincit, Catholic Coloring Book For Children
Author: Pablo Claret
Get it as a Paperback:
https://vcrey.com/coloring-book

VIVA
CRISTO
REY.ORG

LIBROS &
AUDIOLIBROS
EN ESPAÑOL

CATALOG OF BOOKS AND AUDIOBOOKS

Title: Rosario Para Principiantes. Tutorial Detallado
Author: Pablo Claret
Get it as an Ebook:
https://vcrey.com/rosario-ebook
Get it as a Paperback:
vcrey.com/rosario-libro
Get it as an Audiobook:
vcrey.com/rosario-audio

Title: Evangelio de Jesucristo según San Marcos, discípulo de San Pedro Apóstol, Papa. Basado en la versión de Torres Amat, traducción de la Vulgata, 1823. Con Imagenes, Comentarios y Mapas.
Author: San Marcos, El Espiritu Santo.
Editor: Pablo Claret
Get it as an Ebook:
https://vcrey.com/evangelio-san-marcos-ebook
Get it as a Paperback:
vcrey.com/evangelio-san-marcos-libro
Get it as an Audiobook:
vcrey.com/evangelio-san-marcos-audio

CATALOG OF BOOKS
AND AUDIOBOOKS

Title: El Vaticano vs Hitler. Como Roma condeno la Alemania Nazi, el Racismo del III Reich, la propaganda del Nacional-Socialismo y su idolatría del Estado antes de la II Guerra Mundial.
Author: Papa Pio XI
Editor: Pablo Claret
Get it as an Ebook:
https://vcrey.com/vs-hitler-ebook
Get it as a Paperback:
vcrey.com/vs-hitler-libro
Get it as an Audiobook:
vcrey.com/vs-hitler-audio

Title: San Alfonso Maria de Ligorio sobre la Paciencia e Imitacion de Cristo. Con Sabiduria Biblica de los Evangelios, Salmos, Proverbios, Eclesiástico + citas de San Francisco de Asís, y muchos más.
Author: St. Alphonsus Liguori
Editor: Pablo Claret
Get it as an Ebook:
https://vcrey.com/paciencia-ebook
Get it as a Paperback:
vcrey.com/paciencia-libro
Get it as an Audiobook:
vcrey.com/paciencia-audio

CATALOG OF BOOKS AND AUDIOBOOKS

Title: San Alfonso Maria de Ligorio sobre como aceptar y amar la voluntad de Dios y su Divina Providencia, incluye citas de San Juan, Isaias, el Cantar de los Cantares, San Bernardo, etc
Author: St. Alphonsus Liguori
Editor: Pablo Claret
Get it as an Ebook:
https://vcrey.com/providencia-ebook
Get it as a Paperback:
vcrey.com/providencia-libro
Get it as an Audiobook:
vcrey.com/providencia-audio

Title: Cristo y el Árbol de la Vida. Beneficios de la Lectura de la Sagrada Biblia y Libros de Santos para las almas que desean conocer al Espíritu Santo.
Author: St. Alphonsus Liguori
Editor: Pablo Claret
Get it as an Ebook:
https://vcrey.com/cristo-ebook
Get it as a Paperback:
vcrey.com/cristo-libro
Get it as an Audiobook:
vcrey.com/cristo-audio

CATALOG OF BOOKS AND AUDIOBOOKS

Title: Pureza moral y de intención. El honor y gloria de cultivar la virtud de la honestidad para llegar a la presencia de Dios y conocer el amor de Cristo. Con citas de los santos padres.
Author: St. Alphonsus Liguori
Editor: Pablo Claret
Get it as an Ebook:
https://vcrey.com/pureza-ebook
Get it as a Paperback:
vcrey.com/pureza-libro
Get it as an Audiobook:
vcrey.com/pureza-audio

Title: De Corazón a Corazón en la Presencia de Dios. Meditaciones Bíblicas sobre el Silencio y la Soledad Cristiana. Recibe abundante Luz Divina, Abandona el Pecado y vence a los Demonios.
Author: St. Alphonsus Liguori
Editor: Pablo Claret
Get it as an Ebook:
https://vcrey.com/corazon-ebook
Get it as a Paperback:
vcrey.com/corazon-libro
Get it as an Audiobook:
https://vcrey.com/corazon-audiolibro

CATALOG OF BOOKS
AND AUDIOBOOKS

Title: De la entrega total a Dios. Sabiduria Catolica Para Entrar Por la Puerta Angosta, Recibir La Corona de la Vida, Dejar el Pecado, y Obtener la Amistad del Rey de Reyes, Jesucristo.
Author: St. Alphonsus Liguori
Editor: Pablo Claret
Get it as an Ebook:
https://vcrey.com/entrega-a-dios-ebook
Get it as a Paperback:
vcrey.com/entrega-a-dios-libro

Title: La Verdadera Esposa de Jesucristo. Extracto sobre la Oración ferviente, espiritual y agradable al corazón de Dios. Con conmovedoras enseñanzas del Espíritu Santo, Los Profetas, etc
Author: St. Alphonsus Liguori
Editor: Pablo Claret
Get it as an Ebook:
https://vcrey.com/oracion-ebook
Get it as a Paperback:
vcrey.com/oracion-libro

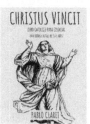

Title: Christus Vincit, Libro Catolico Para Colorear, Para Niños y Niñas de 2 a 8 Años
Author: Pablo Claret
Get it as a Paperback:
vcrey.com/libro-colorear

CATALOG OF BOOKS
AND AUDIOBOOKS

Title: Bienaventurados los que lavan sus túnicas para tener derecho al árbol de la vida. (Apocalipsis 22:14) Paquete 2 en 1 de Religion Católica y Mejora Espiritual, para las almas sedientas de la verdad.
Author: St. Alphonsus Liguori
Editor: Pablo Claret
Get it as an Ebook:
vcrey.com/2-en-1-kindle
Get it as an Audiobook:
https://vcrey.com/bienaventurados-au-diolibro

Title: Dios es amor, paquete 2 en 1 de religión católica. Pon a tu alma en libertad con la misericordia de Jesus de Nazaret, Dios y Hombre Verdadero.
Author: St. Alphonsus Liguori
Editor: Pablo Claret
Get it as an Ebook:
https://vcrey.com/dios-es-amor-ebook

Final Credits

In the creation of this book, we are debtors of the following people and entities:

- We thank God, who has given us enough life, and the efficient desires to bring this work to light.
- We thank the Blessed Virgin. Because her free consent has been the joy of all the generations of men of good will since the Incarnation of Christ.
- We thank the Catholic Church. Because the constant source of its light teaches us that *"Outside the Catholic Church there is absolutely no Salvation."* And that doctrine compels us to try, according to our weak strength, to do something for our neighbors.

Made in United States
Orlando, FL
21 December 2024

56290307R00212